Pascal
An introduction
to methodical programming

Pascal
An introduction
to methodical programming

Third edition

William Findlay
and David A. Watt

Computing Science Department,
University of Glasgow

Pitman

London · Boston · Melbourne · Toronto

PITMAN PUBLISHING LIMITED
128 Long Acre, London WC2E 9AN

PITMAN PUBLISHING INC.
1020 Plain Street, Marshfield, Massachusetts 02050

Associated Companies
Pitman Publishing Pty Ltd, Melbourne
Pitman Publishing New Zealand Ltd, Wellington
Copp Clark Pitman, Toronto

© William Findlay and David A. Watt 1978, 1981, 1985

First published in Great Britain 1978
Second edition 1981
Reprinted 1981, 1982, 1984 (twice)
Third edition 1985

British Library Cataloguing in Publication Data

Findlay, William
    Pascal: an introduction to methodical
    programming—3rd ed.
    1. PASCAL (Computer program language)
    I. Title   II. Watt, David A.
    001.64'24   QA76.73.P2

    ISBN 0-273-02188-5

Library of Congress Cataloging in Publication Data

Findlay, William, 1947–
    Pascal: an introduction to methodical programming.
    Bibliography: p.
    Includes index.
    1. PASCAL (Computer program language)   I. Watt,
David A. (David Anthony)   II. Title.
QA76.73.P2F5   1985   001.64'24   84-25522

ISBN 0-273-02188-5

Printed and bound in Great Britain at The Pitman Press, Bath

Preface to the third edition

This book is intended for use in conjunction with a first course in computer programming based on the programming language Pascal. The reader is assumed to have had no previous exposure to computers, and to have only elementary mathematics. Programming principles, good style and a methodical approach to program development are emphasized, with the intention that the book should be useful even to those who must later write programs in a language other than Pascal. Thus one objective is simply to teach readers how to write good programs.

A second objective is to present an introduction to Pascal. In this respect the book should be useful not only to novices but also to readers with some experience of programming in another language.

Pascal was introduced in 1971 by Professor Niklaus Wirth. His aim was to make available a language which would allow programming to be taught as a systematic discipline and in which the techniques of both 'scientific' and 'commercial' programming could be convincingly demonstrated. The adoption of Pascal has been rapid and widespread, to the extent that it has become the *lingua franca* of computing science and the basis for many new developments, such as Ada.

For our present purposes what is really important is the clarity with which fundamental programming concepts may be expressed in Pascal. Most of the book is devoted to a treatment of these fundamentals, presented in such a way that the reader should be convinced of the need for each language feature before we show how it is realized in Pascal. Since Pascal contains only a few features which are not truly fundamental, these remaining features are also covered, briefly, for the sake of completeness.

Use of the book

The best way to acquire a methodical approach to programming is subconsciously, by imitation, and the best time to start is right at the beginning. The technique of programming by stepwise refinement is therefore imparted mainly by consistent example throughout the book. Nevertheless, three chapters are devoted exclusively to programming methodology. The first, Chapter 7, introduces the methodology by means of a simple example and a case study, and is placed early enough to encourage good programming habits from the start. The second, Chapter 15, shows how subprograms fit into the methodology, illustrating this with another case study. The third, Chapter 18, applies the methodology to realistically-sized problems involving data structures, by means of two further case studies.

The main text falls naturally into six parts. Part I (First Steps in Programming) aims to bring the novice as soon as possible to the stage of writing and testing complete programs in a methodical manner. This part covers the Integer and Boolean data types, input and output, and the basic control structures of sequencing, selection and repetition. Its highlights are the first complete program, in Chapter 4, and the introduction of a methodology, in Chapter 7. Part II (Further Simple Data Types) covers the data types Char and Real, and ordinal types in general. The chapter on Char includes a detailed treatment of text input and output. The chapter on ordinal types also covers the related control structures, **for** and **case**. Part III (Arrays and Strings) introduces the simple data structures common to most programming languages. Part IV (Subprograms) introduces functions, procedures and parameters, and demonstrates their importance in program development. This is the pivot of the book—the reader who has mastered the material up to this point can reasonably claim to be a programmer. Part V (Further Data Structures) continues the coverage of Pascal's rich variety of data structures with records and files, and relates the choice of suitable data structures to the methodical development of a program. Part VI (Additional Topics) completes the coverage of Pascal with sets, pointers and linked lists, recursion, functional and procedural parameters, conformant array parameters, and the **goto** statement.

Some sections can be skipped on a first reading. They may be omitted altogether if time is short. This is pointed out in the text, wherever relevant. The title of such a section is marked with an asterisk in the table of contents.

The topic sequence implied by reading the chapters in order, from first to last, is one that we can confidently recommend. However, many alternative paths through the book are possible. Readers may choose to follow one that suits their particular interests. For example, Chapter 10 on Real arithmetic may be read directly after Chapter 6 by those whose main interest is in numerical methods. Similarly, much of Chapters 16 and 17 may be taken at an early stage by those with an interest in commercial data processing. The following diagram shows how topics relate to each other. An arrow from topic A to topic B means that A must be read before B.

Examples

Every non-trivial example used in this book has been tested on a computer. We challenge readers to find any errors in them!

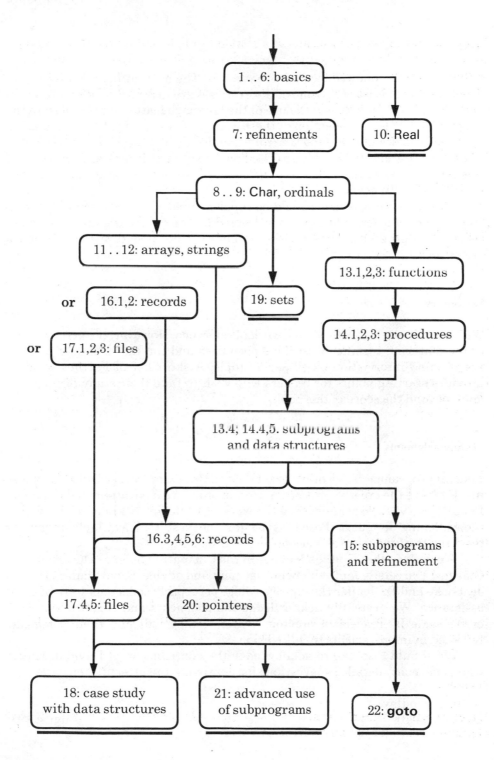

Exercises

Each chapter is followed by a set of exercises. The more difficult exercises are marked with asterisks (*). Some of the exercises are intended to be answered on paper, to provide practice in the use of the language features introduced in the chapter. Answers to a selection of these exercises are provided. The remaining exercises are designated *programming exercises,* which involve the writing of complete programs to be run and tested on a computer. Practical experience of this nature is essential to every programmer. (Not all the programming exercises need be attempted.)

A programming course should be supplemented by a programming laboratory, in which a series of exercises selected by the course organizer is undertaken. The programming exercises herein may be used to assist in such a selection.

References

We have not attempted to write a work of reference. However, the arrangement of the material, together with the Appendices and the Index, should make it easy to find information on a specific topic. A short list of Further Reading provides starting points for readers who wish to take their study of programming beyond the scope of this book.

Acknowledgments

Like all programmers, we owe a great debt to Professor Edsger Dijkstra, whose insights into the creative aspects of programming we have attempted to reflect. Equally, we wish to acknowledge the work of Professor Niklaus Wirth, whose programming language Pascal is by far the best tool available today for teaching the fundamental concepts of programming.

We wish to thank our colleagues in the Computing Science Department of Glasgow University for their encouragement and advice; in particular Dr John Jeacocke and Dr Jenifer Haselgrove whose perceptive comments were of great assistance. We gratefully acknowledge the comments and constructive criticisms made by readers of previous editions; they will find their comments reflected in improvements to this edition.

We should also like to acknowledge the contribution of David J. Hatter who made many detailed suggestions for improving the presentation.

William Findlay
David A. Watt   August 1984

Contents

Sections marked with an asterisk may be omitted on a first reading.

Part I
First steps in programming

1

Computers and programming

This chapter introduces:

* computers and programming
* hardware and software
* algorithms and heuristics
* programming languages
* syntax and semantics
* the high-level language Pascal
* compilation and execution
* compilers and interpreters

1.1 INTRODUCTION

There can be few people, at least in the industrialized countries of the world, who have never had any contact with computers. Computers are now routinely used for mundane tasks such as producing bank statements, financial reports, electricity bills and payslips. Hotel and airline reservation systems have been made possible by computers. In industry, computers control machine tools and chemical plant. Scientists use computers to analyse experimental data, doctors generate 'cross-section' X-ray pictures, psychologists simulate mental processes. Manned and unmanned space exploration would hardly be possible without the assistance of computers. On the frivolous side, computers have been programmed to play games such as backgammon and chess. More ominously, military applications have a long history.

Computing has grown rapidly, from its origins before 1950 to its present position as one of the world's largest industries. There is no sign of this expansion slowing down. Indeed, the development of cheap integrated circuits means that domestic and personal computers are now practical. These will more and more invade everyday life as domestic appliances, motor vehicles, communications systems and the like come increasingly to depend on them. This accelerating process has rightly been called the Second Industrial Revolution. Nobody can yet foresee with any certainty what the ultimate consequences for society may be, but it is already clear that vast changes lie ahead for us all.

Consider the impact of pocket calculators on accepted ideas about education and numeracy. Computer technology will soon have a similar effect in all areas of clerical and skilled manual work. Many books are now edited and typeset by their authors, aided by computers. As a result they are much less expensive than would be possible with traditional printing technology. On the other hand the craft of the compositor is thereby made redundant, and the end product often lacks the elegance he might have given it. Concerns like these make it imperative that computers be understood as widely as possible.

One of the most common misconceptions is that computers are 'problem-solving' machines. Nothing could be further from the truth. In fact the successful application of computers is made possible only by finding solutions to problems which computers themselves have created. The most obvious of these is that a computer is useless without programs to control it. The writing of good computer programs is both a vital part of the modern economy and a fascinating intellectual exercise. Such is the topic of this book.

1.2 HARDWARE AND SOFTWARE

Early computers filled large rooms with tall metal racks on which were fixed thousands of vacuum tubes, tanks of mercury and panels of flashing lights. The resemblance to an ironmonger's store was so compelling that the computer engineers of the time wryly talked about their creations as 'hardware'. Nowadays a considerably more powerful computer fits easily in a briefcase, but the principles of its operation remain the same.

The hardware of every digital computer consists of a processor, a store and an assortment of peripheral devices. The *processor* is the unit which actually performs the calculations. It contains a *control unit* to direct operations, as well as an *arithmetic unit*. The latter is equivalent to an electronic calculator, but much faster, being capable of a million or more operations per second. To make use of this speed the processor must be able to access its data equally quickly. Retaining data for rapid access by the processor is the job of the computer's *store*. Some calculators have a handful of 'registers', or locations in which numbers can be kept. The store of a modest computer contains tens of thousands of locations. A calculator's numeric keys and display correspond to the *peripherals* or input/output devices of a computer. These allow data to be placed in the store and results to be taken out. Though very fast by human standards, peripherals are usually much slower than the processor and store.

A calculator is given instructions by pressing its function keys. However the great speed of a computer would be wasted if it could not be supplied with instructions as quickly as it obeys them. To make this possible the computer's instructions, encoded in numerical form, are held in store along with the data. The computer works in a cycle as follows.

(1) The control unit fetches the next instruction from store.
(2) The instruction is decoded into electronic signals by the control unit.
(3) In response to these signals the arithmetic unit, the store, or a peripheral device carries out the instruction.
(4) The whole cycle repeats from step (1).

In this way long sequences of instructions can be obeyed automatically at the full speed of the processor. Such a sequence of instructions is called a *program*.

Individual computer instructions are very simple in their effect, the following examples being typical.

(a) Read an item of data into store from an input device.
(b) Copy an item of data from one location to another.
(c) Add the contents of two locations and place the sum in a third.
(d) If the content of a location represents a negative number, take the next instruction from a different part of the program; otherwise continue with the next instruction in sequence.
(e) Write an item of data from store to an output device.

Nearly all computers in existence today are electronic computers. That is, their processors and stores are made from electronic devices such as transistors, diodes and capacitors. Integrated circuit technology allows many thousands of these devices to be fabricated cheaply within a small piece of silicon, a *chip*. It is the low cost of chips that has made possible the use of computers in applications, such as video games, that were previously uneconomical.

When you think of a computer, you probably think in terms of electronics and silicon chips. But non-electronic computers are possible. Mechanical computers, made from gears and levers, were designed during the nineteenth century by an English mathematician, Charles Babbage. Electro-mechanical computers, made from relays, were actually built during the 1940s and 1950s. There have even been proposals for pneumatic and hydraulic computers!

Whether powered by electricity, air or water, any computer has the same basic structure: processor, store and peripherals. It is the functions performed by these units, and their interconnections, that make a machine a computer rather than a radio or a windmill. In fact the idea of *structure* is an essential one in computing. You will see it applied to computers themselves, to the programs they run, and to the data they process.

Many different programs can be written to perform a given task. They may run faster or slower, use more or less store, or be intended to run on different makes of computer. But, so long as they follow the same general method, we say that they are all implementations of the same *algorithm*. An algorithm is a method for carrying out a specific calculation that is guaranteed to produce a result in a finite number of steps. These steps may be as simple as the machine instructions described above, or even simpler. Amazingly, it has been proved that some results cannot be computed by any algorithm whatsoever! This places a fundamental restriction on the abilities of computers.

Even when an algorithm for computing a certain result is known to exist, it may not be feasible to use it in practice. For example, it may be too slow, or need too much store. An example of this would be an algorithm to play a perfect game of chess. Methods that usually work, but are not guaranteed, are called *heuristics*. Chess machines use heuristics, and can therefore be beaten.

Computer programs are working models of algorithms and heuristics. An important topic in computer science is the invention and study of algorithms. The invention and study of heuristics is more controversial—it goes by the name of *artificial intelligence.*

The collection of all the programs available in a computer system constitutes its *software*. This word was invented to emphasize that the programs are just as important as the hardware. It also contrasts them effectively. Hardware is visible, solid and substantial; software is somewhat intangible. The hardware of a computer system is not easily changed; the software is usually in a state of flux.

One of the most important parts of the software is the *operating system,* a set of control programs which are kept permanently in store. The operating system carries out many of the routine tasks needed to prepare and run a user's program; e.g. deciding which program to run next, making ready its input, bringing the program into store, allocating it some processor time, and so on. There are many different operating systems and you will have to familiarize yourself with the features of the one you will be using to help you with your own programs.

1.3 PROGRAMMING LANGUAGES

The earliest computers were programmed in machine code: in other words, by giving them instructions directly in numerical form. However the drawbacks were soon recognized.

(a) Because of the very primitive nature of machine instructions, machine-code programming is both tedious and error-prone.
(b) For the same reason, machine-code programs are difficult to understand and to modify.

(c) Programming is a time-consuming and expensive business. It would be a great saving to be able to use the same program on different computers, but a machine-code program is specific to one model of computer and will not work on any other.

For these reasons machine code is now seldom used.

Why not write programs in English? Computer programming is not unique in needing to describe sequences of actions precisely and in detail. The same requirement is often met in daily life. However, anyone who has struggled with the sometimes mystifying instructions in car maintenance handbooks, do-it-yourself manuals, or recipe books will agree that English is not ideally suited to the task. In fact the glories of English—its vast scope, its subtlety, its potential for ambiguity and metaphor—must be considered severe disadvantages when the aim is literalness, accuracy and completeness. The same is true of Dutch, Greek, Japanese and all other *natural* languages.

English is at the opposite extreme from machine code and precisely for that reason must be rejected as a medium for practical computer programming. What is needed is a middle way: one which combines the readability and generality of English with the directness and precision of machine code. Languages of this sort are called *high-level programming languages.*

Knitting patterns offer an interesting example where a similar problem has been faced. A knitting pattern is comparable in complexity with a modest computer program, so it is understandable that a special 'knitting language' has evolved. It borrows many words from English, but these are used in stereotyped ways and with definite meanings. Another noteworthy feature of a knitting pattern is its division into two parts: a list of the materials and tools needed, followed by a list of instructions stating how to use them. The programming language used in this book, Pascal, shares both of these characteristics.

Any language can be studied from two points of view: that of its grammar, or *syntax,* and that of its meaning, or *semantics.* A good understanding of both is needed to use it properly. We will find that the semantics of Pascal can be described adequately in English. On the other hand a description of its syntax in English would be very tedious. Instead we will use a pictorial device, the *syntax diagram.* This is best explained by an example.

Stated in English, the Pascal definition of an integer number is the following. 'An integer number is a sequence of one or more decimal digits. A decimal digit is the character "0", or "1", or "2", or "3", or "4", or "5", or "6", or "7", or "8", or "9".' Exactly the same information is conveyed by Figure 1.1. This can be understood by following the arrows through the diagram, from entry to exit, and writing down a specimen of everything you pass. When you come to a fork, either path may be chosen. For instance, the integer number 365 is produced by going through Decimal Digit three times, choosing the fourth, seventh and sixth forks respectively. However the form 1,000 is *not* a

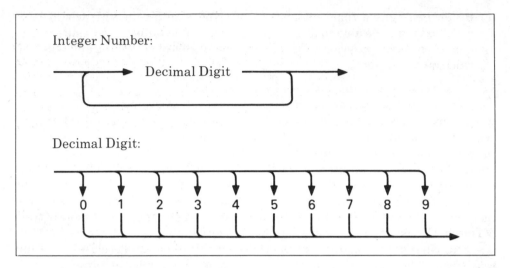

Figure 1.1. Syntax of Integer Numbers

valid integer number, according to Figure 1.1, because no path through the diagram includes a comma symbol.

As a slightly more complicated example, Figure 1.2 defines an identifier, widely used in Pascal for naming things. The English equivalent of this diagram is 'An identifier is a sequence of characters beginning with a letter and followed by zero or more letters or decimal digits.' The definition of letter is omitted; it is tedious in any form. For instance, X is an identifier produced by passing straight through Letter and out. In Letter, we choose the 24th fork! Similarly, A1D is produced by passing through Letter (and taking the first fork therein), then circling back through Decimal Digit (taking its second fork) and finally circling back through Letter (taking its fourth fork).

The identifiers A1D, A1d, a1D and a1d are all equivalent, because corre-

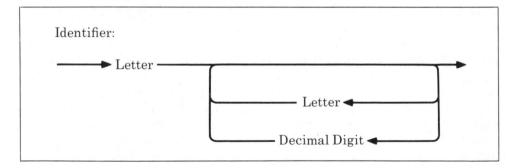

Figure 1.2. Syntax of Identifiers

sponding upper- and lower-case letters are interchangeable in identifiers and other Pascal words.

A program written in Pascal cannot be directly performed by the hardware of a computer. To make it executable it must be translated from Pascal into an equivalent set of machine code instructions. This translation can be specified rigorously enough to make it a suitable task for a computer. Three programs are involved here: the translator program, or *compiler*; the user's Pascal text, or *source program*; and the equivalent machine code, or *object program*. Thus a Pascal program is run in two distinct stages.

(1) *Compilation*. The Pascal compiler is brought into store and obeyed. It causes the computer to read the source program, check it for errors, and convert it into the corresponding object program.

(2) *Execution*. The object program resulting from stage (1) is brought into store. It is obeyed in turn and reads input, performs computations, and writes output, in exactly the manner specified by the Pascal source program. This stage can be repeated as often as necessary. Recompilation is needed only when the source program is changed.

Programs often contain errors in the use of the programming language and these are reported by the compiler during stage (1). The report usually takes the form of an error message or a number which refers to a list of error messages. These error messages are often helpful in finding the cause of the trouble. (However, the compiler may be misled by an error into taking later, perfectly correct, parts of a program as erroneous. Thus one genuine error can cause a whole group of messages to be output, many of which are spurious. Nothing more forcefully reminds a programmer that computers do not *understand* the programs which drive them.)

The compilation phase, during which the program is translated from source code to object code, is often called *compile time*. The execution phase, when the object program is running, is often called *run time* or execution time. Confusingly, the same terms are often used for how long it takes to compile and run a program.

A final point about compilation. On some types of computer, especially microcomputers, the machine code for a program may take up so much space that the object program does not fit into store. Faced with this problem, compiler designers have invented more compact representations of the object program. These representations are, in effect, the machine code of a hypo-thetical computer. They then write compilers to translate Pascal into the hypothetical machine code. But there is no actual computer that runs this hypothetical code. Instead, there is another program, called an *interpreter,* that simulates the behaviour of the hypothetical machine. The interpreter takes as data both the hypothetical object program, and *its* data, and produces the same output that we would get from the hypothetical machine!

Now there are four programs involved: the source program, the compiler, the object program in hypothetical code, and the interpreter. The interpreter is written in the machine code of the real machine it runs on (as is the compiler).

The main disadvantage of this technique is that interpreting a hypothetical code is slower than running real machine code, usually by a factor of between five and 50. A big advantage is that interpreters often detect errors in the program that the hardware of the real machine would not be able to discover in a machine-code object program.

EXERCISES 1

1.1 Which of the following are valid identifiers, according to the syntax of Figure 1.2?

(a) Seven, (b) VII, (c) Nmr7, (d) 7, (e) Kermit, (f) Joe 90,
(g) ABCDEFGHIJKLMNOPQRSTUVWXYZ

1.2. Write down examples of sentences generated by the following syntax diagrams.

Sentence:

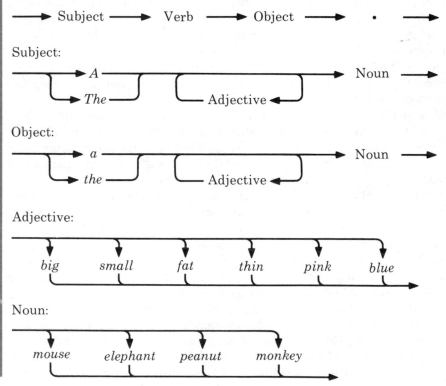

Subject:

Object:

Adjective:

Noun:

Verb:

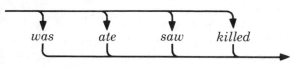

1.3. Which of the following are valid sentences, according to the syntax of the previous exercise?

(a) *The big fat monkey ate a peanut.*
(b) *The pink elephant was killed.*
(c) *The monkey saw a pink elephant.*
(d) *The small, thin elephant killed a mouse.*
(e) *The mouse ate.*
(f) *A elephant was a elephant.*

1.4. Draw a syntax diagram which defines exactly, and solely, the Roman numerals from 1 to 10 (i.e. *I, II, III, IV, V, VI, VII, VIII, IX* and *X*). Your diagram should not consist merely of ten alternatives.

1.5*. Write down examples of chemical formulas generated by the following syntax diagrams.

Chemical Formula:

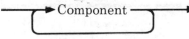

Component:

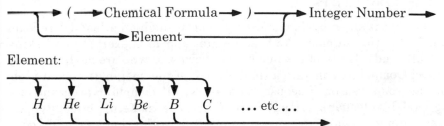

Element:

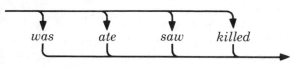

2

Data: types, constants, and variables

This chapter introduces:

* data and data types
* values and their representations
* constants and variables
* constant definitions
* variable declarations
* the assignment statement

2.1 DATA AND DATA TYPES

Who has not spent an enjoyable hour browsing through an atlas? There is an enduring fascination in maps. An even greater appeal is exerted by working models of all kinds. Think of the number of grown-ups who are model railway enthusiasts! Computers can gain a similar hold on the imagination, and probably for the same reason. Because, in a sense, all computer programs are working models. Mechanical models are difficult to make or to modify. But with a computer we are able to represent miniature worlds that we can shape at our will.

An example that shows this very clearly is weather forecasting by computer. Using information such as temperature, humidity, pressure and so on (gathered by weather stations), and rules about the way these properties change (derived from the laws of physics), a fast computer can model the behaviour of the atmosphere. The result is a description of the atmosphere a few days in the future. Inaccuracies in the forecast are explained by the incompleteness of the original information and by the approximate nature of the rules that the computer applies.

Such a model works just as well with hypothetical data as with observed data, allowing us to answer questions such as: 'How would the weather change if temperatures were two degrees lower?'. This is not something we could find out by experiment.

The interpreter programs described in Section 1.3 provide an example of modelling within computing itself. Here the computer is being used to model the behaviour of another (hypothetical) computer.

Perhaps the most vivid illustration of the computer's ability to model is given by video games. Most of these simulate worlds that exist only in the realms of fantasy. Nevertheless, the same principles apply as in weather forecasting programs and in interpreters:

(1) The computer is provided with data that describes some system to be modelled.
(2) The computer is provided with a program whose operations model events within the system.
(3) Running the program models the activity of the system.
(4) The output from the program models the resulting state of the system.

All this is done because the model is easier to handle than the system itself.

Later in this book you will learn much about the operations that programs can apply to data. This chapter is more concerned with the data itself.

The word 'data' means 'the things given'. We use the term to refer to the information which must be supplied to a program (or piece of program) before it can produce any results. Data may originate outside the computer, in which case it must be read from an input device, or it may already be available in the computer's store, having been placed there as a result of a previous computation.

An item of data represents some fact, observation or idea. People can recognize data in speech, in pictures, in printed text and in many other forms. However, the input devices of a computer are much less adaptable than human sensory organs and most data presented to computers is in the form of a *text,* a sequence of characters from some character set. Until recently, texts were punched on cards for input by means of a card reader. Nowadays texts are more often typed directly into the computer at a terminal. There are devices which permit the input of sound and pictures to computers, but they are less common, and many of them work by converting the data to what is basically a form of text.

Printed material has traditionally used a large set of symbols. The alphabet is often available in bold letters, in italics, and in many sizes and styles. There is also a huge assortment of symbols for use in mathematics and other specialized fields. For economic reasons computer input is much more restrictive. In fact most computers can process only a small, fixed set of characters. This will certainly include the capital letters, the decimal digits, the usual punctuation marks and a few of the mathematical signs.

Even this restricted set of characters allows a vast range of data to be input to the computer. With just two characters we can distinguish between true and false. The digits allow us to write integer numbers and these can represent a great variety of things, for example populations, votes, dates, sums of money, and so on. The digits together with the decimal point allow us to write numbers containing fractions (real numbers). Thus we can represent smoothly-varying quantities such as distances, times, weights, volumes, and probabilities. Adding letters, punctuation marks and mathematical signs allows us to input human-language text: both natural languages such as English and programming languages such as Pascal.

A very important characteristic of a data item is its *type,* as this determines its meaning and constrains what can sensibly be done with it. In Pascal the values True and False constitute the Boolean type; the whole numbers constitute the Integer type; the numbers with fractional parts constitute the Real type; and the computer system's character set constitutes the Char type. Furthermore, the programmer can add to this list by defining new types.

It is very easy to make a computer do totally meaningless calculations. One of the ways high-level languages help to avoid this is by *type checking*: that is, by ensuring that the types of the data involved in a computation are compatible with the operations to be performed.

In Pascal every item of data is considered to be of some specific type and there are rigid rules concerning how each type may be used. When a program is translated into machine code the compiler checks it to verify that these rules have been followed. For example, the compiler would reject a program which attempted to multiply a Char value (such as the ampersand symbol '&') by an Integer value (such as the number 7). Multiplication is simply not a meaningful operation on Char values.

In practice only radical differences of type are recognized. For instance, in Pascal all Integer values are treated alike. Adding an Integer value which represents a population and one which represents a sum of money would *not* be detected as an error by a Pascal compiler, even though the result would not represent any 'fact, observation or idea'. (Pascal does, however, permit finer distinctions of type to be made than most other programming languages. This is a major factor contributing to its popularity.)

Outside the computer values of all types can be represented by texts, that is by sequences of characters. For example, integer numbers can be represented by sequences of decimal digits, and real numbers by digits and the decimal point character. Characters, interestingly, represent themselves.

Inside the computer things are very different. The hardware of an electronic computer is made of devices with two easily distinguishable physical states. For example, a transistor may be conducting an electrical current, or not. A device with two states is said to store one binary digit, or *bit*. A group of N such devices has 2^N different states and stores N bits. It is called an *N-bit word*.

An 8-bit word has 256 different states. This is enough to allocate one state to each character in a typical character set. We say that each state *encodes* a character. There is little to choose between many different encodings, but having chosen one it is wise to stick with it! In fact, several different character codes are in use. By far the most common are the codes called ASCII and EBCDIC. (These are defined by the tables in Appendix 5.)

A 16-bit word has 65536 states. This is enough to encode all the integer numbers from -32768 to $+32767$. Other data types, such as real numbers, may be encoded as bit patterns in a similar way.

Now that you know how a computer is able to store characters, numbers and other data, you can relax and forget it! One of the greatest advantages of a high-level language like Pascal is that it allows us to program *as if* the computer actually held characters or numbers, rather than bit patterns. We shall exploit this advantage to the full.

2.2 CONSTANTS AND VARIABLES

Some of the data used in a program never change. For example, the ratio of the circumference of a circle to its diameter is approximately 3.14159 and this is an invariable fact. Such data are modelled in a program by *constants*, in other words by stating their values literally. It is often useful to give a symbolic name to a constant. The name can then be used throughout the program whenever the value of the constant is required. A suggestive name such as Pi, rather than the obscure 3.14159, makes a program easier to read.

Other data are intrinsically subject to change. For example, in a program summing a list of numbers, the running total changes every time the next item from the list is added to it. Such data are modelled in a program by *variables*.

In programming a variable is best thought of as a *container* for a value. We will speak loosely about 'the value of a variable', but we should really say, in more precise language, 'the value contained in a variable'. Like a physical container a variable may be empty, in which case we will say that its value is *undefined*. Attempting to use an undefined value from an empty variable is one of the most common mistakes in programming. Its effect is to make the program behave unpredictably. On different runs it may give correct results, or an error may be detected, or it may even give wrong results without any sign that something is wrong.

Variables can be both created and destroyed in a program: the value of a newly-created variable is undefined. Once a value has been placed in a variable it stays there until the program deliberately alters it, or until the variable itself is destroyed. Values of different types require variables of corresponding types to hold them. Again, we speak loosely of 'an Integer variable' when we really mean 'a variable capable of holding an Integer value'.

Like constants, the variables in our programs have names. This is essential, not a convenience as it was with constants. We must be able to refer to specific variables independently of their values, since their values may change. In a program a variable is created by a *declaration*. To declare a variable it is necessary to specify both its type and its name.

The instruction which alters the value of a variable is called an *assignment statement*. An assignment statement specifies a variable and an expression. When it is obeyed the expression is evaluated and the result is copied (assigned) to the variable. There are many other kinds of statement: some of them can be used to change variables, others use the existing values of variables.

More generally, definitions and declarations describe data types and data objects; whereas statements specify actions to be taken by the computer when the program is obeyed. (The term 'statement' is rather misleading but unfortunately has become universal, for historical reasons. Statements would better be called 'commands' or 'instructions'.)

You may like to think of the various types of data as each having a characteristic shape. Variables would then be thought of as suitably-shaped boxes. We will often represent variables by boxes in this book. Unfortunately it is not practical to print boxes of several shapes, so all our boxes will be rectangular, regardless of type. When we picture a variable as a box, we will label the box with its identifier.

2.3 DEFINITIONS AND DECLARATIONS

A constant definition looks like an equation. On the left is the name of the constant to be defined, this is followed by the '=' sign, and this is followed in turn by the value to be ascribed to the constant. All of this can be summarized very concisely in pictorial form, by means of a syntax diagram: see Figure 2.1.

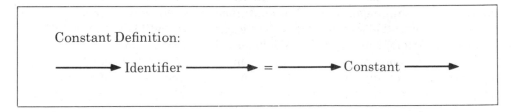

Figure 2.1. Syntax of Constant Definitions

This diagram does not give the syntax of a constant, as that would take us into other matters prematurely.

Several constant definitions may be given, or none. If there are any they must be separated from each other by semicolons, and the complete group must be introduced by the symbol **const**.

Example 2.1

```
const
   WorkingDays = 5;
   WeeksPerYear = 52;
   Pi = 3.14159;
   SpeedOfLight = 299792.0;
   CmPerInch = 2.54;
   Ampersand = '&';
   Asterisk = '*'
```

These constant definitions establish two identifiers for integer constants (WorkingDays and WeeksPerYear), three identifiers for real constants (Pi, SpeedOfLight and CmPerInch) and two identifiers for character constants (Ampersand and Asterisk).

There is no ambiguity about the type of a constant identifier. It is the same as the type of the value to the right of the '=' sign and Pascal has been designed so that this type is always obvious.

Variable declarations are a little more complicated than constant definitions and quite different in appearance. The variable declaration part of a program begins with the symbol **var**. This is followed by a group of one or more variable declarations, these being separated by semicolons. Each variable declaration consists of a list of identifiers, separated by commas, then a colon, and finally a type. See Figure 2.2 for the syntax diagram. Again, it would be

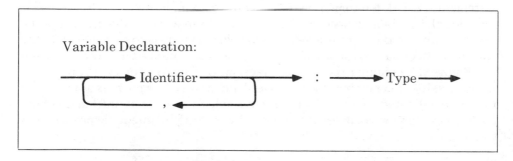

Figure 2.2. Syntax of Variable Declarations

premature to disclose the syntax of types, so take it on trust that Boolean, Char, Integer and Real are allowable.

{The following is a reliable general rule in Pascal: *within* definitions, declarations and statements, commas are used to separate the components of a list. *Between* definitions, declarations and statements, semicolons appear.}

Example 2.2

```
var
   WeeklyPay, YearlyPay: Integer;
   Radius, Circumference, Orbit: Real;
   Punctuation, Initial: Char;
   Untaxed: Boolean
```

Here we declare two Integer variables (WeeklyPay and YearlyPay), three Real variables (Radius, Circumference and Orbit), two Char variables (Punctuation and Initial) and one Boolean variable (Untaxed). In terms of our 'boxes', we can picture the effect of these declarations as follows, where the question marks act as reminders that the values of newly-declared variables are undefined:

WeeklyPay ⬚ ?   YearlyPay ⬚ ?

Circumference ⬚ ?   Radius ⬚ ?   Orbit ⬚ ?

Punctuation ⬚ ?   Initial ⬚ ?

Untaxed ⬚ ?

2.4 ASSIGNMENT STATEMENTS

A value is copied into a variable when the computer obeys an assignment statement. Pascal assignment statements have a simple syntax. On the left is specified the variable whose contents are to be replaced, following this is the ':=' sign, and on the right is an expression whose value is to be assigned to the variable. This reads naturally if the ':=' sign is pronounced as 'becomes equal to'. Figure 2.3 contains the syntax diagram. (An expression is a formula by which a value is computed. Its syntax is defined fully in Appendix 1.3, but it is rather complicated, and it would be inadvisable to study that until more of the background has been covered. We begin by looking at Integer expressions in Chapter 3.)

Figure 2.3. Syntax of Assignment Statements

Example 2.3

Using the constants and variables introduced in Examples 2.1 and 2.2, the assignment statements:

```
WeeklyPay := 100;
YearlyPay := WeeklyPay * WeeksPerYear;
Untaxed := False;
Initial := 'W'
```

(where '*' is the multiplication sign of Pascal) will leave the values of the variables as follows:

WeeklyPay | 100 | YearlyPay | 5200 |

Circumference | ? | Radius | ? | Orbit | ? |

Punctuation | ? | Initial | 'W' |

Untaxed | false |

Now consider the curious-looking assignment statement:

```
WeeklyPay := WeeklyPay + 5
```

This assignment statement takes the *current* value of WeeklyPay, adds 5, and finally assigns the result to WeeklyPay. Thus the effect of this assignment statement is to increase the value of WeeklyPay by 5:

WeeklyPay | 105 | YearlyPay | 5200 |

There are two important points to note here.

(a) When a value is assigned to a variable, its previous value (if any) is lost forever.
(b) The computer does *not* automatically change the value of YearlyPay when we change the value of WeeklyPay. The computer will obey only *explicit* instructions. If we wish the value of YearlyPay to be changed accordingly, we must ensure that the assignment statement YearlyPay := WeeklyPay * WeeksPerYear is obeyed *again*.

It is important not to be misled by the superficial similarity of assignment statements and constant definitions. The latter are static, giving a name to a fixed value (at compile time), and have no effect when the program is obeyed by the computer. Assignment statements on the other hand are dynamic. Each time an assignment is performed by the computer (at run time) the value copied into the variable may be different. It is precisely to point out this crucial difference that the ':=' sign is used in assignments in place of the '=' sign.

Type checking is particularly effective at finding errors in assignments. The type-compatibility rule for assignments states: a value may be assigned only to a variable of the *same type*. Thus we are guaranteed that the value always 'fits' its container. For example, we can assign the value 100, but not Ampersand nor the contents of Untaxed, to the Integer variable WeeklyPay. (The rule is actually more complicated than this. The simplified version above will be adequate for the present.)

EXERCISES 2

2.1. Many properties of a data item are either True or False (i.e. themselves values of type Boolean). For example, the property 'is positive' is True of the Real value 1.2 but False of the Real values 0.0 and −1.2; the property 'has a non-zero fraction part' is True when applied to the Real value 1.414 but False when applied to the Real value 5.0. Write down at least three such properties (a) of Integer values; and (b) of Char values.

2.2 What is likely to be the most important type in a program (a) to compute spacecraft trajectories; (b) to edit an author's manuscript; and (c) to calculate bank balances?

2.3. If I is an Integer variable, C is a Char variable, R is a Real variable, and B is a Boolean variable, which of the following assignment statements are legal?

(a) I := 1
(b) I := R
(c) I := '&'
(d) C := 1
(e) C := I
(f) C := '&'
(g) B := False
(h) B := C
(i) B := 1
(j) R := B
(k) R := '&'
(l) R := 1.0

2.4. Explain *variables* (containers), *values*, and *undefined*, in terms of *words* and *bit-patterns*.

3

The data type **Integer**

This chapter covers:

* the Integer data type
* arithmetic with Integer data
* Integer overflow

3.1 Integer VALUES

The Integer type in Pascal allows us to represent, store and process integer (whole) numbers. In theory the set of integer numbers extends outward from zero to numbers with arbitrarily large positive or negative values. But this is a finite world, modelled by an even more finite computer, and infinite sets must be cut down to a practical size. Pascal recognizes this by providing, automatically, a constant identifier MaxInt, whose value is the largest number which can be held in an Integer variable. Typical values of MaxInt would be 32767 on a microcomputer and 2147483647 on a large computer. Indeed, the Integer type consists of all the integer values in the range:

$$-\text{MaxInt}, \ldots\ldots, -1, 0, +1, \ldots\ldots, +\text{MaxInt}$$

(MaxInt is an example of a *predefined constant*; you can use it without having to define it yourself.)

Arithmetic on Integer values will be performed correctly by the computer if all the operands, and all the intermediate results, lie in the range from −MaxInt to +MaxInt. If the allowable range is exceeded the result of the arithmetic is unpredictable. This is called *overflow* and the program must be considered to have failed. When an overflow occurs, on some computers, an error message is output and the program stops at once. Other computers do not

21

detect overflow, so that the program may generate worthless results without any warning being given. Thus overflow is a serious matter, and it is the programmer's responsibility to try to avoid it.

Integer numbers are written as a sequence of decimal digits, optionally preceded by a sign: '−' indicates a negative number, '+' or no sign indicates a positive number. See Example 3.1.

Example 3.1

```
const
    Positive = +1;
    Negative = −Positive;
    Biggest = MaxInt;
    Smallest = −MaxInt;
    Emergency = 999;
    Decrement = −15
```

Note that the value specified in a constant definition may itself be a previously-defined constant identifier, or its negative.

3.2 Integer EXPRESSIONS

From two Integer values we can calculate a new Integer value by addition, subtraction, multiplication or division. Pascal uses the conventional notation for arithmetic operators, modified to suit the computer's character set. Addition is denoted by '+', subtraction by '−', multiplication by '*' and division by the symbol **div**. It is also possible to obtain the remainder from a division, using the symbol **mod** (short for 'modulo') in place of **div**.

Dividing one integer number by another does not always give an integral result; there may be a fractional part. To ensure that **div** always yields an integer any fractional part in the result is discarded. For example:

$$(+7) \textbf{ div } (+2) = +3$$
$$(-7) \textbf{ div } (+2) = -3$$
$$(+7) \textbf{ div } (-2) = -3$$
$$(-7) \textbf{ div } (-2) = +3$$

It is an error to attempt to divide any number by zero. It is also an error to attempt to compute a remainder using **mod**, for a negative or zero divisor. The expression $x \textbf{ mod } y$, where y is greater than zero, yields a value for the remainder which is greater than or equal to zero and less than y. This is the smallest number which, subtracted from x, makes it an integral multiple of y.

For example:

$$(+7) \textbf{ mod } 4 = +3 \quad \text{because } (+7) - (+3) = +4 = (+1) * 4$$
$$(-7) \textbf{ mod } 4 = +1 \quad \text{because } (-7) - (+1) = -8 = (-2) * 4$$

Multiplication and division by the same number do not always cancel out for Integer values, because **div** drops any fractional part. Thus the order in which they are done can affect the result. For example:

$$(7 \textbf{ div } 2) * 2 = 3 * 2 = 6$$
$$(7 * 2) \textbf{ div } 2 = 14 \textbf{ div } 2 = 7$$

Similarly, it is not possible to cancel out common factors in multipliers and divisors:

$$(128 \textbf{ div } 20) * 15 = 6 \ * 15 = 90$$
$$(128 \textbf{ div } \ 4) * \ 3 = 32 * \ 3 = 96$$

The normal algebraic conventions apply in Pascal, so multiplications and divisions in an expression take priority over additions and subtractions. Thus in the expression A+B*C the multiplication of B and C is done first and A is added to the result. If this is not what is wanted then parentheses, '(' and ')', can be used to override the priority rules. For example in (A+B)*C the addition of A and B is done first and the result is multiplied by C.

It is allowable to prefix a sign to the first term of an expression. The '−' sign is the negation operator: the value of −x is the negative of x. The '+' sign is the identity operator: the value of +x is the same as the value of x, so the '+' may always be omitted. Multiplication and division take priority over identity and negation, which have the same priority as addition and subtraction. For example the expressions −X+4*Y and +4*Y−X are both equal to the expression (4*Y)−X.

Pascal has no operator for raising one number to the power of another, chiefly because it is difficult to specify such an operator in a way that is both simple and consistent with the type rules. In partial compensation Sqr(x), a function which returns the square of x, is provided. It is often more efficient to evaluate Sqr(x) than (x*x), particularly if x is a complicated expression.

One other useful function is Abs(x), which returns the absolute value of x. That is, if x is negative Abs(x) equals −x, otherwise Abs(x) equals x. For example, Abs(−5) and Abs(5) both give +5.

Sqr and Abs are examples of *standard functions,* which are provided in Pascal to augment the more common operators.

Example 3.2

On each of the following lines is a group of three equivalent expressions. The first in each group is written in the simplest way possible, the rest show alternative formulations. As these examples illustrate, the sparing use of parentheses may clarify a complicated expression and overuse may have the opposite effect. Judicious spacing further improves readability.

$-$X	$(-$X$)$	$(-($X$))$
X$+$Y	$($X$+$Y$)$	$(($X$)+($Y$))$
X$*$Y$+$Z	$($X$*$Y$)+$Z	X$*$Y$+$Z
X **mod** Abs$($Y$)*$Z	X **mod** Abs$($Y$)*$Z	$($X **mod** Abs$($Y$))*$Z
Sqr$($Sqr$($X$))$	Sqr$($X$*$X$)$	X$*$X$*$X$*$X

Because of the danger of overflow, it is not always desirable to rearrange an expression into a mathematically equivalent form. For example, the expressions $($A$-$B$)*($A$+$B$)$ and Sqr$($A$)-$Sqr$($B$)$ are mathematically equal, but the latter is much more prone to overflow when A and B are large.

Be careful with expressions of the form x/y. Even when x and y both have type Integer, and even when y divides x exactly, the quotient is of type Real. For example, 8 **div** 4 has the Integer value 2, but 8/4 has the Real value 2.0. If you are interested in applications where Real arithmetic is important, you might like to preview Chapter 10, although you may not be able to understand it fully until you have finished Chapter 6.

EXERCISES 3

3.1. Write constant definitions for the Integer constants DaysInWeek, InchesPerFoot (or CmPerMetre) and YardsPerMile (or MetresPerKm).

3.2. Write declarations for Integer variables named GrossPay, Tax, UnionDues and NettPay.

3.3. What are the resulting values of these variables when the following assignment statements are obeyed in sequence? Draw suitable box diagrams.

UnionDues := 20; GrossPay := 4900; Tax := GrossPay **div** 3;
NettPay := GrossPay $-$ Tax $-$ UnionDues

3.4. Write assignment statements to calculate (a) UnionDues at £10 plus a hundredth of GrossPay, (b) Tax at a quarter of GrossPay, and (c) NettPay, for any value of GrossPay. Draw suitable box diagrams.

3.5. Write declarations and statements to calculate the minimum number of bank-notes and coins needed to pay out Sum in cash, assuming Sum is given as a multiple of the smallest unit of currency. Draw suitable box diagrams for each stage of the calculation.

3.6*. A non-negative number greater than MaxInt can be held in a computer as *two* Integer values. For example, if MaxInt is 32767 we can represent a number, *n*, with value up to 100 million, in the form of two Integer variables NM and NL, such that:

$$n = 10000*\text{NM}+\text{NL}$$

where NM = n **div** 10000 gives the most significant digits and NL = n **mod** 10000 gives the least significant digits. Suppose two large numbers, x and y, are stored in this way in the Integer variables XM, XL and YM, YL. Write statements to place in ZM, ZL (a) the sum, (b) the difference and (c) the product of x and y. In what circumstances can overflow occur in your Pascal statements?

4

Towards the complete program

> This chapter gets us on to a first complete program. It introduces:
>
> * Pascal input and output statements
> * the structure of a complete program
> * the use of comments
> * good programming style
> * formatted input and output

4.1 INPUT AND OUTPUT

So far we have seen how to write constant definitions, variable declarations and assignment statements. The latter can be used to compute new values from constants and from values which have been computed previously. These program elements allow us to specify computations of a restricted kind, but they provide no means to vary the data on which the computations are performed.

Example 4.1

The following statements, obeyed in sequence, compute the total number of seconds since midnight, given that the time of day is 9:12:30:

```
 H := 09;
 M := 12;
 S := 30;
TotalSecs := 3600*H + 60*M + S
```

The fourth statement is quite general, but if we wish to repeat the computation for some other time of day, we have to modify the first three statements of the 'program' itself.

Now, the whole point of programming a computer is to be able to write a program *once*, and then make it work with *many* different sets of data. In our example, we would prefer the values assigned to H, M and S somehow to be supplied *on each occasion the program is run*, rather than being part of the program itself and therefore fixed. This would allow us to supply different values on each run.

Another limitation of our 'program' is that the computed value is simply placed in a store location (TotalSecs), where it remains invisible. Thus we also need a means of getting results out of the computer.

The separation of a program and its data is a fundamental idea in computing. We should perceive a program as a general set of instructions for performing some computation. A program can be run many times, each time being supplied with different input data. The individual data items supplied in this way are read into the computer in response to explicit input instructions in the program; and results of the computation are written out, in some suitable form, in response to explicit output instructions. All computers are equipped with input devices which allow data to be read by a program, and with output devices which allow data to be written.

In some computer systems the input data is prepared in advance by the computer user, perhaps by punching the data on cards. These cards are read by a card-reader when the program is run on the computer. The program's output is printed on paper, by a line-printer, and the printed results are returned to the user after the program has completed its run. This is the *batch* mode of computing.

Alternatively the computer user might have a terminal connected to the computer. *While the program is running*, the user types the input data on the terminal's keyboard. This data is read by the program, and the program's output returns directly to the terminal, where it is either printed on paper or displayed on a screen. The terminal acts as a combination of an input device (the keyboard) and an output device (the printer or screen). This is the *interactive* mode of computing.

Whatever mode you use, your programs will contain input instructions which cause data to be read from some input device, and output instructions which cause data (results) to be written to some output device.

4.2 INPUT OF INTEGERS

The role of an input instruction is to read an item of data and store it in a variable, so that subsequently it can be used in some computation. In Pascal this role is performed by the *Read statement*.

Example 4.1 (continued)

We can vary the data on which our 'program' works by replacing the first three assignment statements by Read statements:

```
Read (H);
Read (M);
Read (S);
TotalSecs := 3600*H + 60*M + S
```

Suppose we supply the following input data:

    12 25 0

The input data is read from left to right. The statement Read(H) causes the data item '12' to be read and the value 12 to be assigned to H; then the statement Read(M) causes the data item '25' to be read and the value 25 to be assigned to M; then the statement Read(S) causes the data item '0' to be read and the value 0 to be assigned to S. Thus in this case the 'program' computes the number of seconds from midnight to 12:25:0. We can make the 'program' deal with a different time of day simply by running it again with different input data.

In general, the effect of the Read statement Read(V), where V is an Integer variable, is to scan forwards through the input data, skipping any blank characters, until a data item is found; the value of this data item (which must be an integer *number*, possibly signed) is then assigned to V.

The three consecutive Read statements in Example 4.1 could be combined into a single Read statement with the same effect:

```
Read (H, M, S);
TotalSecs := 3600*H + 60*M + S
```

H, M and S are *parameters* of the Read statement. A Read statement may have any number of parameters, all of which must be variables, and for each of these variables one data item is read.

4.3 OUTPUT OF INTEGERS

The role of an output instruction is to get results out of the computer in some suitable form, e.g. printed on paper or displayed on a screen. In Pascal this role is performed by the *Write statement*.

Example 4.2

Continuing from Example 4.1, we could write out the total number of seconds since midnight by the following Write statement:

```
Write (TotalSecs)
```

The following statements, executed in sequence, will read the number of hours, minutes and seconds since midnight, compute the total number of seconds since midnight, and write out all four numbers:

```
Read (H, M, S);
TotalSecs := 3600*H + 60*M + S;
Write (H, M, S, TotalSecs)
```

For example, if the input data is:

9 12 30

then the output would look like this:

9   12   30 33150

Observe that a Write statement, like a Read statement, may have any number of parameters. However, each parameter of Write may be an *expression*, not necessarily a simple variable, and it is the value of this expression which is written.

Example 4.3

Assuming that M and N are integer variables, the following statement writes the values of M and N followed by their sum, difference and product:

```
Write (M, N, M+N, M−N, M*N)
```

4.4 THE COMPLETE PROGRAM

To build a complete Pascal program, we must collect together all the necessary definitions, declarations and statements.

Example 4.4

Here is an example of a complete Pascal program which performs a simple tax calculation:

```
program ComputeTax (Input, Output);

    (* This program computes a taxpayer's tax payment
        for a year, given as input the taxpayer's annual
        income and number of children. It is assumed
        that tax is calculated at one-third of income
        less tax allowances, where the allowances consist
        of a personal allowance of £5000 plus a child
        allowance of £1000 per child. *)

const
    PersonalAllowance = 5000;
    ChildAllowance    = 1000;
var
    NumberOfChildren         : Integer;
    Income, TaxableIncome, Tax: Integer;

begin
Read (Income, NumberOfChildren);
TaxableIncome := Income — PersonalAllowance —
            NumberOfChildren * ChildAllowance;
    (* ... taxable income is income less allowances *)
Tax := TaxableIncome div 3;
    (* ... tax is calculated as a whole number of £ *)
Write (Income, TaxableIncome, Tax, Income — Tax)
end.
```

This program first reads the taxpayer's income (in £) and number of children; then it computes the taxable income and tax; and finally it writes the income, taxable income, tax and nett income after tax. For example, if the input data is:

    11000 4

then the written output from the program would look like this:

    11000   2000   666 10334

This example illustrates all the parts of a complete program.

(1) '**program** ComputeTax' gives an identifier, ComputeTax, to the program.

(2) '(Input, Output)' specifies that this program performs both input and output. Input and Output are called *program parameters*. Program parameters will be treated fully in Chapter 17. Meanwhile, assume that Input must be present if the program reads any input, and that Output must be present if the program writes any output.

(3) The program parameters are followed by the program's *declarative part*.

This consists of a group of constant definitions headed by **const**, followed by a group of variable declarations headed by **var**.

(4) The words **begin** and **end** enclose the program's *statement part*. This contains a sequence of statements, separated by semicolons, and these statements are obeyed one after another in *exactly* their order of occurrence. The period following **end** marks the end of the program text.

Each piece of text enclosed between the special brackets '(*' and '*)' is called a *comment*. Although part of the program text, these comments are entirely ignored by the compiler and are included only to help explain the program to a human reader. A comment may be placed anywhere within a Pascal program text, except in the middle of a symbol such as a word or number.

The order of the program parts is summarized by the syntax diagrams of Figures 4.1, 4.2 and 4.3. Notice that **const** would be omitted in the absence of any constant definitions, and that **var** would be omitted in the absence of any variable declarations.

program, **const**, **var**, **begin** and **end** are all *reserved words*. They are so called because, although they look like identifiers, they must not be chosen as identifiers for constants, variables or anything else. They have special, fixed, meanings in Pascal, implied by their occurrence in the syntax diagrams. Pascal

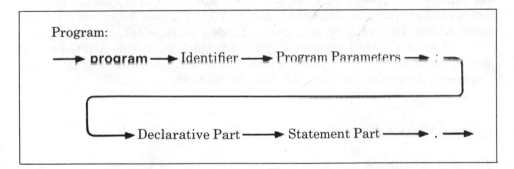

Figure 4.1. Syntax of Programs

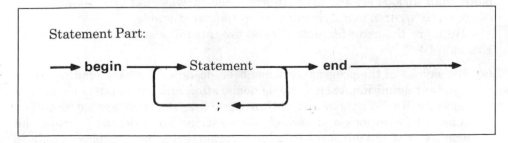

Figure 4.2. Syntax of Statement Parts

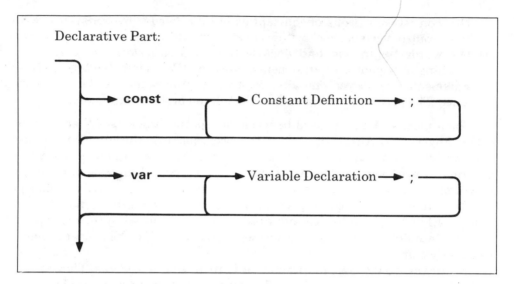

Figure 4.3. Syntax of Declarative Parts (simplified)

has thirty-five reserved words in all, which are listed in Appendix 2.1; they include the operators **div** and **mod** introduced in Chapter 3 (but not **Read** and Write, which are ordinary identifiers). In this book we shall always write reserved words in **bold** lower case. This will help you distinguish them from identifiers, which we shall write in mixed case or upper case. (But remember this is only a convention: the case is immaterial to the compiler.)

4.5 PROGRAMMING STYLE

You probably found the first complete program, in Example 4.4, easy to understand. Partly this was because the program was very short, with only four statements. (By comparison, some programs have been written which contain more than 100000 statements!) Another reason was that the program was deliberately written in a style intended to make it readable.

Here are the main features of good programming style, as illustrated by Example 4.4.

(a) The layout of the program text has been designed for easy reading. Each constant definition, each variable declaration and each statement is on a separate line. The symbols within each line are well spaced out. The constant definitions and variable declarations are indented to make the words **const** and **var** stand out. The program text is 'paragraphed' by blank lines separating its major parts.

(b) All the identifiers have been chosen to suggest the significance of the data they represent. For example, the variable NumberOfChildren is clearly intended to hold a value which is the number of children.

(c) Comments are used in the program text to summarize the function of the program and to explain how it performs its function.

It must be emphasized that these stylistic features are intended solely for the benefit of the human reader. The layout of the program text is of no concern to the compiler (except that consecutive words and numbers must be spaced apart, just as in ordinary English: **begin** A := B **end** is interpreted very differently from beginA := Bend). Comments also are entirely ignored by the compiler. Finally, any significance suggested to the human reader by an identifier like NumberOfChildren is quite lost on the compiler (which understands no English); the compiler would accept the program just as well if another identifier such as N were used instead.

Example 4.5

As an illustration of *bad* programming style, let us rewrite the program of Example 4.4 without concern for layout, without comments, and with short meaningless identifiers.

```
program ComputeTax(Input,Output);const
PA=5000;CA=1000;var N:
Integer,I,TI,T:Integer;begin Read(I,N);TI:=I−PA−N*CA;T:=
TI div 3;Write(I,TI,T,I−T)end.
```

This version of the program is certainly much more concise than the original version, and moreover it will produce exactly the same results as the original when run on a computer. Its only drawback, but a major one, is that it is difficult and unpleasant for human readers.

Throughout this book a reasonably consistent programming style has been adopted. We do not suggest that you should imitate this style slavishly; feel free to develop your own style. What is important is that all your programs should be written in a style which makes them easily understood, by other programmers as well as by yourself.

4.6 FORMATTED INPUT AND OUTPUT

Examine the sample output from the program of Example 4.4:

    11000   2000   666 10334

What would you make of this output if you had never seen the program which produced it? It is just a line of numbers with no indication of their significance.

Since computer output is intended ultimately to be read by ordinary people (i.e. non-programmers), it is essential that the output should be self-explanatory, with appropriate headings, captions, etc. For this purpose we need a means of writing text as well as numbers. In Pascal we can cause a piece of text to be written by enclosing it in apostrophes and supplying it as a parameter in a Write statement. This text is written out, without the apostrophes, when the Write statement is obeyed.

Example 4.6

The statement:

```
Write ('tax due is £', Tax)
```

would produce output like this:

tax due is £   666

The text enclosed in apostrophes is called a *character string*, or simply a *string*. If the string itself is to contain an apostrophe, this apostrophe must be doubled to distinguish it from the apostrophe which ends the string. Thus the statement:

```
Write('That''s the question')
```

would write the following output:

That's the question

The output in Example 4.6 still looks rather strange, because of the blank characters between the currency sign and the number. These are present because each number is written in a *field* of a certain width, and if the number has too few digits then the field is filled with blank characters to the left of the number. We can control the layout by specifying explicitly what field width we require for any parameter in a Write statement.

If no field width is specified explicitly, some default field width will be assumed. For an Integer parameter the default is typically 6 spaces (as above), but this default will vary from one compiler to another. For a string parameter the default field width is always just enough to accommodate the entire string.

Example 4.7

We could modify the Write statement of Example 4.6 as follows:

```
    Write ('tax due is £', Tax:4)
```

The suffix ':4' of the parameter 'Tax:4' specifies that the value of **Tax** is to be written in a field of 4 spaces. Now we can expect output like this:

tax due is £ 666

If we replace the **Write** statement of Example 4.4 by the following:

```
    Write ('income: £',   Income:5,   '   taxable: £',
           TaxableIncome:5,   '   tax: £',   Tax:5,   '      nett: £',
           (Income—Tax):5)
```

then we can expect output like this:

income: £11000   taxable: £ 2000   tax: £   666   nett: £10334

Replacing each ':5' by ':1' makes the output look like this:

income: £11000   taxable: £2000   tax: £666   nett: £10334

since all the numbers are too large to fit into a field of only one space.

The last part of Example 4.7 shows that when you specify a field width too small for the number being written, the number is written in full but without any preceding blanks.

All data written by **Write** statements, whether numbers or strings or anything else, are written on a single line, as illustrated by Example 4.7. If we want to write output on *several* lines, we must use the *WriteLn statement* which forces subsequent output on to a new line.

Example 4.8

If we replace the **Write** statement of Example 4.4 by the following statements:

```
    Write ('income              £', Income:5);
    WriteLn;
    WriteLn;
    Write ('taxable income      £', TaxableIncome:5);
    WriteLn;
    Write ('tax due             £', Tax:5);
    WriteLn;
    Write ('nett income         £', (Income—Tax):5);
    WriteLn
```

then we can expect output like this:

income   £11000

taxable income   £ 2000
tax due   £   666
nett income   £10334

Note that the effect of two consecutive WriteLn statements is to leave a completely blank line.

We may also consider the input data to consist of a number of lines. (If the input data is punched on cards, then each card is considered to be a line of data.) This point is of no concern when using the Read statement to read numbers, since Read will automatically move on to a new line of input data if there is no more data on the current line. Thus program ComputeTax would happily accept its input data on two lines:

11000
 4

For some purposes it is desirable to force the input data to be read a line at a time. For this purpose the *ReadLn statement* is useful: it causes the unread part of the current line of input data to be skipped, so any subsequent input will be taken from the next line.

Example 4.9

Consider the statements:

```
Read (NumberOfSheep); ReadLn;
Read (NumberOfGoats); ReadLn
```

where NumberOfSheep and NumberOfGoats are Integer variables. If the input data is:

10 sheep
 4 goats

then the values 10 and 4 will be read and assigned to the two variables; the textual data on both lines will be ignored. If the ReadLn statements were omitted, on the other hand, the second Read statement would fail, by attempting to interpret 'sheep' as an integer number.

A last word about input and output. The input data is always read from left to right within each line, and from one line to the next. Once a data item has been read, it cannot subsequently be re-read. {By comparison, a person reading a book can go back and re-read any passage.} Likewise, output data is written from left to right within each line, and from one line to the next. Once data has been written, it is not possible to go back and erase it, nor to write some more data about it. {By comparison, a person writing on paper can erase any part of the previous work, or write from the bottom of the page to the top.} These restrictions, which reflect the properties of the common computer input and output devices, have an important influence on many programs, as we shall see in later examples.

EXERCISES 4

4.1. Show what output you would expect from program ComputeTax if the following input data were supplied:

8000   6   8000, -3000 - 1000   9000.

4.2. Consider the following program:

```
program BalanceOfPayments (Input, Output);

(* This program computes a country's trading balance, given its
   import and export bills and its balance on 'invisible' trade. *)

var
    Imports, Exports, VisibleBalance,
        InvisibleBalance, TotalBalance: Integer;
begin
Read (Imports, Exports);
VisibleBalance := Imports — Exports;
Read (InvisibleBalance);
TotalBalance := VisibleBalance + InvisibleBalance;
    (* ... positive for a surplus, negative for a deficit *)
Write ('  imports    exports   visible    invisible     total');
WriteLn;
Write ('       £M         £M        £M          £M        £M');
WriteLn;
WriteLn;
Write (Imports:10, Exports:10,
    VisibleBalance:10, InvisibleBalance:10, TotalBalance:10);
WriteLn
end.
```

Show exactly what output this program would produce, if the following input data were supplied:

(a)
   9120   9670   750

(b)

    555   405
       −12

4.3. Write down statements which output your name and address in the form
you would print them on an envelope.

4.4. Write a program which reads a number and which outputs the number
together with its square, cube and fourth power.

4.5. Write a program which reads three integers representing a date (day,
month and year), and which outputs the date neatly in the form 'day/month/
year' (writing only the last two digits of the year).

PROGRAMMING EXERCISES 4

4.6. Write a program which reads the number of seconds since midnight and
outputs the time in the form 'hours:minutes:seconds', allowing two digits for
each component of the time. Test your program by running it several times,
with various numbers in the range 0 to 86399 as input data.

4.7. A business employs four grades of staff, of which grade A staff are paid
monthly and grades B, C and D are paid weekly. Four lines of input data are
supplied: the first line contains the number of grade A staff and their monthly
pay rate; the remaining lines contain the number of staff and the weekly pay
rate in each of grades B, C and D. Write a program which reads this data and
outputs the total weekly pay bill, the total monthly pay bill and the total
annual pay bill, with appropriate captions. Test your program by running it at
least with the following input data:

     5   1500   A
    10   150   B   .
    20   200   C
    50   125   D

5

The data type **Boolean**

This chapter covers:

* the **Boolean** data type
* comparisons and **Boolean** expressions
* Boolean Algebra (optional on a first reading)

5.1 CONDITIONS IN PROGRAMMING

Valuable results can certainly be obtained with the simple statements introduced in the previous chapters: the assignment, reading and writing of **Integer** values. However these limited means effectively restrict the computer to the role of a calculator. For most applications the program being obeyed by the computer must be able to vary the course of the computation. It is sometimes necessary to select one of several alternative actions, depending on some stated condition. At other times it is necessary to repeat an action over and over again, so long as some continuation condition is satisfied.

Take as an example a program which is processing a company's payroll file and printing each employee's payslip. The calculation of an employee's tax deduction illustrates the need for selective action, as the tax payable might depend on gross pay (with different rates of tax at differing income levels), marital status, number of children, etc. To take account of these factors the program must be able to adapt its behaviour to the circumstances of the employee. Repetition is also needed: the program must be able to repeat the same calculation for every employee, stopping when all the payslips have been printed.

To make full use of the speed, reliability and flexibility of the computer in applications such as this we must have a way of expressing *in the program* conditions which the computer is to test.

Most of the conditions encountered in programming are very simple in nature: either they hold or they do not. If a condition holds it has the value **True**. Otherwise it has the value **False**. **True** and **False** are constant identifiers denoting the only two values of the **Boolean** type.

The name **Boolean** commemorates George Boole (1815–1864) who first placed the study of logic on a sound mathematical basis. His book *The Laws of Thought* described an algebra of logical values, now called Boolean Algebra, which underlies the manipulation of **Boolean** values in the same way that the conventional algebra of arithmetic underlies the **Integer** type. To make progress in the study of programming a good understanding of the elements of Boolean Algebra is vital. Do not despair! As you will discover in the following sections, Boolean Algebra is largely a formal restatement of common sense.

5.2 COMPARISONS

The most familiar way of computing a **Boolean** value is by a *comparison*. In Pascal the values to be compared may be of any suitable type. It is not generally possible to compare values of different types, nor would it make any sense to do so. For example, it makes no sense to ask whether a **Char** value (such as the letter 'A') is equal to an **Integer** value (such as the number 9). For the present, take it that any two **Integer** values or any two **Boolean** values can be compared.

The normal arithmetical rules for comparing signed numbers apply to **Integer** values, so that the comparisons $-1 < 6$, $100 > 99$ and $-23 < -20$ all have the value **True**. Similarly, $7 < 3$, $-44 > -37$ and $13582 < 9$ all have the value **False**. The result of comparisons such as $X = Y$ and $A + B < C$ will, of course, depend on the values of X, Y, A, B and C.

Comparing **Boolean** values is an unusual operation, but it can sometimes provide a very elegant formulation of a complicated condition. This is discussed in Section 5.5.

A full range of comparison operators is available in Pascal. Unfortunately several of the conventional mathematical symbols are absent from the character sets of most computers. To meet this problem the following notational conventions are used:

=	means 'is equal to'
<>	means 'is not equal to'
<	means 'is less than'
<=	means 'is less than or equal to'
>=	means 'is greater than or equal to'
>	means 'is greater than'

The expressions introduced in Chapter 3, and all expressions other than

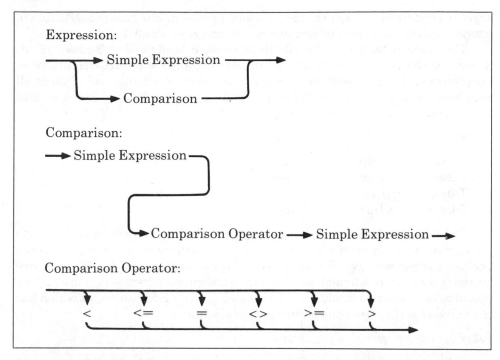

Figure 5.1. Syntax of Expressions

comparisons, are more correctly called simple expressions. An expression is either a simple expression or a comparison (see Figure 5.1). This syntax has two important consequences.

Firstly, comparison operators have the lowest priority of all operators in Pascal. Thus the expression 2*A<>B+C is entirely equivalent to the expression (2*A)<>(B+C).

Secondly, the convenient notations X<Y<Z, A>B>C, and so on, are not allowed in Pascal. We shall see in the next section how a double comparison such as Freezing<Temperature<Boiling can be expressed properly.

It must be clearly understood that, in a program, a comparison makes the computer produce a True or False result. When we write a comparison such as Temperature>Boiling we are *not* stating a fact. Rather, we are defining a condition which may or may not hold and which must be tested at that point in the program.

5.3 THE Boolean OPERATORS

It is often necessary to be able to construct Boolean expressions which involve more than a single comparison. The operators **and**, **or** and **not** allow us to express a condition of any complexity, along lines similar to the construction of Integer expressions. (**and**, **or** and **not** are all reserved words.)

The operator **and** takes two Boolean operands and yields a Boolean result which has the value True if and only if both operands are True. Definitions of Boolean operators are most easily given in the form of a 'truth table' listing all possible operand values and the corresponding results. For the operator **and** the truth table is:

x	y	x **and** y
False	False	False
False	True	False
True	False	False
True	True	True

The word 'or' has two meanings in English. In the inclusive sense we have phrases such as 'These clothes are suitable for summer or winter wear.' In the exclusive sense we have 'Either the world is flat or it is round.' The inclusive meaning has been adopted in Boolean Algebra and hence in Pascal. The operator **or** takes two Boolean operands and yields a Boolean result which has the value True if at least one of the operands is True:

x	y	x **or** y
False	False	False
False	True	True
True	False	True
True	True	True

The operator **not** takes a single Boolean operand and yields a Boolean result which is the opposite of the operand. For **not** the truth table is particularly simple:

x	**not** x
False	True
True	False

Using **and** we can recast the double comparison of the previous section in an acceptable form, as:

```
(Freezing < Temperature) and (Temperature < Boiling)
```

Note that the parentheses are necessary here, the reason being that the comparison operators are of lower priority than **and**. Without parentheses we would have:

```
Freezing < Temperature and Temperature < Boiling
```

which is equivalent to:

Freezing < (Temperature **and** Temperature) < Boiling

This is meaningless, because the operands of **and** must be Boolean, and syntactically incorrect, because the double comparison has been inadvertently reintroduced. To avoid such errors, comparisons used as operands of **and**, **or** and **not** must always be parenthesized in Pascal.

5.4 USING Boolean DATA

Boolean data may be used in all the ways previously described for Integer data. Boolean constants may be defined, for example:

Forever = False

Boolean variables may be declared, for example:

IsVoter, IsPeer, IsPrisoner, IsInsane: Boolean;

Boolean expressions may be computed and their values assigned to Boolean variables, for example:

IsVoter := (Age > 18) **and**
            not (IsPeer **or** IsPrisoner **or** IsInsane)

and Boolean values may be output by means of Write, for example:

Write (IsVoter)

The effect of writing a Boolean value is, naturally enough, to write either 'true' or 'false'.

We rely on the internal consistency of Pascal to avoid much tedious reworking of these ideas in the new context. Unfortunately, there is one minor restriction in Standard Pascal: Read cannot be used to read Boolean values. Although a nuisance, this does not create insuperable difficulties.

Refer to the collected syntax diagrams of Appendix 1.3 to see how Boolean operators fit into the syntax of expressions. The following are some of the most important consequences.

Firstly, **and** has the same priority as '*', **or** has the same priority as '+', and **not** has the highest priority of all operators in Pascal. Contrast the arithmetic expression −A*B+C, which is equivalent to (−(A*B))+C, with the Boolean expression **not** A **and** B **or** C, which is equivalent to ((**not** A) **and** B) **or** C.

Secondly, parentheses may be included to override these priorities and to clarify complicated expressions. For example, A **and** B **or** C **and** D is equivalent to (A **and** B) **or** (C **and** D).

Thirdly, any of the following may stand by itself as a **Boolean** expression: a **Boolean** constant, a **Boolean** variable, or a **Boolean** function.

A useful standard function is **Odd**, which takes an **Integer** parameter, yielding **True** if the parameter is an odd number and **False** otherwise. In fact $\text{Odd}(x)$ is equivalent to $((x) \bmod 2 <> 0)$.

Example 5.1

The following program writes out the truth table for the **Boolean** expression A **and not** B.

```
program TruthTable (Output);

var
   A, B: Boolean;

begin
Write ('A       B       A and not B'); WriteLn;
WriteLn;
A := False; B := False;
Write (A, B, A and not B); WriteLn;
B := True;
Write (A, B, A and not B); WriteLn;
A := True; B := False;
Write (A, B, A and not B); WriteLn;
B := True;
Write (A, B, A and not B); WriteLn
end (* TruthTable *).
```

5.5 THE RULES OF BOOLEAN ALGEBRA

{This section may be omitted on a first reading.}

There are many rules, or 'laws', defining relationships between **not**, **and** and **or** which are of importance in formulating, simplifying and understanding **Boolean** expressions. Several of these rules are closely analogous to rules in the algebra of arithmetic, which may be helpful in grasping their significance. Others have no helpful analogy.

The laws of Boolean Algebra are summarized below, the corresponding rules of arithmetic being given where possible. The symbol '$\equiv$' means 'is equivalent to'. In the cases which seem strange, it is a good idea to construct truth tables and so demonstrate their validity.

Redundancy laws

(R1) x **and** False $\equiv$ False   {c.f. $a \times 0 \equiv 0$}
(R2) x **and** True $\equiv x$ {c.f. $a \times 1 \equiv a$}
(R3) x **or** False $\equiv x$ {c.f. $a + 0 \equiv a$}
(R4) x **or** True $\equiv$ True   {There is no analogy in arithmetic}
(R5) x **and** $x \equiv x$ {No analogy}
(R6) x **or** $x \equiv x$ {No analogy}
(R7) x **and not** $x \equiv$ False   {No analogy}
(R8) x **or not** $x \equiv$ True   {No analogy}

Commutative laws

(C1) x **and** $y \equiv y$ **and** x {c.f. $a \times b \equiv b \times a$}
(C2) x **or** $y \equiv y$ **or** x {c.f. $a + b \equiv b + a$}

Associative laws

(A1) (x **and** y) **and** $z \equiv x$ **and** y **and** $z \equiv x$ **and** (y **and** z)
     {c.f. $(a \times b) \times c \equiv a \times b \times c \equiv a \times (b \times c)$}
(A2) (x **or** y) **or** $z \equiv x$ **or** y **or** $z \equiv x$ **or** (y **or** z)}
     {c.f. $(a + b) + c \equiv a + b + c \equiv a + (b + c)$}

Distributive laws

(D1) (x **and** y) **or** (x **and** z) $\equiv x$ **and** (y **or** z))
     {c.f. $(a \times b) + (a \times c) \equiv a \times (b + c)$}

E.g. (Married **and** (Salary $<=$ Limit)) **or** (Married **and** (Children > 1))
    $\equiv$ Married **and** ((Salary $<=$ Limit) **or** (Children > 1))

(D2) (x **or** y) **and** (x **or** z) $\equiv x$ **or** (y **and** z)
     {There is no analogy in arithmetic}

E.g. (British **or** SpeaksGaelic) **and** (British **or** SpeaksIrish)
    $\equiv$ British **or** (SpeaksGaelic **and** SpeaksIrish)

Involution law

(I1) **not** (**not** x) $\equiv x$ {c.f. $-(-a) \equiv a$}

E.g. **not** (**not** Married) $\equiv$ Married

De Morgan's laws

{Neither of these laws has an analogy in arithmetic}

(DeM1) **not** $(x$ **and** $y) \equiv$ **not** x **or not** y

E.g. **not** ((Freezing < Temperature) **and** (Temperature < Boiling))
    $\equiv$ **not**(Freezing < Temperature) **or not** (Temperature < Boiling)
    $\equiv$ (Freezing >= Temperature) **or** (Temperature >= Boiling)

(DeM2) **not** $(x$ **or** $y) \equiv$ **not** x **and not** y

E.g. **not** ((Salary <= Limit) **or** (Children > 1))
    $\equiv$ **not** (Salary <= Limit) **and not** (Children > 1)
    $\equiv$ (Salary > Limit) **and** (Children <= 1)

When Boolean values are compared by an operator implying relative magnitude (i.e. '<=', '<', '>=' or '>'), the result follows from the fact that, in Pascal, False is considered to be less than True. Since the results of such comparisons are themselves Boolean values, they can be defined by truth tables and have corresponding Boolean expressions. The table for '<=' follows as an example:

x	y	$x <= y$
False	False	True
False	True	True
True	False	False
True	True	True

From any truth table we can derive an equivalent expression in terms of **and**, **or** and **not**. Then, using the rules of Boolean Algebra, this can be converted to its simplest equivalent form. For the example of '<=' we work as follows; $x <= y$ has the value True if:

(a) x and y are both False, i.e. (**not** x **and not** y) is True; or
(b) x is False and y is True, i.e. (**not** x **and** y) is True; or
(c) x and y are both True, i.e. (x **and** y) is True.

Thus we can write:

$x <= y \equiv$ (**not** x **and not** y) **or** (**not** x **and** y) **or** (x **and** y)

We can now simplify this expression:

$x <= y \equiv$ **not** x **and** (**not** y **or** y) **or** (x **and** y)	{D1}
$\equiv$ **not** x **and** True **or** (x **and** y)	{C2, R8}
$\equiv$ **not** x **or** (x **and** y)	{R2}
$\equiv$ (**not** x **or** x) **and** (**not** x **or** y)	{D2}
$\equiv$ True **and** (**not** x **or** y)	{C2, R8}
$\equiv$ **not** x **or** y	{C1, R2}

The laws applied at each step are indicated on the right.

More simply, we can use the single False case: $x <= y$ is False only when x is True and y is False, i.e. only when (x **and not** y) is True. Thus we can write:

$$x <= y \equiv \textbf{not }(x\textbf{ and not }y) \equiv \textbf{not }x\textbf{ or }y \qquad \{\text{DeM1, I1}\}$$

Manipulations of expressions more complicated than this are unlikely to occur in practice. Indeed, complicated Boolean expressions may be symptomatic of flaws in the design of a program.

EXERCISES 5

5.1. Let Number be an Integer variable, and let Positive, Zero and Negative be Boolean variables. Write statements which will assign to Positive, Zero and Negative values which are True if the value of Number is, respectively, greater than zero, equal to zero, and less than zero.

5.2. Let Left be a Boolean variable and let PageNumber be an Integer variable. Write a statement which will assign to Left a Boolean value meaning 'the value of PageNumber is even'.

5.3. Let English, French and Monoglot be Boolean variables, where English means 'speaks English' and French means 'speaks French'. Write a statement which assigns to Monoglot a Boolean value meaning 'speaks English or French, but not both'. Note that this is an example of the exclusive sense of the word 'or', as mentioned in Section 5.3.

5.4. Write a program which reads two Integer numbers, and outputs 'true' if the first is a multiple of the second, and 'false' otherwise.

5.5. Write a program which reads two integers representing a date (month and day of the month), and outputs 'true' if that is the date of Christmas Day, and 'false' otherwise.

5.6. Assuming that an Integer variable Year contains the number of a year, write a statement which assigns to a Boolean variable LeapYear a value meaning 'the year is a leap year'. (a) Assume that any year whose number is a multiple of 4 is a leap year. (b*) More accurately, take into account the fact that years whose numbers are multiples of 100, but not of 400, are *not* leap years. (Thus 2000 will be a leap year, but 1700, 1800 and 1900 were not.)

{The following exercises should not be attempted until Section 5.5 has been read.}

5.7. Construct Boolean expressions for the other five comparison operators when applied to Boolean operands, as was done in Section 5.5 for ' $<=$ '.

5.8. Simplify the Boolean expressions $x=$ True, $x=$ False, $x<>$ True, and $x<>$ False. What conclusions can be drawn about the advisability of writing such expressions in programs?

5.9. Simplify the following Boolean expressions:

(a) $(a$ **or** $x)$ **and** $(b$ **or** $x)$ **and** $(c$ **or** $x)$
(b) b **or** **not** $(a$ **and** $b)$
(c*) a **and** x **or** b **and** x **or** c **and** x **or**
      a **and** y **or** b **and** y **or** c **and** y **or**
      a **and** c **or** b **and** c **or** c

6

Fundamental control structures

This chapter covers:

* the fundamental control structures—
  sequencing, repetition and selection
* the **while** statement
* the **if** statement
* nested control structures
* the compound statement
* the **repeat** statement (optional on a first reading)

6.1 CONTROL STRUCTURES

The programs in Chapters 4 and 5 had the simplest possible structure. Their statements were executed in textual order, so that every statement was obeyed once and only once. However, we have seen that selective and repetitive execution are necessary for practical use of a computer. We now turn to the language structures which allow this. They are called *control structures* because they control the order in which statements are obeyed.

In some programming languages (especially earlier ones such as FORTRAN and BASIC) it is necessary to describe selective and repetitive control structures in terms of very primitive statements, which are almost at the level of machine-code instructions. More modern languages, among them Pascal, have been designed to make life easier. They have notations—the **while** and **if** statements—that correspond exactly with repetitive and selective control structures.

6.2 REPETITIVE EXECUTION: THE while STATEMENT

The fundamental repetitive control structure in Pascal is the *while statement*. Its syntax is given in Figure 6.1. Note that **while** and **do** are both reserved words.

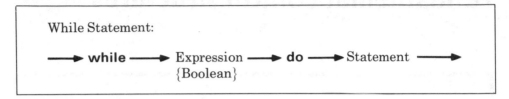

Figure 6.1. Syntax of the While Statement

The statement following **do** is called the *component statement* and specifies the action to be repeated. The expression following **while** gives the condition that must be satisfied if the statement is to be obeyed. In detail, the sequence of operations is as follows:

(1) Test the condition. If it is False: continue from step (4).
(2) Obey the component statement, knowing the condition to be True.
(3) Repeat from step (1).
(4) Knowing the condition to be False, go on with the rest of the program.

Because of the link back from step (3) to step (1) repetitive control structures have come to be called *loops*. The component statement must be such that eventually (i.e. on the last repetition) it does something to make the condition False. Failure to do this results in an *infinite loop* which is obeyed indefinitely, thus preventing further progress through the program.

The syntax of the **while** statement requires the repeated action to be given by a *single* statement, but we often want to repeat a group of statements. This requirement is met by the *compound statement*, whose only significance is to cause a sequence of statements to be treated as a single statement for syntactic

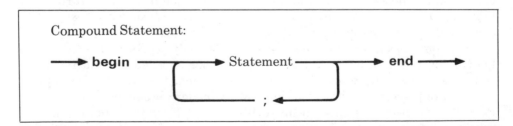

Figure 6.2. Syntax of the Compound Statement

purposes. This is done by bracketing the statement sequence between the reserved words **begin** and **end** (see Figure 6.2).

Example 6.1

Pascal does not provide an operator to calculate powers of numbers. The following will calculate the B-th power of A for non-negative values of B (so that the result is an integer). A, B, I and Power are Integer variables.

```
Power := 1; I := 0;
while I < B do
  begin
  Power := Power * A;
  I := I + 1
  end
```

We can check this solution by tracing through it with at least two test cases. Let us try B=0, and some B greater than 0, e.g. B=2. In either case Power is initially set to 1 and I to 0. Suppose A contains 7.

If B is 0 the **while** condition, I < B, already has the value False, so that the body of the loop is not obeyed. Thus the final value of Power is 1, which is correct.

If B is 2 the **while** condition has the value True and the body of the loop is obeyed. This alters Power to 7 and I to 1. Again the condition is tested and found to be True. The body of the loop then alters Power to 49 and I to 2. On the third repetition the **while** condition is found to be False and the loop terminates. The final value of Power is 49, which is also correct.

Study this program fragment carefully and convince yourself that the loop will always terminate and deliver the correct result, for any non-negative value of B. In particular, trace through it with A=3, B=1 and A=3, B=4.

It is usually more convenient to set down the results of tracing in a tabular form. A column is used to represent the successive values of each variable, the current value being that written lowest-down in the column. Each row shows the outcome of obeying a statement or testing a condition. The current statement or condition is shown in the first column, the second column being used for the value of the condition. If you feel it tedious to write and rewrite the same statements you may prefer to number them and record their numbers in the first column. Figure 6.3 repeats the checks on Example 6.1, in tabular form.

Example 6.2

The following program reads a list of numbers and writes their sum. To allow for varying amounts of data, the first data item is a number giving the size of

(a) A=7, B=0

Position	Condition	I	Power
Power := 1			1
I := 0		0	
{**while**} I < B	false		

(b) A=7, B=2

Position	Condition	I	Power
Power := 1			1
I := 0		0	
{**while**} I < B	true		
Power := Power*A			7
I := I+1		1	
{**while**} I < B	true		
Power := Power*A			49
I := I+1		2	
{**while**} I < B	false		

Figure 6.3. Checking Example 6.1

the list which follows it; for example:

    4
    15   21   13   6

```
program SumByCount (Input, Output);

var
    Sum, Summand, Count, Size: Integer;

begin
Sum := 0;
Count := 0;
```

```
(* read the size of the list *)
Read (Size);

while Count < Size do
   (* read the next Summand and add it to Sum *)
   begin
   Read (Summand);
   Sum := Sum + Summand;
   Count := Count + 1
   end;

Write ('Sum of integers read is', Sum); WriteLn
end (* SumByCount *).
```

The variable Count is used to keep track of how far through the data the program has reached. Just before the statements:

```
Read (Summand);
Sum := Sum + Summand
```

are executed, the value of Count is the number of entries in the list that have already been processed. After these statements, the program increases Count to correct it for the entry that has just been processed. Since Count starts at zero, and increases by one each time round the loop, it will become equal to Size after Size repetitions. Therefore Count < Size will be False, and the loop will terminate, after having read and processed exactly Size entries.

The method of indicating the end of a list used in SumByCount has the disadvantage that someone has to count the data. This is liable to error and may be impractical if there is a large quantity of data. An alternative approach is to mark the end of the list in some way the program can detect. If all the data are known to be positive numbers, a negative number could be used as an end-marker; for example:

    15   21   13   6   −1

Example 6.3 illustrates the idea.

Example 6.3

```
program SumToMarker (Input, Output);

var
   Sum, Summand: Integer;
```

```
begin
Sum := 0;

(* read the first integer in the list *)
Read (Summand);
while Summand >= 0 do
   (* add a Summand to Sum and read the next *)
   begin
   Sum := Sum + Summand;
   Read (Summand)
   end;

Write ('Sum of Integers read is ', Sum); WriteLn
end (* SumToMarker *).
```

SumToMarker is simpler than SumByCount: no auxiliary variables such as Count and Size are needed. However, in SumToMarker the variable Summand has two distinct meanings at different times. Usually it contains a data item to be added to Sum, but right at the end of the list it contains an end-marker which must *not* be added to Sum. The logic of the **while** statement takes care of this, although the repeated statement looks a little strange: it first adds Summand to Sum and *then* reads a number into Summand! This can work only if there is already a number in Summand when the loop is first entered, as is the case here.

A deficiency of SumToMarker is that it cannot process negative numbers, which it treats as end-markers. In general, it is difficult to find an end-marker that could never be confused with data. Fortunately, Pascal provides a way to detect the end of the input which is independent of the data itself: this is the standard **Boolean** function EOF ('End Of File'). EOF(Input) has the value True if and only if all the input data has been read. Its use is illustrated by Example 6.4.

Beware! SumToEOF, unlike SumByCount and SumToMarker, requires each number to be on a separate line of input. This is because, when reading numbers, the EOF test should be used only if the most recent input operation was ReadLn, rather than Read. This requirement will be explained in Section 8.2. Typical input to SumToEOF would be:

15
21
13
 6

Example 6.4

```
program SumToEOF (Input, Output);
```

```
var
   Sum, Summand: Integer;

begin
Sum := 0;

while not EOF(Input) do
   (* read the next Summand and add it to Sum *)
   begin
   Read (Summand);
   Sum := Sum + Summand;
   ReadLn
   end;

Write ('Sum of integers read is ', Sum); WriteLn
end (* SumToEOF *).
```

Note that SumToEOF combines the natural structure of SumByCount and the simplicity of SumToMarker.

Examples 6.2, 6.3 and 6.4 illustrate themes which appear in almost all programs. For this reason they are worth careful study. Hand-test them yourself, in the manner shown for Example 6.1. In particular, verify that they are correct: (a) when the list of numbers to be read is empty; (b) when there is just one number in the list; and (c) when there are several.

6.3 SELECTIVE EXECUTION: THE if STATEMENT

In Pascal, selective execution is programmed using the *if statement*, which has the syntax given in Figure 6.4. **if**, **then** and **else** are all reserved words.

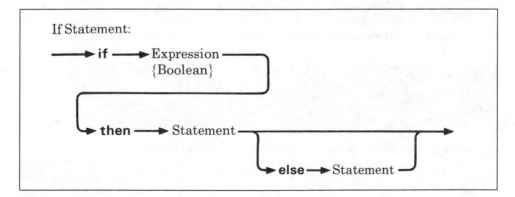

Figure 6.4. Syntax of the If Statement

The expression following **if** represents the condition to be tested. The statement following **then** is executed only if the condition has the value True; otherwise the statement following **else** is executed (or none, if there is no **else** part). In more detail the sequence of operations is as follows:

(1) Test the condition.
(2) If it is True; obey the **then** part, and continue from step (4).
(3) If it is False; obey the **else** part, and continue from step (4).
(4) Go on with the rest of the program; nothing can be assumed about the value of the condition.

When the **else** part is absent this simplifies to:

(1) Test the condition.
(2) If it is True: obey the **then** part.
(3) Go on with the rest of the program; nothing can be assumed about the value of the condition.

The syntax, like that of Figure 6.1, forces the alternative actions to be specified by single statements. If either alternative action is required to consist of a number of statements, the remedy is the same: use **begin ... end** brackets to make a sequence of statements into a single (compound) statement.

Example 6.5

The following statement sets X to the larger of Y and Z:

```
if Y > Z then
   X := Y
else
   X := Z
```

Replacing Z by X throughout, we get a statement which sets X to the larger of Y and itself:

```
if Y > X then
   X := Y
else
   X := X
```

Since the **else** part has no useful effect, it should be omitted:

```
if Y > X then
   X := Y
```

Example 6.6

The following statements write suitable messages according to the value of
Score:

```
if Score > 70 then
   Write ('excellent');
if Score < 30 then
   Write ('dismal');
if (Score <= 70) and (Score >= 30) then
   Write ('typical')
```

There is much redundancy in these statements. When **Score** exceeds 70
there is no point in making the two further tests of its value, both of which must
give **False**. Similarly, once **Score** is known to be less than 30 the test in the final
if statement is futile. This is an example of a very common situation: testing for
one of several *mutually exclusive* conditions, with an appropriate action for
each. It can be written more concisely using **else**:

```
if Score > 70 then
   Write ('excellent')
else
if Score < 30 then
   Write ('dismal')
else
   Write ('typical')
```

In this form the expression Score < 30 is evaluated only if necessary and no
test at all is required for the third alternative.

In Example 6.6 the use of separate **if** statements with mutually exclusive
conditions was clumsy rather than erroneous. Example 6.7 illustrates a situation in which separate **if** statements *are* erroneous.

Example 6.7

The following statement increments A if it is negative and decrements A if it is
positive or zero:

```
if A < 0 then
   A := A + 1
else
   A := A - 1
```

Compare its effect with that of the following two sequences:

```
if A < 0 then                    if A >= 0 then
   A := A + 1;                      A := A - 1;
if A >= 0 then                   if A < 0 then
   A := A - 1                       A := A + 1
```

when the value of A is initially (a) 0; and (b) −1. (The reason for the difference is that the component statements change the values of the variables being tested.)

Example 6.8

A common and quite subtle error is to try something along these lines:

```
if (Tally <> 0) and (Total div Tally > Threshold) then
   Write ('acceptable average')
else
   Write ('unacceptable average')
```

The mistake is that, when Tally is zero, Total **div** Tally causes an attempt to divide by zero (usually with disastrous results). In cases like this the two parts of the condition must be separated:

```
if Tally <> 0 then
   if Total div Tally > Threshold then
      Write ('acceptable average')
   else
      Write ('unacceptable average')
```

An ambiguity lurking in the syntax of Figure 6.4 now comes to light! In a statement with the following structure:

```
if ... then if ... then ... else ...
```

to which **if** does the **else** correspond? Pascal has the reasonable (though arbitrary) rule that in such a case the **else** goes with the closest **if**. We have anticipated this in the indentation of Example 6.8. Compare that with Example 6.9.

Example 6.9

```
if Tally <> 0 then
   begin
```

```
   if Total div Tally > Threshold then
       Write ('acceptable average')
   end
else
   Write ('nothing to find the average of')
```

It is advisable, in all doubtful cases, to make the meaning perfectly clear by liberal use of the statement brackets **begin** and **end**.

6.4 NESTED CONTROL STRUCTURES

Very often a programming problem will demand both repetition and selection for its solution. There is no difficulty about this. Remember that the **while** and **if** constructs both *contain* statements and *are themselves* statements. Thus a **while** can govern an **if** or another **while** and an **if** can govern a **while** or another **if** (as we have already seen). Structures of any complexity can be built up in this way, each statement being *nested* within another. When it is necessary to govern a sequence of statements, rather than just one, the compound statement allows this to be done.

Example 6.10

Program Display is to read a sequence of integers, terminated by a negative end-marker. When a positive number is read, that many asterisks are to be written. Zeros are to be written numerically. {The effect is to display the data as a bar-chart, or histogram, thus making it easier for the user to assimilate.}

```
program Display (Input, Output);

var
   StarCount, WidthOfBar: Integer;

begin
(* read the first WidthOfBar *)
Read (WidthOfBar);
while WidthOfBar >= 0 do
   begin
   (* output a representation of WidthOfBar *)
   if WidthOfBar = 0 then
      (* output WidthOfBar in numerical form *)
      Write (WidthOfBar: 1)
```

```
    else
      (* output a row of WidthOfBar asterisks *)
      begin
      Write ('   ');
      StarCount := 0;
      while StarCount < WidthOfBar do
        begin
        Write ('*');
        StarCount := StarCount + 1
        end
      end;
    (* start a new line of output *)
    WriteLn;
    (* read the next WidthOfBar *)
    Read (WidthOfBar)
    end
  end (* Display *).
```

Note the layout of program Display. Here, as in the preceding examples, the repeated statements in loops have been indented relative to the **while** symbol. Similarly, the alternative statements in selections have been indented relative to the **if** and **else** symbols. This convention shows clearly how much of the text is actually included in each construct and makes the program much easier to read.

It is essential to adopt a methodical approach when writing relatively complicated programs like Display. Methodical programming is the topic of the following chapter.

6.5 THE repeat STATEMENT

{This section may be omitted on a first reading.}

We have already seen that with the **while** construct it is possible for the number of repetitions to be zero. For example, in:

```
while R >= N do
  R := R-N
```

the statement $R := R-N$ will not be executed at all if the condition $R >= N$ is initially False.

Usually this does exactly what we need. However, there are circumstances in which the special case with no repetitions is known to be impossible, and it would be more natural to use a construct that guarantees at least one repetition. In Pascal this is the *repeat statement*.

The syntax of **repeat** statements is given in Figure 6.5. Note that several

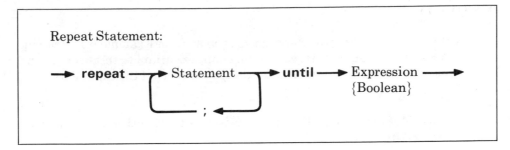

Figure 6.5. Syntax of Repeat Statements

statements may be placed inside the loop, without **begin . . . end** brackets, since **repeat** and **until** themselves act as statement brackets. **repeat** and **until** are both reserved words.

The sequence of operations is as follows:

(1) Obey the statement(s) between **repeat** and **until**.
(2) Test the condition. If it is False: repeat from step (1).
(3) Knowing the condition to be True, go on with the rest of the program.

Compare this sequence of operations with that of the **while** statement (see Section 6.2). The principal difference is this: in the **while** statement the loop condition is tested *before* each repetition of the loop; in the **repeat** statement the loop condition is tested *after* each repetition of the loop. This distinction is emphasized by the position of the **while** clause at the beginning of the **while** statement and the position of the **until** clause at the end of the **repeat** statement. Note also that the **repeat** loop terminates when its condition is found to be True, the opposite of the case with the **while** statement.

Example 6.11

In program Display, Example 6.10, the inner loop outputs a row of asterisks. Each time the **while** statement is obeyed the component statement is executed at least once, so the loop could be rewritten as a **repeat** statement:

```
repeat
    Write ('*');
    StarCount := StarCount + 1
until StarCount >= WidthOfBar
```

The advantage of this version is that it exhibits very clearly the fact that at least one asterisk will be output. Using **while**, it is necessary to analyse almost the whole program to deduce the same fact.

EXERCISES 6

6.1. Work systematically through program Display from Example 6.10, tracing the actions of the computer as it reads data, changes variables, tests conditions and writes output. Show exactly what output is produced if the input data is:

    5   17   9   6   0   1   −1

{Check your solutions to the following exercises by tracing through them with suitable input data.}

6.2. What does program Display do if a large number is included in the input data? Modify the program to make it write numerically any number which is too large. Choose as a limit a value which does not exceed the width of a line on whatever output device you use.

6.3. Write a program fragment which computes the factorial of N, given that the value of N is a positive integer. (The factorial of N is the product 1*2*...*(N−1)*N.)

6.4. Given that the value of N is a positive integer, write a program fragment which determines how many decimal digits are needed to write down the value of N. (For example, 99 needs two digits, and 100 needs three digits.)

6.5. Write a program fragment which outputs 'positive', 'negative' or 'zero', depending on the value of N.

6.6. Write a program fragment which reads three integers representing today's date (day, month and year), followed by three integers representing a person's birth-date, and which outputs that person's age in years.

6.7. Write programs to read a list of positive integers and output the largest of them: (a) when the size of the list is given as the first datum; (b) when the list is terminated by a negative number; (c) using EOF.

6.8. If you have read Section 6.5, recast your answers to Exercise 6.7 so that the programs will output a suitable message if the list to be examined is empty.

PROGRAMMING EXERCISES 6

6.9. Modify your program of Exercise 4.6 to write the time in terms of the 12-hour clock rather than the 24-hour clock. (For example, write '10:50:30 P.M.' rather than '22:50:30'.)

6.10. (a) Write a program which reads an integer N and produces a table of the first N positive powers of 2. (b) Write a program which reads an integer N and produces a table of the positive powers of 2 which are less than or equal to N.

6.11. Details taken from an invoice are supplied as input data. Each line of input contains the number of units of one item invoiced, followed by the unit price of that item (in pence or cents). Write a program which will read this data, output the data in tabular form, and finally output the total amount invoiced. Use EOF(Input) to detect the end of the input data.

7

Programming methodically

This is a very important chapter. It introduces themes that are developed throughout the rest of the book:

* methodical program development
* stepwise refinement
* how to make refinements
* how to test programs
* how to correct errors

You should familiarize yourself with this material before going on to learn much more Pascal, and you may want to review it after reading Chapter 18

7.1 STEPWISE REFINEMENT

So far in this book we have looked at some of the basic features of Pascal. These are, if you like, the building blocks of the language, and we have demonstrated their use by writing a number of programs. We have also touched on the matter of programming style, showing how it affects the readability of programs.

It is one thing to *read* a simple example program and understand what it does. But the real question is, how do we go about *writing* a program from scratch, to satisfy a given problem specification? For very small programs, a little careful thought, coupled perhaps with a flash or two of insight, might be sufficient to produce a rough solution. This can then be tried out on a computer. The program is likely to contain errors, however, and these have to be discovered and corrected. Often this is tedious and haphazard.

Such an *ad hoc* approach might be all right for very small programs (up to about 50 lines, say). But when we attempt to write larger programs, a more methodical approach becomes essential. We now consider how to achieve this.

First of all we must be clear about our objectives in writing programs. A program must, above all, be *correct*. There can be no argument about this: correctness is the overriding, indisputable objective. A program that produces wrong results is unacceptable.

A second objective is *efficiency*. It is little use having a program that calculates a weekly payroll perfectly correctly if it takes nine days to process the data! Nor would a cash-dispenser program or an airline reservation program be very useful if it took an hour to perform each transaction.

A third objective is that a program should be *easy to modify*. Modifiability is important because, during the life of the program, it might have to be adapted to deal with changes in the 'real world'. As a simple example, suppose that a company has five departments. The payroll program has been written with numerous occurrences of the constant 5 (for example, in **while** DeptNo <= 5 **do** ...). If the company now sets up another department, the programmer will have to go through the program line by line, changing each 5 to 6. (Not *every* occurrence of 5, of course—some occurrences might relate to the number of working days in a week!) It would have been preferable if the program had been written in the first place using a constant identifier NrOfDepts (for example, **while** DeptNo <= NrOfDepts **do** ...), with a constant definition NrOfDepts = 5 at the head of the program. Then only this single occurrence of 5 would have to be changed. The program would be more easily modifiable. Associated with this objective is *readability*. This is dependent on the programming style. A readable program is relatively easy to understand and hence to modify.

In many cases the objectives of efficiency, modifiability and readability must be traded off one against another, until a working compromise is achieved. However, there can never be any compromise about correctness.

These objectives are not easy to achieve. You are faced not only with the problem of getting the program to work correctly, which requires thorough testing. You must also bear in mind that, in the future, the program will have to be modified in unforseen ways. And, as if that is not enough, you must also make sure that the program is reasonably efficient. The task is daunting. For that reason, a wise programmer adopts any methods that will simplify the task.

Several different techniques of methodical programming have been devised. Really, the particular method chosen matters less than the fact that it is used consistently. In this book we advocate a method that is both simple and effective. It is known as *stepwise refinement*.

The basic idea of stepwise refinement is to break a problem down into a set of smaller *subproblems*. Assume for the moment that each of these subproblems will eventually be solved. Then we have achieved an outline solution to the original problem. We call this the *Level 1 outline* of the solution.

We now examine each of the subproblems in turn. If a subproblem is trivial, then we can write down its solution directly. If a subproblem is non-trivial, then we break it down further, into a set of smaller subproblems. If all the new subproblems can eventually be solved, then we have achieved a more detailed outline solution, the *Level 2 outline*.

We repeat the refinement process as long as necessary to reduce the original problem down to trivial subproblems. This completes the solution of the original problem.

Now we look at a simple example to illustrate programming by stepwise refinement.

THE STEPWISE REFINEMENT OF PROGRAM Display

The Display program from Example 6.10 was developed along the following lines. The program is to read and process a sequence of numbers, terminated by a negative end-marker. This at once suggests a loop, in fact the sort of loop used in Example 6.3. Each repetition of the loop processes a number, let us call it WidthOfBar (remembering it will have to be declared as an Integer variable). The value of WidthOfBar is to be represented by writing it out as a row of the histogram. To give the correct format each number should be represented on a separate line. Having output one number, the loop must read in the next. These considerations lead to the following sketch of the program.

Level 1 outline

```
program Display (Input, Output);
declarations;
begin
read the first WidthOfBar;
while not end of data do
  begin
  output a representation of WidthOfBar;
  start of a new line of output;
  read the next WidthOfBar
  end
end (* Display *).
```

This is intended to be a self-explanatory outline of the program. Material in upper case is already formalized in terms of Pascal. Material in lower case is informally descriptive of some action to be performed or some expression to be evaluated—the context should make clear which. For example, 'not end of data' must represent a Boolean expression which we are to interpret in terms of the end-of-data condition. At the moment it does not matter how the condition is to be detected: any valid implementation will result in a correct program. In the same way, 'output a representation of WidthOfBar' represents a statement which, we are to assume, will write out one row of the histogram.

The whole program can now be checked before any further refinements are made. This is done by tracing through it with sample data, just as we would do with the final program. Only when satisfied that the outline is correct do we continue with the refinement. Should any error be found it must be corrected in the Level 1 outline, *before* going on to produce Level 2. Program outlines should not be treated as provisional drafts of a solution, nor should refinements be thought of as amendments and corrections. Each outline of the program should be both correct and complete, given its level of detail. Check Level 1 now, using the data given in Exercise 6.1.

Refinements from Level 1

The most complex step in Level 1 is 'output a representation of WidthOfBar', so we shall refine that first. When WidthOfBar is positive a row of that many asterisks is to be written; when it is zero its value is to be output numerically.

Refinement 1.1: output a representation of WidthOfBar

```
if WidthOfBar = 0 then
    output WidthOfBar in numerical form
else
    output WidthOfBar asterisks
```

Each of the remaining components of Level 1 can be trivially expanded into Pascal. They are then complete and need no further development.

Refinement 1.2: read the next WidthOfBar

```
Read (WidthOfBar)
```

Refinement 1.3: start a new line of output

```
WriteLn
```

Refinement 1.4: not end of data

```
WidthOfBar >= 0
```

Refinement 1.5: read the first WidthOfBar

```
Read (WidthOfBar)
```

Replacing each of these components in the Level 1 outline by its refinement we get a more detailed outline of the program at Level 2. To show how it was derived we include appropriate comments.

Level 2 outline

```
program Display (Input, Output);
declarations;
begin
(* read the first WidthOfBar *)
Read (WidthOfBar);
while WidthOfBar >= 0 do
  begin
  (* output a representation of WidthOfBar *)
  if WidthOfBar = 0 then
    output WidthOfBar in numerical form
  else
    output WidthOfBar asterisks;
  (* start a new line of output *)
  WriteLn;
  (* read the next WidthOfBar *)
  Read (WidthOfBar)
  end
end (* Display *).
```

This must be checked before continuing the refinement. Try it now, using the same data as before.

Refinements from Level 2

Only two components of Level 2 can be refined at this point. Again, we start with the more complex: 'output WidthOfBar asterisks'. A single asterisk is easily output by the statement Write('*'); to output several we must include this in a count-controlled loop (compare Example 6.2). This will require more than one statement, so it will all have to be enclosed in **begin** and **end** brackets.

Refinement 2.1: output WidthOfBar asterisks

```
begin
prepare to output the row;
while WidthOfBar asterisks have not yet been written do
    output another asterisk
end
```

Refinement 2.2: output WidthOfBar in numerical form

    Write (WidthOfBar:1)

Level 3 outline

```
program Display (Input, Output);
declarations;
begin
(* read the first WidthOfBar *)
Read (WidthOfBar);
while WidthOfBar >= 0 do
   begin
   (* output a representation of WidthOfBar *)
   if WidthOfBar = 0 then
      (* output WidthOfBar in numerical form *)
      Write (WidthOfBar:1)
   else
      begin (* output WidthOfBar asterisks *)
      prepare to output the row;
      while WidthOfBar asterisks have not yet been written do
         output another asterisk
      end;
   (* start a new line of output *)
   WriteLn;
   (* read the next WidthOfBar *)
   Read (WidthOfBar)
   end
end (* Display *).
```

Once again, check this before we go on to Level 4.

Refinements from Level 3

To record the number of asterisks that have been output by the inner **while**
loop the program must keep a tally of them in a suitable variable. Thus we
introduce the Integer variable StarCount (remembering that it will have to be
declared). Each time a row of asterisks is begun StarCount will start off at zero;
each time an asterisk is output it will be incremented by one. Thus the value of
StarCount represents the number of asterisks already output in the current
row.

Refinement 3.1: WidthOfBar asterisks have not yet been written

StarCount < WidthOfBar

Refinement 3.2: output another asterisk

```
begin
  Write ('*');
  StarCount := StarCount + 1
end
```

The preparation for each row must include zeroizing **StarCount**. Another point: zeros are output in a field of one column (see Refinement 2.2). To preserve the format of the bar-chart a blank should therefore be output before each row of asterisks.

Refinement 3.3: prepare to output the row

```
Write ('  ');
StarCount := 0
```

The whole program has now been converted to Pascal code, with the exception of the declarations. Since we know all the variables needed we can finally write:

Refinement 3.4: declarations

```
var
  StarCount, WidthOfBar: Integer
```

This completes the stepwise refinement of program **Display**. Checking the complete program has already been set as Exercise 6.1.

Perhaps you feel that writing such a small program in this manner is taking a sledgehammer to crack a nut. Indeed, programs the size of **Display** can be written by skilled programmers after only a moment's forethought. This is just an application of the rule in stepwise refinement that, if a subproblem is trivial, you can write down its solution directly. Exactly what constitutes a trivial subproblem depends on the circumstances. While you are still unfamiliar with the Pascal language and with stepwise refinement, you will probably want to carry out refinements in detail, writing complete program outlines at each level. As you gain experience and confidence, much of this will become unnecessary and the refinement process can be much more concise.

Be assured that, for programs of a more realistic size and complexity than **Display**, stepwise refinement is immensely helpful. In the meantime the discipline it imposes may be tedious. Persevere, and you will reap the rewards later.

7.2 CASE STUDY I: THE TRAFFIC SURVEY PROBLEM

PROBLEM SPECIFICATION

A traffic survey is conducted automatically by placing a vehicle detector at the roadside, connected by data link to a computer. A clock in the detector is started at the beginning of a survey. Every second thereafter the detector transmits a signal which the computer reads as the number 1. Whenever a vehicle passes, the detector transmits a signal which is read as the number 2. At the end of the survey the detector transmits a terminator signal which is read as the number 0. (Assume that no two signals exactly coincide.)

The following diagram illustrates a possible sequence of events, 'V' indicating the passage of a vehicle:

```
start  V            VV   V V         V            end
  ↓    ↓            ↓↓   ↓ ↓         ↓             ↓
  ├────┼────┼────┼────┼────┼────┼────┼────┼──────→ time (marked off
                                                       in seconds)
```

The corresponding sequence of signals sent to the computer would be:

2 1 1 2 2 1 2 2 1 1 2 1 1 0

Due to transmission errors a signal may occasionally be received as a number greater than 2.

The problem is to write a program which reads such a set of signals and outputs the following:

(a) The length of the survey period.
(b) The number of vehicles recorded.
(c) The length of the longest interval in which no vehicles pass. The length of a vehicle-free interval is to be taken simply as the number of timing signals received during this period. For example, the above data contains one 1-second interval, two 2-second intervals and one 3-second interval.
(d) The number of transmission errors. An error signal is to be taken as terminating a vehicle-free interval. (This prevents corrupted vehicle signals from exaggerating the length of vehicle-free intervals.)

Thus with the input data cited above, the expected results are:

(a) 8, (b) 6, (c) 3, and (d) 0.

If the third of the vehicle signals were corrupted, however, the expected results would be:

(a) 8, (b) 5, (c) 3, and (d) 1.

SOLUTION

One of the most helpful ways to start on the development of a program is to think carefully about the data it must process. Once you have a good understanding of the data, you can go on to write a Level 1 outline that has an appropriate structure.

In this case, perhaps the simplest way of looking at the data is as a random sequence of timing signals, vehicle signals and error signals—a simple list of positive numbers, terminated by a zero. This immediately suggests a **while** loop of the form used in Example 6.3.

An alternative understanding of the data is possible, and leads to a different program. The version developed here we shall call Traffic(a). The alternative, which we call Traffic(b), is developed in Exercise 7.2.

Level 1a outline

```
program Traffic (Input, Output);
declarations;
begin
prepare to process signals;
while not end of data do
    process one signal and read the next;
output the results
end.
```

As an exercise, devise some test data and use it to work through the Level 1a outline. What properties of the program can you check at this stage?

Refinements from Level 1a

Since the other elements seem to be quite simple, we tackle 'process one signal and read the next' first. The signal to be processed could be a timing signal, a vehicle signal or an error signal. This suggests that the refinement should be in terms of **if** statements, with 'process a timing signal', 'process an error signal' and 'process a vehicle signal' as the components.

Refinement 1.1a: process one signal and read the next

```
begin
if it is a vehicle signal then
    process a vehicle signal
else
if it is an error signal then
    process an error signal
```

```
else
    process a timing signal;
read the next signal
end
```

Level 2a is derived by substituting this in Level 1a. As an exercise, write out the Level 2a outline in full, and check it with your test data.

Refinements from Level 2a

Remembering that one objective is to measure vehicle-free intervals, we see that 'process a vehicle signal', 'process an error signal' and 'process a timing signal' must interact in such a way that the start and end of each interval can be recognized. Define the *current interval* to be that which has elapsed since the most recent vehicle signal or error signal, and let Interval be an Integer variable whose value is the length in seconds of the current interval. Interval must be set to zero at the start of each vehicle-free interval (i.e. on receiving each vehicle or error signal), and 'process a timing signal' must increment it by one (as the timing signals come once a second). To count the vehicles and the errors, and to note the total elapsed time, we need three more Integer variables: Vehicles, Errors and Seconds.

Refinement 2.1a: process a timing signal

```
begin
Seconds := Seconds + 1;
Interval := Interval + 1
end
```

A vehicle signal marks the end of one vehicle-free interval and the start of another. It is necessary to check the length of the interval just ended.

Refinement 2.2a: process a vehicle signal

```
begin
Vehicles := Vehicles + 1;
check the length of the interval;
Interval := 0
end
```

Processing an error signal is analogous to Refinement 2.2a.

Refinement 2.3a: process an error signal

```
begin
Errors := Errors + 1;
```

```
check the length of the interval;
Interval := 0
end
```

Substituting these refinements in Level 2a gives us Level 3a. As an exercise, write out Level 3a in full, and check it with your test data.

Refinements from Level 3a

The length of the current interval is held in Interval. At the end of each interval we must check to see whether this is greater than the longest interval so far recorded. We introduce the Integer variable Longest to hold the latter.

Refinement 3.1a: check the length of the interval

```
if Interval > Longest then
    Longest := Interval
```

We now introduce an Integer variable, Signal, to hold the current signal number. To make the program more flexible, and easier to understand, we also introduce constants Terminator (equal to 0), TimingSignal (equal to 1) and VehicleSignal (equal to 2).

Refinement 3.2a: it is a vehicle signal

```
Signal = VehicleSignal
```

Refinement 3.3a: it is an error signal

```
Signal > VehicleSignal
```

Refinement 3.4a: not end of data

```
Signal <> Terminator
```

Refinement 3.5a: read the next signal

```
Read (Signal)
```

Refinement 3.6a: output the results

The details depend entirely on the layout required, but this has not been specified. One possibility is shown in the complete program below.

Refinement 3.7a: prepare to process signals

```
Vehicles := 0;
Errors := 0;
```

```
Seconds := 0;
Longest := 0;
Interval := 0;
Read (Signal)
```

Refinement 3.8a: declarations

```
const
   Terminator = 0;
   TimingSignal = 1;
   VehicleSignal = 2;
var
   Vehicles, Errors, Seconds,
            Longest, Interval, Signal : Integer
```

Putting all of this together, we get a complete Pascal program.

Complete program for ***Traffic***(a)

```
program Traffic (Input, Output);
const
   Terminator    = 0;
   TimingSignal  = 1;
   VehicleSignal = 2;
var
   Vehicles, Errors, Seconds, Longest, Interval, Signal : Integer;
begin
(* prepare to process signals *)
Vehicles := 0;
Errors := 0;
Seconds := 0;
Longest := 0;
Interval := 0;
Read (Signal);
while Signal <> Terminator do
   begin (* process one signal and read the next *)
   if Signal = VehicleSignal then
      begin (* process a vehicle signal *)
      Vehicles := Vehicles + 1;
      if Interval > Longest then
         Longest := Interval;
      Interval := 0
      end
   else
```

```
    if Signal > VehicleSignal then
        begin (* process an error signal *)
        Errors := Errors + 1;
        if Interval > Longest then
            Longest := Interval;
        Interval := 0
        end
    else
        begin (* process a timing signal *)
        Seconds := Seconds + 1;
        Interval := Interval + 1
        end;
    (* read the next signal *)
    Read (Signal)
    end;
(* output the results *)
Write ('            No. Of        No. Of        Elapsed        Longest');
WriteLn;
Write ('            Vehicles        Errors        Time        Gap');
WriteLn;
Write (Vehicles:12, Errors:12, Seconds:12, Longest:12);
WriteLn
end (* Traffic(a) *).
```

We have presented the development of Traffic(a) in detail so that you can see exactly what is happening. In future examples we shall be less rigorous, presenting only the important features of the development process. Feel free to take the same approach yourself.

7.3 MAKING REFINEMENTS

The question we must now examine is, how do we choose refinements? Although choosing refinements becomes easier with practice, like many skills, the novice needs some guidelines to get started. The first point to remember is to look for familiar themes. Some common themes (for example, sorting and searching) crop up again and again as subproblems. If you identify a subproblem that you have previously solved, you can use the same solution again. A word of warning, though. Sometimes a small difference in the problem requires a very different solution. Always guard against using a stock solution without carefully thinking about whether it is suitable for the current problem.

Here is an encouraging observation. Every solution is composed from three basic structures, which we have already met. These are the sequence, selection and repetition. There is no problem that cannot be solved in terms of these structures. Making a refinement step now appears at least somewhat easier. The choice is from only three possibilities, and that makes the programmer's task more manageable.

Care is still needed, of course. Apparently the simplest kind of refinement is to split an action into several steps, to be performed in sequence. For example:

```
read all input data;
perform calculations;
write all results
```

This implies that all the input data and all the results are held in storage throughout the calculation step. For some problems, this solution is perfectly appropriate. But for other problems it would be absurd. Consider a payroll program performing a simple calculation on each of thousands of employee records! In such cases it would be more appropriate to choose a loop in which the reading, calculation and writing are interleaved:

```
while input data remains to be read do
   begin
   read some input data;
   perform calculations;
   write some results
   end
```

Another point worth watching is whether the sequencing is correct. For example, the following is obviously wrong:

```
write results;
perform calculations;
read input data
```

However, other sequencing errors are less obvious, so care is needed.

A common pattern is of the form:

```
preparation;
while continuation condition do
   repeated action;
finalization
```

Here the loop does most of the work, but the preparation may be needed to start things going, and the finalization may be needed to tidy up afterwards.

In refining such a pattern, it is usually best to start with the continuation condition, then refine the repeated action, and last of all the preparation and finalization. The repeated action must be programmed to make the continuation condition False eventually (otherwise the loop would continue forever). The preparation must:

(a) establish an initial value for the continuation condition; and
(b) initialize any variables whose values are used by the loop.

Point (a) does not always require explicit action. For example EOF(Input) always has a value, so we often see a loop **while** not EOF(Input) **do** . . . without any explicit preparation.

It might seem strange that the preparation should be refined last. However, it is not until the loop is fully refined that we know what is required to prepare for it.

When deciding between sequential, conditional and repetitive structures for a refinement, it is often helpful to take into account the structure of the input that must be accepted and the output that must be generated. Sometimes the structure of the input will determine the control structure to be used (for example Refinement 1.1a of program Traffic, Section 7.2); sometimes the structure of the output is the important factor (for example Refinements 1.1, 2.1, etc., of program Display, Section 7.1).

Whatever its form, a good refinement usually has the following desirable properties:

(a) *Modularity*. A program is said to be modular if its various components are relatively independent of each other. Choose refinements whose components interact as little as possible. This reduces the complexity of the refinements to be made at the next level down. In Traffic(a) 'process a vehicle signal' and 'process an error signal' both use and change variables concerned purely with timing. As you will find when you do Exercise 7.2, a more modular solution exists without these interactions.

(b) *Localization*. A program displays good localization when related statements are written close to each other in the text. This improves readability by reducing the need to scan back and forth through a program to see how things connect together. In the Traffic program all of the output is written by a group of adjacent statements. It would have been possible to write the headings as part of 'prepare to process signals', but this would have made it more difficult to check that the headings and the numerical output correspond in position and layout. In the given versions this can be seen at a glance.

(c) *Consistency*. When you have to do the same sort of thing several times, do it the same way on each occasion (unless there is good reason to vary). In Traffic(a) we refined 'process a vehicle signal' and 'process an error signal' into analogous Pascal statements. In either case it would have been correct to increment the counter after checking the length of the interval, but if we had been inconsistent the reader would have been left with a puzzle. When you *must* vary from a pattern, include a comment at that point to say why.

(d) *Delayed decisions*. Choose refinements which incorporate only those design decisions that cannot be postponed. This avoids committing the design prematurely to specific implementation ideas, increases the ease with which modifications can subsequently be made, and reduces the distracting effect of minutiae. Referring again to the Traffic program, the exact output format was a detail that could be postponed to the very end of the development process.

(e) *Simplicity*. It is very difficult to keep in mind more than about half a dozen facts or inter-relationships. Avoid overloading yourself by choosing refinements with at most five or six components (two to four would be preferable). This reduces the likelihood of confusion and error.

From time to time every programmer finds that ideas stop flowing and a difficult problem blocks all further progress. When this happens, suspect that a design error at a higher level has set you an impossible task. However, if the design seems to be sound, there are a few things worth trying. First of all, look for a solution by someone else. This may be found in the literature of the subject, or there may be a ready-made program in a software library. Even if no solution of exactly the current problem turns up, you may still be able to find solutions to closely related problems. These are a fertile source of ideas. Failing that, try to simplify the problem, solve the simpler problem and then work back to the original.

When you find yourself staring blankly at the title of a refinement, bogged down with useless ideas, that is the time to put the problem aside. Relax, or work on something quite different. Unconscious mental processes will continue to grind away at the problem, free from conscious preconceptions. Often a solution will come to mind when you least expect it. Reading Robert Pirsig's novel *Zen and the Art of Motorcycle Maintenance* would be a profitable way to pass the time while you wait for inspiration. As well as being a good story, this book contains many insights into problem solving, most of which are directly relevant to programming by stepwise refinement.

It is important to use a consistent notation for stepwise refinement and to be thorough about writing down design decisions. In this way the written record of the design process acts as an extension of our limited memory, and allows more factors to be taken into account than would otherwise be possible.

Each program outline is written in terms of a set of actions and expressions whose implementation has not yet been determined. These actions and expressions should be given descriptive names that will suggest exactly what the program is doing, even to a casual reader of the program outline. Accuracy is much more important than conciseness, because a misleading or vague name is both a symptom and a cause of sloppy thinking. The aim in writing a program outline should be to make it so clear that it reads 'like a book'.

As a general rule, material to be refined into Pascal statements should be described in terms of a command (e.g. 'prepare...' or 'output...' or 'calculate...'). Similarly, material to be refined into an expression should be described in terms of a word or phrase defining an object (e.g. 'next summand') or a situation (e.g. 'at end of data').

In the search for clarity it is often tempting to name part of a program in terms of one possible implementation. Guard against this, for it biases all your later ideas and may blind you to an alternative, and better, implementation.

Our notation for refinement steps has been chosen with two points in mind. Firstly, a refinement expands an expression or action from the program outline at the level above and it should be made clear how it fits into that context. For this reason the refinements are numbered systematically, level by level. Secondly, a refinement introduces a new set of expressions and actions. These will form part of the program outline at the next level down and it should be made clear what they are implementing. For this reason each refinement is headed by its own descriptive name, given in full. By reading just the refinement step it is possible to see *what* is being done, *how* it is being done, and *where* it belongs in the overall structure. Omitting either the name or the number reduces this self-explanatory quality of the notation.

Using the numbers of the refinement steps we can draw a diagram which shows the structure of the complete program in a vivid way. The structure diagram of Traffic(a), developed in Section 7.2, is shown in Figure 7.1.

Each level of a program outline contains all the refinements of the previous level, as well as all the unrefined material, which is simply carried forward. Also, every refinement lies on a path down through the structure diagram, starting at Level 1. If no such path can be found for a refinement then it must be structurally invalid.

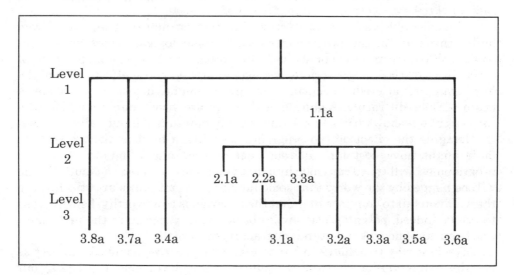

Figure 7.1. The structure of program Traffic(a)

7.4 TESTING AND CORRECTING

In programming there are many opportunities for errors. Even a modest-sized program is a complicated piece of text. We can cause it to fail by inserting or deleting a single punctuation mark.

We can distinguish several kinds of errors. The most elementary is a syntax error. This means that the program or part of it is ill-formed; it does not follow the syntax diagrams. For example, the statement 'if N < 0 N := 0' contains a syntax error. (What is it?) Syntax errors are simple to discover, because they are signalled by the compiler.

The next kind of error is one concerned with identifier declarations or the type rules. For example, the statement N:=0 is syntactically well-formed, but it contains an error if N has not been declared, or if N has been declared as a constant identifier, or if N is a Boolean variable. Again, such errors are simple to discover, because they are signalled by the compiler.

Some semantic errors, however, will escape the compiler and will appear only at run-time. Consider the following program fragment:

```
if (N > 0) and (Sum div N > 50) then
    Write ('OK')
```

This will successfully compile, but it *could* fail at run-time, if the value of N is 0. Errors like this are easy to spot when the statement is actually executed, because the program halts immediately (and produces a suitable error message, hopefully). They are much more troublesome than compile-time errors, however, since they might not show up for a long time. In the example, it might be rare for N to be 0.

The most elusive errors are errors of logic or structure. These arise from faulty thinking on the programmer's part. Some logical errors are rather obvious. We have all heard of utility billing programs that demand payment of £0.00 or £1,000,000. More serious are logical errors whose effects are subtle. For example, a credit company's program might incorrectly reduce a customer's credit rating. Again, logical errors are very troublesome because they might not show up until some unusual combination of input values occurs.

Imagine the effect on the program user when a fault is discovered. The fault might have cost him a great deal of time and/or money. You, the programmer, will try to convince him that you have corrected the fault. But he will be nagged by the worry that some further dormant faults are still lurking there. If you fail to convince him that the program is trustworthy, he will cease to use it. Indeed, potential users will not buy your program in the first place, until you convince them that the program is trustworthy.

The best way to achieve this is to make the program as nearly correct as possible. However much care we put into the development process, our programs will contain mistakes. The problem is to find them, and correct them. This we do by *testing*, a process that begins as soon as we have a Level 1 outline.

The traditional jargon calls errors 'bugs', malevolent little creatures that creep into good programs and spoil them. The programmer gets rid of bugs by 'debugging', and is happy when testing shows no evidence of their presence. For this reason, it does not pay to test programs too rigorously—you never know what nasty little bug you might find!

So much for tradition. The negative attitude towards testing that it encourages is the result of trying to deny responsibility for mistakes. Our aim is to be both more honest and more constructive. For us, a successful test is one that discovers an error, and so helps us to eliminate it. We take pride in the thoroughness and ingenuity we lavish on testing.

We have already seen how tracing, or hand-testing, allows us to check a program (or program outline) manually. Hand-testing is practicable only on a small scale, however. Worse, it is unreliable. A programmer will often miss errors, by assuming that the program does what he wanted it to do rather than what he actually programmed it to do! More comprehensive tests are indispensable. Thus the program must be tested on a computer, with large and varied sets of data.

Choosing good test data is not at all easy. In fact, it is a big enough subject to warrant a book of its own. Myers' *The Art of Software Testing* (Wiley, 1979) can be confidently recommended. The following advice on testing is sufficient only for the present. You should read much more on the topic before you undertake a programming project of any substance.

Start by considering the control structures of the program. Aim to test all statements and paths through the program.

Obviously it is essential for every statement to be executed at least once during testing. We cannot expect to show up an error in an untested statement! There is a rumour that a very expensive spacecraft fell into the Sun because of a software fault. This was traced to a punctuation error that altered the meaning of a statement. This statement had never been tested before the flight!

But even testing every statement is not enough. Consider the program fragment:

```
Read (X, Y);
if X > Y then
   Max := X;
Write (Max)
```

There are two paths through this fragment. One path includes the statement Max:=X—this path is followed if the condition X > Y is True. The other path omits that statement, and is followed if the condition is False. Both paths must be tested. We could test only once, with inputs 3 and 2 respectively, and force every statement to be executed. Nevertheless, the error will not show up unless we test the second path, when Max remains undefined.

In the case of a loop, we must test what happens both when the loop body is repeated several times and when it is not executed at all. Consider the following program fragment. (It is based on Example 6.3, but modified to compute the mean of the numbers read.)

```
Sum := 0;
Count := 0;
Read (Summand);
while Summand >= 0 do
  begin
  Sum := Sum + Summand;
  Count := Count + 1;
  Read (Summand)
  end;
Mean := Sum div Count
```

The loop body is repeated once for each non-negative number read. The program fragment will work correctly when at least one such number is read. But when there are none, the last statement will fail by attempting division by zero. As a rule of thumb, running a program with no input data is a good tough test for the program.

Each expression must be tested, to be sure that it represents the correct formula. In arithmetic expressions, try large and small, positive, zero and negative numbers. In **Boolean** expressions, try all combinations of **True** and **False**. Complicated expressions are error-prone and difficult to test thoroughly, so you should try to avoid them. Indeed, try to avoid any constructs that will be difficult to test thoroughly.

In all testing, you will be comparing the actual results with the expected results. Work out the expected results *in advance*, using the program specification. It makes sense to choose input data for which the expected results are easy to predict.

Take the example of program Traffic(a), in Section 7.2.

(1) The outermost control structure is a loop controlled by the end-of-data condition. There are two cases: (a) when the body of the loop is not obeyed at all; and (b) the normal case in which the body is repeated once for each signal read. These cases will require separate test runs.

(2) The next structure to come out of the refinement was the chain of **if** statements in 'process one signal and read the next'. To test this we need data in which only one kind of signal occurs (only timing signals, or only vehicle signals, or only error signals); data in which just two kinds of signal out of three occur (again, three cases); and data in which all three kinds of signal occur (one case).

(3) The last control structure to emerge was the **if** statement in 'note the end of an interval'. This occurs in two places in the program. We must ensure that there are runs in which both, each, and neither of these are obeyed.

With these considerations in mind, we might select data sets for Traffic(a) as follows:

(1a) 0
(1b) the following data sets cover this case.
(2a) 1 1 1 1 1 1 1 1 1 0
(2b) 2 2 2 2 2 2 2 2 0
(2c) 3 4 5 6 7 8 9 0
(2d) 2 1 2 1 2 1 2 1 0
(2e) 3 1 4 1 5 1 6 1 7 0
(2f) 2 3 2 4 2 5 2 6 2 0
(2g) 2 1 3 1 3 2 3 1 2 1 2 3 2 3 1 3 2 1 0
(3a) both **if**s obeyed: data set (2g) covers this case.
(3b) one **if** obeyed: data sets (2d) and (2e).
(3c) neither **if** obeyed: data set (2a).

Although carefully constructed, these data sets by no means exhaust all the possibilities. Devise further test data sets yourself before reading on.

What do we expect the results to be for each case? By inspecting the problem specification, *not* the program, we can deduce that the output for each of these tests should be as follows:

	No. Of Vehicles	No. Of Errors	Elapsed Time	Longest Gap
(1a)	0	0	0	0
(2a)	0	0	9	9
(2b)	8	0	0	0
(2c)	0	7	0	0
(2d)	4	0	4	1
(2e)	0	5	4	1
(2f)	5	4	0	0
(2g)	6	6	6	1

When we run the program we find that all cases give the expected output, except for case (2a), which gives:

No. Of Vehicles	No. Of Errors	Elapsed Time	Longest Gap
0	0	9	0

Our careful choice of test data has paid off: we have discovered an error in Traffic(a)! Trace through Traffic(a) by hand, using test set (2a), before reading on. Can you see why the results are wrong?

Any errors revealed during testing must be corrected as methodically as the program was originally constructed. Never make random changes to your program in the hope that the error will go away. You may succeed in masking the symptoms, but you will not cure the disease. Instead, work through the development of the program again, starting at Level 1, until you find the refinement where the error was introduced. Correct that refinement and carry the correction down to the Pascal coding, retesting each level as you go. Only then should you modify the program text. This approach ensures that the consequences of a change on other parts of the program are reviewed and keeps the program outlines accurate and up to date.

Let us correct Traffic(a). The reason for its failure in case (2a) above is that it has not taken into account the vehicle-free interval at the end of the survey. Often this omission does not show up in the results, but in case (2a) the last (and only) interval happens to be the longest vehicle-free interval.

Careful study of Level 1a shows that it does not cater for this last interval. The wording of 'process one signal and read the next' implies that only one signal will be treated at a time, and its subsequent refinement confirms that checking the length of an interval takes place only when a vehicle or error signal is processed. To rectify this we insert 'check the length of the last interval' immediately after the loop in Level 1a. This is refined as Refinement 3.1a, so the amended program contains the statement:

```
if Interval > Longest then
    Longest := Interval
```

immediately after the loop. Re-testing then shows that the program produces correct results for all the test cases listed above.

When can we be certain that our program is correct? Unfortunately, never! Testing can prove only the presence of errors, not the absence of errors. If a program produces correct results, we know that it works for the particular input data supplied, but no more than that. So a program that has always worked perfectly might still fail with input data not previously encountered. The trouble is that a program is correct only if it produces correct results for *every* possible set of input data. Can we try every possible set of input data? Such *exhaustive testing* is practicable only in trivial cases. Even if the input is a single integer, exhaustive testing would be hopeless. If the input is a sequence of integers, it would be absolutely impossible.

Do not be discouraged. Thorough testing is both essential and useful. If our program survives a series of well-chosen tests, our confidence in it is justifiably increased.

EXERCISES 7

7.1. Systematically modify program Display to read one number per line of input. Negative numbers are to be accepted, and written numerically.

7.2. Another way of looking at the data for the Traffic program is to see it in terms of 'runs' of several consecutive signals of the same kind. This interpretation is a natural one, because we want to measure time *intervals* and each interval is defined by the start and end of a run of timing signals. Runs of vehicle and error signals have no significance in the problem posed, so those signals might as well be processed individually. Timing signals, on the other hand, should be processed in runs of as many consecutive occurrences as possible. For example, the following input data contains four runs of timing signals:

2   1   1   1   2   8   1   2   2   1   1   2   1   1   0

These ideas lead to the following alternative Level 1 outline, and its subsequent refinement. We shall call this version of the program Traffic(b).

Level 1b outline

```
program Traffic (Input, Output);
declarations;
begin
prepare to process signals;
while not end of data do
    process a signal or interval and read the next signal;
output the results
end.
```

Complete the development and testing of this version of the program.

Which version of program Traffic is the more efficient, in the sense of doing less work for the same result?

7.3. Systematically modify both versions of program Traffic so that error signals are counted, but otherwise are ignored (i.e. do not end vehicle-free intervals).

7.4. Systematically modify both versions of program Traffic so that error signals are counted, but otherwise are treated as if they were timing signals.

7.5. Systematically modify both versions of program Traffic so that a warning message is output whenever eight consecutive error signals are received (indicating that there may be a fault in the data link). How is the modularity of the programs affected by these changes?

7.6*. Systematically modify both versions of program Traffic so that the signals are read one per line of input and there is no terminator signal.

7.7. If you have read Section 6.5, systematically modify both versions of program Traffic to use **repeat** statements, where appropriate, instead of **while** statements.

PROGRAMMING EXERCISES 7

7.8. Write a program which reads examination marks, one per line of input data, and outputs the number of passes (marks of 50 or over) and the number of failures (marks of under 50).

7.9. Write a program which reads details of transactions on a bank account and outputs a bank statement summarizing these transactions. The first line of the input data contains the initial balance (in £) of the bank account; the remaining lines of input data each contain a positive or negative number, a positive number indicating the amount (in £) of a credit transaction (deposit) and a negative number indicating the amount (in £) of a debit transaction (withdrawal). The bank statement should consist of the credits and debits, written in separate columns, followed by the initial and final balances of the account. An overdrawn (negative) balance should be indicated by writing the amount of the overdraft followed by the word 'Overdrawn'. For example, given the input data:

```
    1000
   +200
   −500
   +100
   −1000
   −100
```

your program should output a bank statement like this:

Credits (£)	Debits (£)
200	
	500
100	
	1000
	100

Initial Balance (£)	1000
Final Balance (£)	300 Overdrawn

7.10. The takings from each turnstile of a stadium are available as data in the following form:

(a) the identification number of the turnstile;
(b) a series of positive integers, representing the income from the sale of tickets at that turnstile;
(c) a negative integer as terminator.

Write a program to read several such sets of data (one per line of input), calculate and output the total income for each turnstile separately, calculate and output the total income for the stadium, and report the number of the turnstile with the largest taking.

7.11. Air pollution counts (integer numbers in the range 0 to 100) have been measured for several consecutive days. This input data is terminated by a negative number. Write a program to find *peaks* in the pollution counts, that is, counts which are greater than those of the day before and the day after. For each peak the program should output the number of the day on which it occurred (counting from 1) and the pollution count on that day. The total number of peaks found, and the total number of measurements, are also to be output. How will you treat the first and last days in each set of data?

7.12. A cargo consisting of many separate items of differing weights is to be flown to its destination in a single aircraft, first-come first-served. In general, several trips will be required. Write a program to find out how many trips are necessary, and the total payload on each trip, given as input the maximum payload of the aircraft, followed by the weights of the items of cargo (all integer numbers rounded to the nearest kilogram, and all on separate lines). What will your program do (a) if no cargo weights are given; and (b) if a single item of cargo weighs more than the maximum payload?

Part II
Further simple data types

8

The data type Char

This chapter covers:

* characters and character sets
* the data type Char
* legible input/output and textfiles
* the data type Text

8.1 USING CHARACTER DATA

Character data is the most common means of communication between people and computers: a program written in Pascal (or any other programming language), input data typed on a keyboard, and output printed on paper or displayed on a screen, are all expressed in characters.

For technical reasons computer character sets are restricted in size, and unfortunately not all computers use the same character set. The two most common are the ASCII (or ISO) character set, which consists of 128 characters, and the EBCDIC character set, which consists of 256 characters. They are listed in Appendix 5. All character sets include the upper-case letters, the digits, the blank character, some punctuation marks and some mathematical symbols.

To write programs which manipulate characters we need constants and variables whose values are characters. For this purpose Pascal provides the data type Char. A character constant is denoted in a program by enclosing the character between apostrophes, for example 'A' or '7' or '+' or ' ', the last of which denotes the blank character. An exceptional case is the apostrophe character itself, which is denoted by ''''.

Example 8.1

The following constant definitions make Blank a synonym for the blank character and Query a synonym for the character '?':

```
Blank = '   '; Query = '?'
```

The following declares Character and Initial to be variables of type Char:

```
Character, Initial: Char
```

We can now assign to these variables any character values from the character set in use on our computer, for example:

```
Character := Blank; Initial := 'W'
```

after which we can picture the variables as follows:

Character ⎡ '   ' ⎤   Initial ⎡ 'W' ⎤

It is important to distinguish the latter assignment statement from

```
Initial := W
```

in which W is an *identifier* (denoting perhaps a constant or a variable), *not* the character 'W'.

Character values can be transmitted by reading and writing as well as by assignment. The statement Read(C), where C is a Char variable, reads a single character from the input data and stores that character in C. The statement Write(C) writes the character stored in C.

It must be emphasized that blank characters are *not* skipped by Read(C); the next character from the input data, whether blank or not, is the one which is stored in C. It must also be emphasized that a character to be read by Read(C) is *not* to be enclosed in apostrophes in the input data. Nor does Write(C) write apostrophes before and after the value of C. The convention of enclosing characters in apostrophes is used only within the text of a Pascal program, where it is needed to distinguish character values from the symbols of the program.

Example 8.2

The following program fragment reads a person's forename and surname (assuming that each name is followed by one or more blanks, and allowing for blanks preceding the forename as well). It writes the person's surname and initial. It uses the definition of Blank and the declaration of Character and Initial from Example 8.1.

```
Read (Character);
(* skip any blanks preceding the forename *)
while Character = Blank do
  Read (Character);
(* note the initial *)
Initial := Character;
(* skip the rest of the forename *)
while Character <> Blank do
  Read (Character);
(* skip the blanks between the forename and the surname *)
while Character = Blank do
  Read (Character);
(* read and write the surname *)
while Character <> Blank do
  begin
  Write (Character);
  Read (Character)
  end
(* write the initial *)
Write (Blank, Initial, '.')
```

For example, if the input contains:

EDSGER DIJKSTRA

then the output would be:

DIJKSTRA E.

Check this by hand-testing.

As illustrated by Example 8.2, character values may be compared using '='
or '<>'. They may also be compared using the other comparison operators '<',
'<=', '>=' and '>'. You will be familiar with the alphabetic ordering of
letters: 'A' comes before 'B', which in turn comes before 'C', etc. In Pascal, the
comparisons 'A' < 'B', 'B' < 'C' and 'Z' > 'A' all have the value True, whereas the
comparisons 'A' > 'B' and 'Y' > 'Z' have the value False. The comparison
Initial <= 'D' is True if the value of Initial is one of the letters 'A', 'B', 'C' or 'D'; it
is False if the value of Initial is any other upper-case letter. In computers the
alphabetic ordering is extended to the complete character set. Unfortunately,
different character sets have different orderings, as you can see by comparing
ASCII and EBCDIC (Appendix 5). For example, the digits come before the
letters in ASCII, but the opposite is the case in EBCDIC. Nevertheless, all
computer character sets respect the alphabetic ordering and also the numerical
ordering for digits: '0' < '1', '1' < '2', and so on.

Example 8.3

The following program counts the letters and digits in the input data:

```
program CharacterCount (Input, Output);
var
   LetterCount, DigitCount: Integer;
   Character              : Char;
begin
LetterCount := 0;
DigitCount  := 0;
while not EOF(Input) do
   begin
   Read (Character);
   if ('A' <= Character) and (Character <= 'Z') then
      LetterCount := LetterCount+1
   else if ('0' <= Character) and (Character <= '9') then
      DigitCount := DigitCount+1
   end;
Write (LetterCount, ' letters, ', DigitCount, ' digits');
WriteLn
end.
```

This program assumes that, in the computer character set, every character between 'A' and 'Z' inclusive is a letter. This assumption is valid in most character sets including ASCII, but it is not strictly valid in EBCDIC where certain 'control characters' occur among the letters (see Appendix 5.2). These control characters are unlikely to appear in normal data, however, so the assumption is not a bad one. We shall continue to make this assumption in the examples.

If the program must allow for lower-case as well as upper-case letters, the first **if** clause would be replaced by:

```
if ('A' <= Character) and (Character <= 'Z') or
   ('a' <= Character) and (Character <= 'z') then
```

The program also assumes that every character between '0' and '9' inclusive is a digit. This assumption is in fact valid in every character set.

8.2 TEXT INPUT AND OUTPUT IN DETAIL

We have now seen quite a variety of facilities for handling input and output: Read for reading integers and characters; Write for writing integers, characters and Boolean values; ReadLn; WriteLn; and EOF for testing whether all the input data has been read. These facilities have been introduced whenever convenient. It is now time to consolidate and extend our understanding of input and output in Pascal.

Input is the identifier of a set of data to be read by a Pascal program. Output is the identifier of a set of data which is written by a program. Both Input and Output may consist of several lines, with several characters on each line. This is the most convenient form of data for the human user of a computer, whether preparing input or examining output. Any set of input or output data with this structure is known as a *text file*.

To understand the input and output operations in detail, it is useful to visualize a text file as a sequence of characters and *end-of-line markers*, for example:

Input `P A R I S   I N   T H E   S P R I N G - T I M E`

The end-of-line markers serve to terminate the individual lines; they are indicated by ■ in the diagram above. If this text file were punched on cards, it would look like this:

```
      ╱SPRING-TIME
    ╱IN THE
  ╱PARIS
```

If the same text file were printed on paper, or displayed on a screen, it would look like this:

PARIS
IN THE
SPRING-TIME

INPUT AND OUTPUT OF CHARACTERS

When a program reads a text file, the reading position is initially at the very beginning of the text file, as indicated by the arrow:

Input `P A R I S   I N   T H E   S P R I N G - T I M E`
↑

The statement Read(C), where C is a Char variable, reads the character at the reading position, assigns it to C, and advances the reading position by one place:

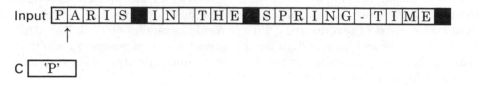

After reading four more characters, in this example, the program reaches the end of the first line:

Input

If the program now obeys Read(C) again, a *blank* character is assigned to C, and the reading position advances to the start of the second line:

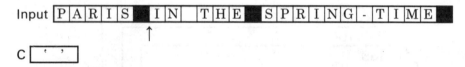

This is rather convenient when processing a text file, such as this one, containing words. The program can ignore any distinction between end-of-line markers and actual blank characters in the text file, both serving to separate words. The program of Example 8.3 also ignores the end-of-line markers, since it is concerned only with non-blank characters.

  Sometimes, however, the program does need to know when the end of the current line of input has been reached. For this purpose Pascal provides the standard function EOLn ('End Of Line'), which is True whenever the reading position is at an end-of-line marker. In our example text file there are three reading positions where EOLn will be True:

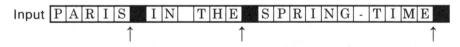

In any of these positions, Read(C) assigns a blank to C.

Example 8.4

Using a Char variable Character, the following program fragment copies to Output the characters of a single line of Input:

```
while not EOLn(Input) do
   begin
   Read (Character);
   Write (Character)
   end
```

As an exercise, trace the action of this program fragment given the above text file as input, assuming that the reading position starts: (a) at the beginning of the first line of input; (b) at the beginning of the last line of input; (c) at the third character of the last line.

The standard function EOF ('End Of File') is True only when the reading position has passed the last end-of-line marker:

Input `PARIS IN THE SPRING-TIME`

When EOF is True, any further attempt to obey Read will fail, since there is no data left to be read.

The effect of ReadLn is to advance the reading position just past the end-of-line marker of the current line. If the reading position is *anywhere* in the second line, for example, ReadLn advances it just past the second end-of-line marker:

Input `PARIS IN THE SPRING-TIME`

before   after ReadLn

If the reading position is anywhere in the *last* line, therefore, ReadLn makes EOF become True.

Example 8.5

The following program exactly reproduces all its input data:

```
program Copy (Input, Output);
var
   Character: Char;
begin
while not EOF(Input) do
   begin
   (* copy one line ... *)
   while not EOLn(Input) do
      (* copy one character ... *)
      begin
```

```
        Read (Character);
        Write (Character)
      end
    WriteLn;
    ReadLn
    end
end.
```

The inner loop is the same as Example 8.4 and is responsible for copying a single line of input. WriteLn terminates the current line of output. ReadLn skips to the start of the next line of input, or makes EOF become True if the last line has just been copied. This is all repeated by the outer loop, which continues as long as EOF is False, i.e. until the last line has been copied.

As an exercise, trace program Copy with the above text file as input. Trace it with different input to convince yourself that it works correctly (a) when supplied with input of no lines at all; and (b) when supplied with input containing an empty line.

As another exercise, trace the program with its statement part replaced by:

```
begin
while not EOF(Input) do
  begin
  Read (Character);
  Write (Character)
  end
end
```

and observe the different behaviour.

Write(C), where C is of type Char, writes a single character, the value of C. Write(C:W) writes the value of C at the right-hand end of a field of W spaces. The following diagrams show what characters are written in various cases:

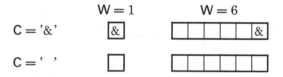

Thus Write(' ':W) simply writes W blanks—a useful trick for spacing your output.

INPUT AND OUTPUT OF NUMBERS

You must understand clearly that when you write down '7' or '365', what you are writing is not itself a number but a *representation* of a number by a sequence of characters. There is nothing inherently meaningful about this representation. We could represent the number *seven* in many ways, for example '7' (decimal notation) or '111' (binary notation) or 'VII' (Roman notation). Decimal notation has been adopted as the standard representation for numbers read from and written to text files, but this was an arbitrary choice. There is nothing to prevent anyone from writing a program which, for example, reads and writes Roman numerals.

Numbers and other data require a representation inside the computer too, and this internal representation may well be different from the external representation. In particular, a binary representation is usually adopted for numbers inside the computer, since this is more efficient for computer arithmetic than decimal. Thus whenever a number is read from a text file it must be converted from character form into its internal representation; and whenever a number is written to a text file it must be converted from its internal representation into characters. These conversions are automatically performed by Read and Write respectively.

We can now describe precisely the effect of the statement Read(I), where I is an Integer variable. The reading position is advanced first over any blanks and end-of-line markers, then over the characters which comprise the decimal representation of an integer number; finally this decimal representation is converted into the number's internal representation which is assigned to I. For example:

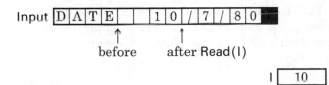

After '10' has been read, the character '/' immediately following it remains to be read subsequently. Instead of Read(I), if we obeyed the statement Read(D,C1,M,C2,Y) where D, M and Y are Integer variables and C1 and C2 are Char variables, then we reach the following situation:

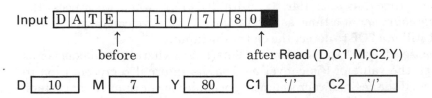

It is now possible to explain the point made in Section 6.2 about the interaction between ReadLn and EOF. Programs such as Example 6.4 which read one number per line of input data have the following outline structure:

```
while not EOF(Input) do
  begin
  Read (Number);
  process Number;
  ReadLn
  end
```

In the following example, the arrows show the reading positions *after* each iteration of the loop, i.e. after ReadLn has been obeyed:

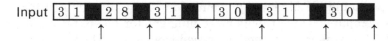

If the ReadLn statement were omitted, the reading position after each iteration would be immediately after the number just read:

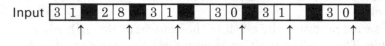

After the sixth iteration, in this example, EOF(Input) would still be False; so the program would then attempt to read a seventh number, causing it to fail. This is avoided by using ReadLn, which advances the reading position past the next end-of-line marker, thus making EOF become True if the reading position was in the last line.

   The use of ReadLn and EOF to detect the end of the input data is not restricted to input data containing one number per line. For example, the same idea could be used to read input data containing *two* numbers per line:

```
while not EOF(Input) do
  begin
  Read (N1, N2);
  process N1 and N2;
  ReadLn
  end
```

The outer loop of program Copy (Example 8.5), which processes a *line of characters* at a time, has a similar structure. It is only when we process the input a *single character* at a time, as in Example 8.3, that we can dispense with ReadLn and still use EOF to detect the end of the input.

   The precise effect of the statement Write(I:W), where I is Integer, is as follows. First, the value of I is converted from its internal representation to decimal. Then, if the decimal representation occupies fewer than W characters, blanks are added to the left to make up W characters exactly. Then all these characters are written on the current line of output. The following examples show what characters are written in various cases:

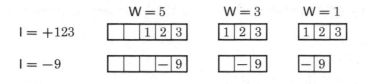

ABBREVIATIONS

Frequently a **Read** statement is immediately followed by a **ReadLn** statement. Pascal allows the two to be combined into a single **ReadLn** statement with parameters. For example, the sequence:

    Read (N1, N2); ReadLn

can be abbreviated to:

    ReadLn (N1, N2)

Similarly, a **Write** statement can be combined with an immediately following **WriteLn**. For example, the sequence:

    Write ('Total is ', Sum); WriteLn

can be abbreviated to:

    WriteLn ('Total is ', Sum)

If you use these abbreviations, remember the order of operations carefully: with **ReadLn**, skipping past the end-of-line marker is always performed *last*; and with **WriteLn**, writing the end-of-line marker is always performed *last*.

If textfiles are of particular importance in the applications that interest you, you may wish to preview Chapter 17, which completes the coverage of type **Text** in its fullest generality.

EXERCISES 8

8.1. Modify program **CharacterCount** (Example 8.3) to count periods, commas, semicolons and colons as well as letters and digits.

8.2. Write a program fragment which reads a line of text and outputs it with 'underlining', that is, with a hyphen under each character (on the following line).

8.3. Write a program fragment which reads a single line of characters and writes them out, replacing every sequence of consecutive blanks by a single blank. Then write a complete program which does the same for every line of input.

8.4. Modify program Copy (Example 8.5) to number each line of output, for example:

1 TO BE
2 OR NOT TO BE...
3 THAT IS THE QUESTION.

8.5. If you have read Section 6.5, recast Example 8.2 using **repeat** statements where appropriate.

PROGRAMMING EXERCISES 8

8.6. A mailing list is supplied as input data. Each line of the mailing list contains one person's name and address, divided up by obliques, e.g.:

HUGH MCSPORRAN/13 LOCH ROAD/TARBERT/SCOTLAND

Write a program which reads the mailing list and writes out the names and addresses, taking a new line at each oblique. Successive addresses are to be separated by two blank lines.

8.7. Write a program which mimics a simple calculator. The input is a series of integers separated by 'operations' ('+', '−' or '*') and terminated by '=', for example:

83+7*37=

The program is to compute the result of the calculation, 3330 in this case. The operations are to be performed from left to right: '*' has no priority over '+' or '−'.

8.8. Write a program which reads natural-language text (consisting of words separated by blanks and punctuation) and writes each word on a separate line. Treat each sequence of letters as a word, and ignore punctuation. (Note: you will not need to use the EOLn function in this program.)

8.9*. Write a program which reads natural-language text (as in the previous exercise), and which computes and writes the average number of letters per word and the average number of words per sentence in the text. These averages are quite good measures of the obscurity of a written text! For the purposes of this exercise, assume that every period ('.') marks the end of a sentence. Try your program on a substantial piece of text from a book.

9

Ordinal types

This chapter covers:

* the enumeration types
* the subrange types
* ordinal types in general
* the **for** statement
* the **case** statement

9.1 ENUMERATION TYPES

So far we have looked in detail at three of Pascal's data types: Integer, whose values are whole numbers; Boolean, whose values are False and True; and Char, whose values are the characters of some character set. Sometimes we need a wider choice than this; for example we might need a data type whose values model days of the week, or a data type whose values model months, or a data type whose values model primary colours. We could extend this list of useful data types indefinitely, and it would be unreasonable to expect Pascal to anticipate all possible needs. Instead Pascal provides a means for us to specify our own data types.

Suppose, for example, we wish to declare variables Today and Tomorrow whose values model days of the week. We *could* declare them as Integer variables, and write down statements like Today := 4 (where it is understood that 0 represents Sunday, 1 represents Monday, 2 represents Tuesday, and so on). This is rather artificial, and we must make an effort to remember which integers represent which days. An improvement is to introduce the constant definitions:

Sunday = 0; Monday = 1; Tuesday = 2; Wednesday = 3;
Thursday = 4; Friday = 5; Saturday = 6

which allows us to replace Today := 4 by the more natural Today := Thursday. Even now we can get into trouble: if Today's value is 6 and the program obeys the (perfectly legal) statement Tomorrow := Today+1, what interpretation can be placed on Tomorrow's new value?

In fact, nearly all programming languages allow no better alternative to declaring Today and Tomorrow as Integer variables. Pascal is richer than most in that it allows us *explicitly* to declare variables whose values will model the days of the week, as follows:

> Today, Tomorrow: (Sunday,Monday,Tuesday,
> Wednesday,Thursday,Friday,
> Saturday)

This declaration has three effects:

(a) it introduces a new data type (Sunday,Monday,Tuesday, . . .);
(b) it implicitly defines Sunday, Monday, etc., to be constant identifiers which denote the values of this new data type (just as False and True denote the two values of the data type Boolean);
(c) it declares Today and Tomorrow to be variables of this new data type.

The new data type is an example of an *enumeration type*, so called because it is specified by enumeration of all its values.

Having declared these variables, we can write statements such as Today := Thursday, after which we can picture the contents of Today as follows:

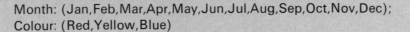

We *cannot* now write statements like Today := 4, since 4 is not a value of the new data type; nor Tomorrow := Today+1, since the value of Today is not a number and therefore cannot be added to anything.

The following are declarations of variables whose values will model months and primary colours respectively:

> Month: (Jan,Feb,Mar,Apr,May,Jun,Jul,Aug,Sep,Oct,Nov,Dec);
> Colour: (Red,Yellow,Blue)

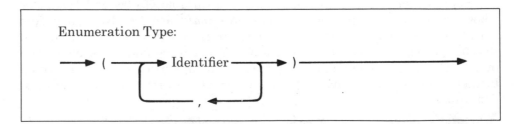

Figure 9.1. Syntax of Enumeration Types

These declarations allow us to write statements like Month := May and Colour := Yellow.

The syntax of enumeration types is summarized in Figure 9.1.

Example 9.1

Assume the variable declaration:

```
Day: (Sunday,Monday,Tuesday,Wednesday,Thursday,Friday,Saturday)
```

In Pascal the constant identifier Sunday is unrelated to the string 'Sunday'. Indeed, no identifier in a Pascal program has any inherent significance. Sunday, Monday, etc. could be replaced by Dimanche, Lundi, etc., or even by A, B, C, D, E, F and G, without affecting the meaning of the program. To emphasize this, Standard Pascal does not allow statements like Write(Day), which you might expect to write one of the words 'Sunday', 'Monday', etc., depending on the value of Day. If you wish to achieve this effect, therefore, you must program it explicitly:

```
if      Day = Sunday        then Write ('Sunday')
else if Day = Monday        then Write ('Monday')
else if Day = Tuesday       then Write ('Tuesday')
else if Day = Wednesday     then Write ('Wednesday')
else if Day = Thursday      then Write ('Thursday')
else if Day = Friday        then Write ('Friday')
else                             Write ('Saturday')
```

(We shall, however, find a better way to do the same thing in Section 9.7.)

The following program fragment reads a day of the week represented in the input data by 'S', 'M', 'T', 'W', 't', 'F' or 's', assuming that Character is a Char variable:

```
Read (Character);
if      Character = 'S'     then Day := Sunday
else if Character = 'M'     then Day := Monday
else if Character = 'T'     then Day := Tuesday
else if Character = 'W'     then Day := Wednesday
else if Character = 't'     then Day := Thursday
else if Character = 'F'     then Day := Friday
else if Character = 's'     then Day := Saturday
else
    WriteLn ('Invalid day-of-the-week representation:', Character)
```

As illustrated by Example 9.1, values of the same enumeration type may be compared with one another. More operations applicable to enumeration types will be introduced in Section 9.4.

9.2 SUBRANGE TYPES

Suppose we wish to declare a variable NrDaysInMonth whose value will be the number of days in some month. We could declare NrDaysInMonth to be an Integer variable, but the trouble with this idea is that NrDaysInMonth can now be assigned values like 32 or −9999 which are meaningless in this context. In fact we know that the variable should take only values in the range from 28 to 31. Pascal allows us to incorporate this knowledge into the variable's type, as follows:

```
NrDaysInMonth : 28 . . 31
```

28 . . 31 is an example of a *subrange type*, specifically the subrange of Integer values from 28 to 31 inclusive. NrDaysInMonth can be used just like an ordinary Integer variable, with this exception: if inadvertently an out-of-range value such as 32 or −9999 is assigned to NrDaysInMonth, it can be detected automatically and a suitable error message can be issued by the computer. This error message will draw attention to a logical error in the program which might have remained undetected if NrDaysInMonth were an Integer variable.

We are not restricted to subranges of Integer. We can specify subranges also of Char or of any enumeration type, for example:

```
Digit          : '0' . . '9';
Weekday        : Monday . . Friday;
SummerMonth: Jun . . Aug
```

The second and third declarations assume prior occurrences of the enumeration types (Sunday,Monday,Tuesday, . . .) and (Jan,Feb,Mar, . . .) respectively. Digit can be used just like an ordinary Char variable, Weekday just like a variable of type (Sunday,Monday,Tuesday, . . .), and so on, except that any attempt to assign an out-of-range value to one of these variables, for example by the statement Weekday := Sunday, can be detected automatically.

Example 9.2

The following program, given as input the number of rainy days in each of the years 1900 to 1980, will write these numbers followed by a total for the whole period.

```
program RainyDays (Input, Output);
const
    FirstYear      = 1900;
    LastYearPlus1 = 1981;
var
    Year              : FirstYear . . LastYearPlus1;
    NrRainyDays       : 0 . . 366;
    TotalRainyDays    : 0 . . MaxInt;
begin
TotalRainyDays := 0;
Year := FirstYear;
while Year < LastYearPlus1 do
    begin
    Read (NrRainyDays);
    WriteLn (Year:5, NrRainyDays:8);
    TotalRainyDays := TotalRainyDays + NrRainyDays;
    Year := Year+1
    end;
WriteLn ('Total', TotalRainyDays:8)
end.
```

Observe that the variable Year is incremented in each iteration of the loop, and on the last iteration it will be incremented to 1981. That is why its declared type must be 1900 . . 1981, not just 1900 . . 1980.

The syntax of subrange types is summarised in Figure 9.2. The lower and upper bounds of the subrange must be *constants*, of the same type, and the lower bound must not exceed the upper bound.

The use of subrange types helps the programmer to find logical errors, since assigning an out-of-range value can be detected automatically and reported to the programmer when the program is run. Subrange types also help to make a program more understandable to the reader. A declaration like N: 1 . . 10 or N: 0 . . MaxInt, stating clearly the expected range of values of N, is much more informative than N: Integer. The latter declaration should preferably be used only when the range of possible values of N is not known.

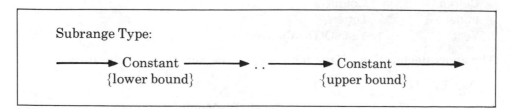

Figure 9.2. Syntax of Subrange Types

9.3 TYPE DEFINITIONS

We have already seen that constant definitions can help to make programs easier to write and to read. By giving a suitable identifier to a constant, as in the constant definition:

```
NrElements = 104
```

we can concentrate on the significance of the constant rather than its actual value.

For similar reasons Pascal provides the *type definition*, which is a means of giving an identifier to a type.

Example 9.3

The following are examples of type definitions:

```
DaysOfTheMonth = 1 . . 31;
DaysOfTheWeek =
   (Sunday,Monday,Tuesday,Wednesday,Thursday,Friday,Saturday);
Weekdays = Monday . . Friday;
Months   = (Jan,Feb,Mar,Apr,May,Jun,Jul,Aug,Sep,Oct,Nov,Dec);
Colours  = (Red,Yellow,Blue);
Letters  = 'A' . . 'Z';
Sexes    = (Male,Female);
YearsOfThisCentury = 1900 . . 1999
```

DaysOfTheMonth, DaysOfTheWeek and so on, are thus defined to be *type identifiers*. We can now use these type identifiers in variable declarations such as:

```
Day                : DaysOfTheMonth;
Today, Tomorrow: DaysOfTheWeek;
Month              : Months;
Workday            : Weekdays;
Colour             : Colours;
Initial            : Letters;
Year               : YearsOfThisCentury
```

The above declaration of **Day**, for example, amounts to the declaration:

```
Day: 1 . . 31
```

but is clearer. Type identifiers like **DaysOfTheMonth**, once defined, may be used in several declarations.

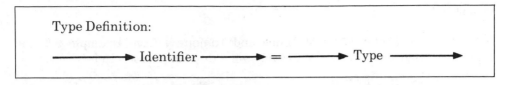

Type Definition:

⟶ Identifier ⟶ = ⟶ Type ⟶

Figure 9.3. Syntax of Type Definitions

It may now be seen that Integer, Boolean and Char are just predefined type identifiers. In fact, we can consider the definition of Boolean to be:

Boolean = (False,True)

The syntax of type definitions is summarized in Figure 9.3. In a program, any type definitions are grouped together and preceded by the reserved word **type**, exactly as constant definitions are grouped together and preceded by **const**. Type definitions (where present) must follow any constant definitions and precede any variable declarations.

9.4 ORDINAL TYPES IN GENERAL

All the data types described so far—Integer, Boolean, Char, enumeration types, and subranges thereof—are collectively called *ordinal types*. The ordinal types have certain properties in common which are not shared by the other data types of Pascal. (Real is an example of a data type which is not ordinal. We shall meet others in the remainder of this book.)

Each value of a given ordinal type has a unique *predecessor* and a unique *successor*. For example:

(a) the predecessor of the Integer value 10 is 9, and its successor is 11;
(b) the predecessor of the Char value 'E' is 'D', and its successor is 'F' (at least in the ASCII and EBCDIC character sets);
(c) in the enumeration type Months (Example 9.3), the predecessor of Feb is Jan, and its successor is Mar—since Jan and Mar immediately precede and succeed Feb in the enumeration (Jan,Feb,Mar,...).

However, one value of each type (e.g. Jan) has no predecessor, and one value of each type (e.g. Dec) has no successor.

Pascal provides two standard functions, Pred and Succ, which take a single parameter of any ordinal type and return the predecessor and successor, respectively, of its value. Thus Pred(Feb) is Jan and Succ(Feb) is Mar. In ASCII and EBCDIC, Pred('E') is 'D' and Succ('E') is 'F'; Succ('I') is 'J' in ASCII but something else in EBCDIC. If N is of type Integer, then Pred(N) is equivalent to N−1 and Succ(N) to N+1.

Example 9.4

Assuming the declarations of Today and Tomorrow from Example 9.3, the following program fragment determines what day Tomorrow will be:

```
if Today = Saturday then
    Tomorrow := Sunday
else
    Tomorrow := Succ(Today)
```

It would be an error to attempt to evaluate Succ(Today) when Today's value is Saturday, since Saturday has no successor.

To every value of a given ordinal type there corresponds a unique Integer value, called its *ordinal number*. (Hence the terminology 'ordinal type'.) The standard function Ord accepts a parameter of any ordinal type and returns its ordinal number. The values of an enumeration type (including Boolean) have ordinal numbers 0, 1, 2, etc. For example, the ordinal numbers of DaysOfTheWeek values and Boolean values are as follows:

```
(Sunday,Monday,Tuesday,Wednesday,Thursday,Friday,Saturday)
    0       1        2         3          4       5        6
```

```
(False,True)
   0     1
```

The ordinal number of each Integer value is itself. Char values have ordinal numbers which depend on the particular character set in use; see Appendix 5.

These ordinal numbers imply an ordering on the values of every ordinal type. We have already seen, in Chapters 5 and 8, that we can compare two Integer values, or two Boolean values, or two Char values, using any of the comparison operators '=', '<>', '<' '<=', '>=' or '>'. The same applies to all ordinal types. The value of the comparison A < B, where A and B are of the same ordinal type, is the same as the value of Ord(A) < Ord(B).

In the case of an enumeration type, the ordering of its values is the same as their order of enumeration. Thus, for the type DaysOfTheWeek (Example 9.3), Sunday < Monday and Friday > Monday are both True; Saturday < Sunday and Monday > Tuesday are both False. The expression Today < Tuesday has the value True if and only if the value of Today is Sunday or Monday.

Example 9.5

The statement Read(Number), where Number is an Integer variable, reads an integer number in the conventional *decimal* notation. The following program fragment could be used to read an unsigned integer number represented in *octal* (base 8) notation. The number may be preceded by zero or more blanks.

```
Read (Character);
(* skip any blanks preceding the number *)
while Character = ' ' do
  Read (Character);
Number := 0;
while ('0' <= Character) and (Character <= '7') do
  begin
  Number := 8*Number+(Ord(Character)−Ord('0'));
  Read (Character)
  end
(* stops after reading a character which is not an octal digit *)
```

This uses a Char variable Character.

The expression ('0' <= Character) and (Character <= '7') is used to test whether the character stored in Character is an octal digit. To compute the value of the octal number we must determine the value *represented* by each octal digit. This value is *not* given simply by Ord(Character), since, for example, Ord('0') is 48 and Ord('7') is 55 in ASCII. However, in every character set the digits have consecutive ordinal numbers, so the value represented by any digit is given by the expression Ord(digit)−Ord('0').

For the type Char only, the inverse of Ord is also provided in Pascal. This is the standard function Chr, which accepts a single Integer parameter and returns the corresponding Char value (if such a Char value exists).

Example 9.6

Assume Number contains an integer between 0 and 9999. Suppose we wish to write out its value as a 4-digit decimal number, for example the value 13 is to be written as '0013'. The statement Write(Number:4) is not quite satisfactory, since it would replace leading zeros by blanks.

We can solve this problem by dividing successively by 1000, 100 and 10; at each step the quotient decides which digit is to be written, and the remainder is retained for the next division. Assuming the variable declarations:

```
Quotient   : 0..9;
Remainder : 0..9999;
PowerOf10: 0..1000;
Pos        : 0..4
```

here is a solution:

```
PowerOf10 := 1000;
Remainder := Number;
Pos := 4;
```

```
while Pos > 0 do
  begin
  Quotient := Remainder div PowerOf10;
  Remainder := Remainder mod PowerOf10;
  Write (Chr(Quotient + Ord('0')));
  PowerOf10 := PowerOf10 div 10;
  Pos := Pos—1
  end
```

The value of Quotient, an integer in the range 0 to 9, is converted to the corresponding numeric character by adding Ord('0') and then applying Chr to the result. Chr(Quotient) would be wrong, since Chr(0) to Chr(9) are *not* the digits '0' to '9' in general, certainly not in ASCII nor EBCDIC.

Verify the solution by hand-testing, assuming that the character set is (a) ASCII, (b) EBCDIC. (Refer to Appendix 5.)

This example is the basis for a number of special ways of formatting numbers for output: see Exercises 9.

When writing a program which manipulates characters, it is tempting to exploit the peculiarities of a particular character set. For example, if the character set is ASCII we might exploit this knowledge in Example 9.5 to write:

```
Number := 8*Number + (Ord(Character)—48)
```

A more subtle error is to assume that the character set has consecutive ordinal numbers for its letters, and use the expression Chr(Ord('A')+I—1) to yield the I-th letter of the alphabet. We might even get away with such errors—unless we tried to run our program on a different computer with a different character set, when the results would be ridiculous! A program which will run correctly on a variety of computers is much more useful than one which is tied to a particular computer. So, whenever possible, write programs that work for any choice of character set. If any part of a program is *unavoidably* dependent on a particular character set, it should be marked clearly by a suitable comment.

9.5 TYPE RULES FOR ORDINAL TYPES

The type rules of Pascal are designed to prevent meaningless operations like assigning a character to a Boolean variable, or comparing a character with an integer. The Pascal compiler will detect all such errors, rather than allow the program to run and perhaps produce strange results.

Now that we have met a variety of ordinal types and operations, it is time to summarize the type rules associated with them.

OPERANDS IN EXPRESSIONS

In general, operators may not have operands of different types. Thus **div** must have two Integer operands, and **or** must have two Boolean operands. However, a variable of a subrange type may always be used as an operand as if it were declared without the range restriction. Functions like Ord and Chr must be used if it is required to convert values from one ordinal type to another.

ASSIGNMENT COMPATIBILITY

In general, the expression in an assignment statement must be *assignment-compatible* with the type of the variable on the left-hand side. Usually this requires the variable and the expression to be of the same type. However, the variable's type may be a subrange of the expression's type (provided that whenever the assignment is performed the expression's value is within the range of the variable's type), or vice versa. If these conditions are satisfied, the expression is said to be *assignment-compatible* with the variable's type.

9.6 COUNT-CONTROLLED REPETITION: THE for STATEMENT

Refer back to Examples 6.2 and 6.3. There is a significant difference between the loops in these examples. In Example 6.3 the number of iterations of the loop cannot be predicted, since it depends on the data read by the loop itself. In Example 6.2, on the other hand, the number of iterations is known in advance of entering the loop: it is the value of Size.

Loops with a predetermined number of iterations are very common, and they all have the same characteristic feature: they use a *control variable* (Count in Example 6.2) to count the iterations. The control variable is first given an initial value; inside the loop it is incremented (or decremented); and the loop terminates when the control variable is found to have reached its final value.

Such loops occur so frequently that Pascal provides a special construct, the *for statement*, to simplify writing them.

Example 9.7

We can simplify the solution of Example 6.2, using a **for** statement, as follows:

```
program SumByCount (Input, Output);
var
   Sum, Summand, Count, Size: Integer;
```

```
begin
  Sum := 0;
  (* Read the size of the list *)
  Read (Size);
  for Count := 1 to Size do
    begin
    Read (Summand);
    Sum := Sum + Summand
    end;
  WriteLn ('Sum of integers read is ', Sum)
end (* SumByCount *).
```

The clause **for** Count := 1 **to** Size **do** means 'Repeatedly execute the following statement with the control variable Count taking consecutive values from 1 up to Size inclusive.' This clause replaces the clause **while** Count < Size **do**, *and* the statements Count := 0 and Count := Count+1, in Example 6.2.

What happens if the value of Size is 0? In Example 6.2, where Count is initialized to 0, the **while** condition Count < Size is already False, so no iterations at all are performed, therefore no more numbers are read and the sum is 0. Using the **for** statement also, no iterations are performed since the control variable's initial value, 1, is greater than its final value, 0. Thus this version of program SumByCount also correctly computes the sum as 0 when Size is 0.

In Example 9.7 the control variable was used solely for counting. If desired, the repeated statement(s) may use the control variable's *value*. For example, we could insert the statement:

```
Write ('Summand ', Count, ' was ', Summand)
```

inside the loop of Example 9.7. However, the repeated statement(s) must not attempt to *alter* the control variable, for example by assigning a value to it. The **for** statement itself has the exclusive right to update the control variable, which it does 'behind the scenes' on every iteration.

There is one, rather subtle, difference between the programs of Examples 6.2 and 9.7. When we leave the **while** statement in Example 6.2 the value of Count is equal to the value of Size, for example:

Size [8]   Count [8]

After leaving the **for** statement in Example 9.7, on the other hand, the value of the control variable Count would depend on the exact manner in which it is updated 'behind the scenes' by the **for** statement, and this might vary from one compiler to another. Consequently, we must assume that the control variable is *undefined* after leaving the **for** statement:

Size [8]   Count [?]

Example 9.8

The program of Example 9.2 can be rewritten more neatly using a **for** statement:

```
program RainyDays (Input, Output);
const
  FirstYear = 1900;
  LastYear = 1980;
var
  Year          : FirstYear . . LastYear;
  NrRainyDays   : 0 . . 366;
  TotalRainyDays: 0 . . MaxInt;
begin
TotalRainyDays := 0;
for Year := FirstYear to LastYear do
  begin
  Read (NrRainyDays);
  WriteLn (Year:5, NrRainyDays:8);
  TotalRainyDays := TotalRainyDays + NrRainyDays
  end;
WriteLn ('Total', TotalRainyDays:8)
end.
```

This solution avoids the problem mentioned in Example 9.2, since Year is no longer assigned the value 1981.

Example 9.9

Assuming the variable declarations:

```
Month         : Months; (* see Example 9.3 *)
NrRainyDays   : 0 . . 31;
TotalRainyDays: 0 . . 366
```

the following program fragment reads and totals 12 *monthly* rainy-day counts:

```
TotalRainyDays := 0;
for Month := Jan to Dec do
  begin
  Read (NrRainyDays);
  TotalRainyDays := TotalRainyDays + NrRainyDays
  end
```

In this example the loop is repeated 12 times, with the control variable Month taking the values Jan, Feb, . . ., Dec.

Occasionally we need to write a **for** statement in which the control variable takes *decreasing* values. For this purpose we use **downto** instead of **to**.

Example 9.10

The solution of Example 9.6 can be simplified using a **for** statement:

```
PowerOf10 := 1000;
Remainder := Number;
for Pos := 4 downto 1 do
  begin
  Quotient := Remainder div PowerOf10;
  Remainder := Remainder mod PowerOf10;
  Write (Chr(Quotient + Ord('0')));
  PowerOf10 := PowerOf10 div 10
  end
```

Example 9.10 could have been written just as well with **to** as with **downto**. Another example using **downto** will be found in Section 11.3.

The syntax of **for** statements is summarized in Figure 9.4. **for**, **to**, **downto** and **do** are all reserved words. The control variable must be declared just like any other variable, and its type must be *ordinal*. The initial and final values of the control variable may be determined by any expressions assignment-compatible in type with the control variable. These expressions are evaluated just once, before entry to the loop.

9.7 MULTI-WAY SELECTION: THE case STATEMENT

The **if** statement allows a program to select one of *two* alternative courses of action—either the statement following **then** or the statement following **else**—depending on the value of the Boolean expression following **if**. Frequently, however, we wish the program to select one of *several* different courses of action, as the following examples illustrate.

Example 9.11

Recall the first program fragment of Example 9.1, where we wished to select one of seven courses of action, depending on the value of Day. The cascade of **if** statements used in that example was clumsy and also rather inefficient, since the value of Day could be inspected as many as six times. When there are more

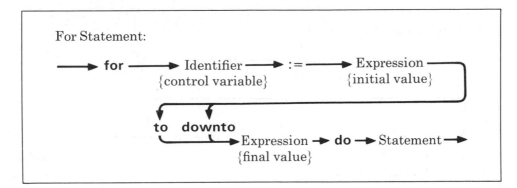

Figure 9.4. Syntax of For Statements

than seven courses of action, this style of programming is even less satis-factory.

What we need is a new construct in which the desired course of action is selected *immediately* after a single inspection of the value of **Day**. For such a purpose Pascal provides the *case statement*:

```
case Day of
    Sunday:     Write ('Sunday');
    Monday:     Write ('Monday');
    Tuesday:    Write ('Tuesday');
    Wednesday:  Write ('Wednesday');
    Thursday:   Write ('Thursday');
    Friday:     Write ('Friday');
    Saturday:   Write ('Saturday')
end
```

Here **Day** is the *case index* of the **case** statement. The constants **Sunday, Monday, Tuesday**, etc., which are the potential values of the case index, are used as *case labels*, each placed in front of a component statement.

If the value of **Day** is **Wednesday**, for example, then the component state-ment Write('Wednesday') is obeyed, and no other.

The effect of a **case** statement is as follows. The case index is evaluated, then *one* component statement is obeyed, namely that component statement which is labelled by the case index's value.

The syntax of **case** statements is summarized in Fig. 9.5. **case, of** and **end** are all reserved words. The case index may be any expression of any ordinal type, and the case labels must all be distinct constants of this same type. Notice that several case labels may be placed in front of the same component state-ment; this is useful when the same action is to be taken for several different case index values.

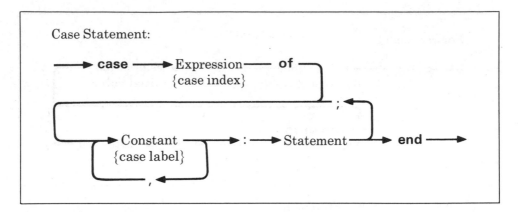

Figure 9.5. Syntax of Case Statements (simplified)

Example 9.12

'Soundex' is a method of encoding names in such a way that slight spelling variations are unlikely to affect the code. The basis of the encoding is the following phonetic grouping of characters:

    group 0: A, E, I, O, U, H, W, Y,
             all non-alphabetic characters;
    group 1: B, F, P, V;
    group 2: C, G, J, K, Q, S, X, Z;
    group 3: D, T;
    group 4: L;
    group 5: M, N;
    group 6: R.

{The characters of the name are first encoded as digits according to the grouping: thus 'SMITH' becomes '25030', and 'SCHMIDT' becomes '2205033'. Then consecutive similar digits are replaced by a single digit, and finally all zeroes are removed: thus both 'SMITH' and 'SCHMIDT' become '253'.}
    Given the variables:

```
Character: Char;
Group    : '0' . . '6'
```

Let us write a program fragment to store, in Group, the group into which Character falls. We assume, for simplicity, that lower-case letters do not occur.
    We can solve this problem using a **case** statement with Character as the case index; the case labels will be character constants.

```
if (Character < 'A') or (Character > 'Z') then
   Group := '0' (* Character is non-alphabetic *)
else
   case Character of
      'A', 'E', 'I', 'O', 'U', 'H', 'W', 'Y':          Group := '0';
      'B', 'F', 'P', 'V':                              Group := '1';
      'C', 'G', 'J', 'K', 'Q', 'S', 'X', 'Z':          Group := '2';
      'D', 'T':                                        Group := '3';
      'L':                                             Group := '4';
      'M', 'N':                                        Group := '5';
      'R':                                             Group := '6'
   end
```

It is essential for every potential value of the case index to occur exactly once as a case label in a **case** statement. If the case index turns out to yield a value which is not present as a case label, the program will fail. In Example 9.12 only the letters were used as case labels, whereas Character could have any character value; hence the prior check which circumvents the **case** statement if the value of Character is definitely not a letter. (It is assumed, however, that the value of Character *is* a letter if it falls between 'A' and 'Z'.)

Example 9.13

The following program fragment updates the score in a table-tennis game. It uses the variables:

```
ServerScore, OtherScore : 0 . . MaxInt;
Finished : Boolean;
Point : (ServersPoint, OthersPoint, Let)
```

It assumes that the first three variables have been initialized, and that the result of the latest play has been recorded in the variable Point.

```
case Point of
   ServersPoint:
      begin
      ServerScore := ServerScore + 1;
      if (ServerScore >= 21) and
            (ServerScore - OtherScore >= 2) then
         Finished := True
      end;
   OthersPoint:
      begin
```

```
      OtherScore := OtherScore+1;
      if (OtherScore> =21) and
              (OtherScore—ServerScore>=2) then
         Finished := True
      end;
   Let:
 end (* case *)
```

Example 9.13 illustrates nesting of compound statements and **if** statements within a **case** statement. It also illustrates how we can arrange to do nothing at all in some cases (Let in the example): we use a *dummy statement* as the relevant component statement. A dummy statement consists of no symbols at all, and one can be 'seen' between 'Let:' and **end** in the example.

EXERCISES 9

9.1. Assuming the variable declarations:

   I : Integer; J : 1 . . 10; C : Char; S : (Male,Female)

which of the following are legal expressions?

(a) I+1   (b) I+J   (c) I=J   (d) I=C   (e) C=S
(f) C='*' (g) S=Male   (h) Ord(C)+I   (i) C=Chr(I)   (j) Ord(S)+1

Which of the following are legal statements?

(k) I := 1   (l) I := J   (m) J := I   (n) C := 'I' (o) C := I
(p) C := Chr(I) (q) I := C   (r) I := Ord(C) (s) S := I   (t) S := Succ(S)

Which of the following are legal **for** clauses?

(u) **for** J := 1 **to** I **do** . . .
(v) **for** S := Male **to** Female **do** . . .
(w) **for** S := 0 **to** 1 **do** . . .
(x) **for** C := 'A' **to** 'Z' **do** . . .

9.2. A university has faculties of Science, Medicine, Law and Arts. (a) Write a declaration of a variable Faculty which can be used to indicate in which faculty a student is studying. (b) Write a program fragment to read a value for Faculty, represented in the input data by a single character, 'S', 'M', 'L' or 'A'. (c) Write a program fragment which outputs, in full, the name of this faculty.
9.3. Assuming that today's date has been stored in the variables

   Day: 1 . . 31; Month: Months; Year: 0 . . 9999

(see Example 9.3 for the definition of Months), write a program fragment which outputs today's date: (a) writing 1 for January, 2 for February, and so on; (b) writing the name of the month in full.

9.4. Continuing from the previous exercise, write a program fragment which updates the variables to tomorrow's date.

9.5. Recast Example 6.1 using a **for** statement.

9.6. Recast the inner loop of Example 6.10 using a **for** statement.

9.7. Modify Example 9.5 so that it reads a *decimal* number rather than an octal number. Further modify it so as to allow (but ignore) commas in the decimal number.

9.8. Modify Example 9.6 so that the output is preceded by a currency sign, e.g. '£0013'. Further modify it so that leading zeros are replaced by asterisks, e.g. '£**13'. (This idea is used in computer printing of cheques, rather than replacing the leading zeros by blanks, as a protection against fraud.)

9.9. Generalize Example 9.6 so that it writes a W-digit decimal number, where W is any positive integer. Then make it insert commas every three digits, e.g. '12,500,000'.

9.10. Assume that the charge for sending a parcel overseas is calculated as follows. First, its weight is rounded *up* to the nearest multiple of 15 grams. Then the charge is taken from the table:

Weight (grams)	Charge (pence)
15	12
30	22
45	31
60	36, plus 2 per *complete* 1000 km
75 and over	40, plus 3 per *complete* 1000 km

Given that its weight in grams and the distance in kilometres have been stored in the Integer variables Weight and Distance respectively, write a program fragment which assigns the charge in pence to the Integer variable Charge. Use a **case** statement.

PROGRAMMING EXERCISES 9

9.11. Write a program which reads an integer N, and outputs the squares and cubes of all the integers from 1 to N inclusive.

9.12. One of the earliest uses of computers was in cryptography. The simplest method of encoding a message is to encode each character by a unique integer (such as its ordinal number). This kind of code is broken rather easily, however, by an analysis based on the known relative frequencies of the characters. A better method is as follows: (a) encode the *first* character of the message by its ordinal number; (b) encode each *subsequent* character by adding its ordinal number to the *previous* character's encoding, and taking this sum modulo Key (where Key is a constant, which is supposed to be secret). For example, if Key=300 and the first few characters of the message have ordinal numbers 100, 255, 35, 220, . . ., then the encoded message would start:

```
100                    .
 55   (=255+100 modulo 300)
 90   (=  35+55  modulo 300)
 10   (=220+90  modulo 300)
```

(a) Write a program which, given a single-line message as input data, uses this method to encode the message as a sequence of integers, terminated by -1.

(b) Devise a method of *decoding* a message encoded as above. Write a program to perform this decoding, and test it with the output from your encoding program. Make sure that your decoding program successfully reconstructs the original message!

9.13. The population and GNP (gross national product, expressed in European Currency Units) for Belgium, Denmark, Eire, France, Germany, Greece, Holland, Italy, Luxembourg and the United Kingdom (in that order) are supplied as input data, in the form of two integers per line. Write a program which reads this data and outputs it as a table showing the name of each country, its population, its GNP and its *per capita* GNP. Include suitable headings, and a final line showing the total population, total GNP and average *per capita* GNP.

10

The data type Real

This chapter covers:

* real numbers and approximate arithmetic
* the Real data type
* programming to avoid loss of accuracy

10.1 Real NUMBERS AND Real ARITHMETIC

So far we have concerned ourselves only with *integer* arithmetic—the arithmetic of whole numbers. These numbers are useful for purposes of counting, but they are inadequate when we wish to deal with quantities that vary continuously, such as distances, time intervals, weights, probabilities and so on. For example, the distance between two points might be expressed as 14.65 metres, and the time interval between two events might be expressed as 9.2 seconds, both measurements involving a fraction. Such values are called *real numbers*.

Just as with integer numbers, the number of digits of a real number which can be stored in a digital computer is limited. As a consequence:

(a) there is a limit to the *magnitude* of real numbers which can be stored in the computer (typically about 10^{30} to 10^{70}); and
(b) there is a limit to the *precision* with which real numbers can be represented in the computer (this limit varies from about 6 to about 17 decimal digits on different systems).

The magnitude range is indeed enormous, and the precision may seem excellent. Nevertheless these limitations must be taken into account. In

123

particular, the limited magnitude introduces the danger of overflow and the limited precision gives rise to a variety of subtle programming problems.

In order to exploit the available precision fully, only the most significant digits of real number are stored. The position of the fractional point relative to the stored digits is held in a separate *scale factor*. Negative scale factors move the point to the left, positive scale factors move it to the right. For example, in a computer capable of storing a real number to 6 decimal digits:

0.0099	is stored as 9.90000 with a scale factor of −3							
0.99	,,	,,	,, 9.90000	,,	,,	,,	,,	,, −1
9.9	,,	,,	,, 9.90000	,,	,,	,,	,,	,, 0
9900.0	,,	,,	,, 9.90000	,,	,,	,,	,,	,, +3
8.7654321	,,	,,	,, 8.76543	,,	,,	,,	,,	,, 0
44530871.6	,,	,,	,, 4.45309	,,	,,	,,	,,	,, +7

This is the *floating-point* representation, so called because the number of stored digits is fixed and the point 'floats' relative to the stored digits. The computer automatically keeps track of the position of the point and takes this into account when performing arithmetic.

The limited precision of the floating-point representation forces numbers with too many significant digits to be *rounded*, as illustrated above. This can give surprising results.

Example 10.1

If we divide 1.0 by 3.0 and then multiply by 3.0, we might expect the result to be 1.0. The mathematical result of the division is 0.3333333333...., but in our 6-digit computer this result must be rounded to 0.333333. Then when we multiply by 3.0, we end up with 0.999999!

Example 10.2

If we subtract 10000.0 from 10000.1 and then add 0.04, we expect the result to be 0.14, and in our 6-digit computer this will indeed be so. If we perform the calculation in a different order, however, we may get a different result. If we first add 0.04 to 10000.1, the mathematical result, 10000.14, is rounded to 10000.1; now when we subtract 10000.0, the result is 0.1!

In some computers, results of arithmetic operations are *truncated* rather than rounded, for example the value 0.66666666666 . . . . would be truncated to 0.666666 (with resulting error 0.00000066 . . . .) rather than rounded to 0.666667 (with resulting error 0.00000033 . . . .). Evidently, truncation causes even more inaccuracy than rounding.

In nearly every digital computer real numbers are stored in a binary base, rather than a decimal base. Nevertheless, the problems illustrated by these examples remain. The use of the binary base does create an additional problem for us, accustomed as we are to expressing numbers in decimal. Many numbers (such as 1/3) cannot be expressed exactly as decimal fractions. Similarly, there are many numbers (such as 0.9) which *can* be expressed exactly as decimal fractions, but which *cannot* be expressed exactly as binary fractions. Thus when we use a constant like '0.9' in a program, or in a set of data, we should be aware that the number actually stored in the computer will only be an approximation to 0.9.

Real numbers obtained by physical measurement can have only limited accuracy, which depends on the device used to measure them. This is the cause of *observational error*, and is important because we cannot expect a calculation to yield results which are more accurate than the original input data. For example, quoting the distance to the moon as '240000 miles, or 386473 kilometres' is just silly, since the original figure was accurate only to 2 significant digits.

Most real numbers, however accurately known or measured, cannot be represented exactly in a computer. This applies to all irrational numbers, to rational numbers which have no exact binary representation, and to numbers with too many significant digits. This phenomenon is called *representational error*, and it forces numbers input to the computer, and those resulting from arithmetic operations, to be rounded or truncated.

Arithmetic operations tend to compound any errors in their operands. For example, if we subtract 4.999996 (represented by 5.00000) from 6.00004 (represented by 6.00000), we get the result 1.00000, in spite of the fact that the mathematical result, 1.000008, rounded to 6 significant digits yields 1.00001. Thus results can be less accurate than the data from which they are derived. This phenomenon is called *computational error*.

Normally, representational and computational errors will be smaller than observational errors; computer users should make sure of this by presenting their real data to a computer which can store more significant digits than their data actually possesses. We shall see, however, that representational and computational errors can accumulate, especially in highly iterative programs, so it is unwise to neglect them.

10.2 Real ARITHMETIC IN PASCAL

Real numbers, within the limitations of magnitude and precision discussed in the previous section, are values of the Pascal data type Real. We may declare variables whose type is Real, and we may assign Real values to such variables.

In Pascal, real numbers may be expressed either in the conventional notation for decimal fractions, or alternatively in the *scientific notation*, which is convenient for expressing very large and very small numbers, for example:

```
55E15      is equivalent to 55000000000000000.0
−3.8e3     „        „        „ −3800.0
1E−4       „        „        „ 0.0001
1.23e−20 „        „        „ 0.00000000000000000000123
```

Here E or e should be read as 'times ten to the power of'. The syntax of real numbers is summarized in Appendix 1.10.

Real expressions may be composed in a similar manner to Integer expressions. The following operators may be used:

$$+ \quad - \quad * \quad /$$

The operator '/' denotes Real division: the result of applying '/' to any two numbers is a Real number as close as possible to the exact quotient of these numbers. Thus 7/3 yields the Real result 2.33333 on a 6-digit computer (compare the expression 7 **div** 3, which yields the Integer result 2). The operator '/' has the same priority as '*'.

A Real value may be assigned to a Real variable by an assignment statement with a Real expression to the right of ':='. Placing a Real variable in a Read (or ReadLn) statement causes a real number to be read from the input data. Including a Real expression in a Write (or WriteLn) statement causes a real number to be written.

Example 10.3

The following program reads the radius of a circle, computes its circumference and area, and outputs all three values:

```
program Circle (Input, Output);
const
   Pi = 3.14159265;
var
   Radius, Circumference, Area : Real;
begin
Read (Radius);
Circumference := 2 * Pi * Radius;
Area := Pi * Sqr(Radius);
WriteLn (Radius, Circumference, Area)
end (* Circle *).
```

Given the input data:

```
3.0
```

the output would look like this:

3.000000E+00 1.884956E+01 2.827433E+01

Note that **Real** values are by default written in scientific notation, with as many fraction digits as possible. Each number is preceded by '—' if negative, or by a blank otherwise. There is no extra spacing.

We can specify a field width explicitly in the usual way, for example:

WriteLn (Radius:8, Circumference:10, Area:10)

which simply decreases (or increases) the number of fraction digits written:

3.0E+00 1.885E+01 2.827E+01

We can also request output in the conventional notation, by specifying the number of fraction digits required as well as the field width:

WriteLn (Radius:8:1, Circumference:10:1, Area:10:1)

would make the output look like this:

3.0   18.8   28.3

Example 10.3 illustrates a use of the standard function **Sqr** in a **Real** expression. Pascal provides a variety of standard functions for performing useful, and sometimes complicated, calculations. Each of the following standard functions accepts a single **Integer** or **Real** parameter, and returns a result of the same type:

Abs(x) computes the absolute value (magnitude) of x.
Sqr(x)   „   „ square of x.

Each of the following standard functions accepts a single **Real** parameter and returns a **Real** result:

Sin(x)   computes the sine of x.
Cos(x)   „   „ cosine of x.
Arctan(x) „   „ arctangent of x.
Exp(x)   „   „ value of e raised to the power of x.
Ln(x)   „   „ logarithm of x to the base e.
Sqrt(x)   „   „ square root of x.

(The parameters of **Sin** and **Cos**, and the result of **Arctan**, are angles expressed in *radians*.) Each of the following standard functions accepts a single **Real** parameter and returns an **Integer** result:

Round(x) computes x rounded to the nearest integer.
Trunc(x)   „ x truncated to its integral part.

Thus Round(2.6) is 3, but Trunc(2.6) is 2; and Round(−2.6) is −3, but Trunc(−2.6) is −2.

Finally, Real expressions may be compared using any of the comparison operators '=', '<>', '<', '<=', '>=' or '>'.

Example 10.4

Given a rectangle with sides Side1 and Side2, and a circle with radius Radius, where Side1, Side2 and Radius are all Real variables, the following program fragment determines which figure has the longer perimeter:

```
if Side1 + Side2 > Pi * Radius then
    Write ('Rectangle')
else
    Write ('Circle');
WriteLn (' has longer perimeter')
```

10.3 TYPE RULES FOR Real

OPERANDS IN EXPRESSIONS

Because there is a real number equivalent to every integer number, a Real expression may contain Integer operands (which are converted automatically to Real). This is illustrated by an expression from Example 10.3:

```
2 * Pi * Radius
```

ASSIGNMENT COMPATIBILITY

It is legitimate to assign an Integer value to a Real variable. Again an automatic conversion takes place. For example:

Radius := 3 has the same effect as Radius := 3.0

On the other hand, Real operands may *not* be used in Integer expressions, nor may a Real value be assigned to an Integer variable. If N is an Integer variable, the statement:

```
N := 3.14159
```

is invalid, because N may take only Integer values and there is no Integer value equal to 3.14159. Note that the statement:

```
N := 3.0
```

is also invalid. The constant '3.0' is of type Real, even though its fraction part happens to be zero.

When reading a value into a **Real** variable, the data item supplied may be either an **Integer** number or a **Real** number.

10.4 PROGRAMMING WITH Real DATA

As a consequence of the inherent approximations in **Real** arithmetic, 'obvious' equalities such as:

$$X / Y * Y = X$$

$$X + Y - Z = X - Z + Y$$

do not hold in **Real** arithmetic. When writing programs which manipulate **Real** data, we must always take arithmetic errors into account, as the following examples illustrate.

Example 10.5

Let us write a program fragment which determines whether a triangle is right-angled, given that the lengths of the sides of the triangle have been stored in **Real** variables **A**, **B** and **C**, and assuming that side **A** is the longest.

Using a **Boolean** variable **RightAngled**, we might be tempted to write down simply:

```
RightAngled := Sqr(A) = Sqr(B) | Sqr(C)
```

which is a direct transcription of Pythagoras' Law.

Unfortunately, exact equality between two computed **Real** values is extremely unlikely on a digital computer: representational and computational errors make it likely that the values being compared will be slightly different even when they would be expected to be equal.

The test is better expressed like this:

```
RightAngled := Abs( (Sqr(B) + Sqr(C))/Sqr(A) − 1 ) < 1.0E−4
```

This version checks whether **Sqr(A)** and **Sqr(B)+Sqr(C)** are equal *to within 4 significant figures*. Observational and computation errors should be taken into account when selecting the tolerance figure (in this case 0.0001).

Example 10.6

Let us write a program which outputs a table of square roots of numbers from 1.0 to 1.1 inclusive, in steps of 0.001. There will be 101 lines of output, one for the starting value and one for each of 100 steps. We might be tempted to write down the following simple program:

```
program SquareRoots1 ( Output );
const
   FirstX = 1.0;
   LastX = 1.1;
   StepSize = 0.001;
var
   StepNumber: Integer;
   X : Real;
begin
StepNumber := 0;
X := FirstX;
while X <= LastX do
   begin
   WriteLn (StepNumber:6, X:12:8, Sqrt(X):12:8);
   StepNumber := StepNumber + 1;
   X := X + StepSize
   end
end.
```

Here are the last few lines of output obtained by running this program on one computer:

```
      . . . . . .      . . . . . .
      . . . . . .      . . . . . .
95   1.09500444   1.04642463
96   1.09600449   1.04690242
97   1.09700453   1.04737985
98   1.09800458   1.04785717
99   1.09900463   1.04833424
```

The stored value of StepSize was only an approximation to 0.001 (in fact it was slightly greater than 0.001) and it was this approximate value which was repeatedly added to X. The output shows that the value of X drifts further and further from what might naïvely be expected. Even worse, because StepSize is too large, X+StepSize is greater than LastX in the 99th iteration, rather than the 100th. As a result the loop terminates one iteration too soon!

The following is an improved version of the program:

```
program SquareRoots2 ( Output );
const
   LastStep = 100;
   FirstX = 1.0;
   StepSize = 0.001;
var
```

```
      StepNumber: Integer;
      X : Real;
  begin
  StepNumber := 0;
  while StepNumber <= LastStep do
    begin
    X := FirstX + StepNumber*StepSize;
    WriteLn (StepNumber:6, X:12:8, Sqrt(X):12:8);
    StepNumber := StepNumber + 1
    end
  end.
```

The last few lines of output in this case were:

```
       . . . . . .      . . . . . .
       . . . . . .      . . . . . .
  95   1.09500003   1.04642248
  96   1.09599996   1.04690015
  97   1.09700000   1.04737771
  98   1.09800005   1.04785502
  99   1.09899998   1.04833198
 100   1.10000002   1.04880893
```

The reason for this improvement is that program SquareRoots2 uses the Integer variable StepNumber for counting, and computes X afresh in each iteration. This avoids the *cumulative* computational error observed with program SquareRoots1, which uses the Real variable X for counting. Even so, the computed values of X can be seen not to be exact.

Example 10.7

Write a program fragment which computes and outputs the roots of the quadratic equation:

$$Ax^2 + Bx + C = 0$$

given the real coefficients A, B and C. Assume that the roots are not complex.
    The two roots are given by the formulas:

$$\frac{-B+S}{2A} \quad \text{and} \quad \frac{-B-S}{2A}$$

where S is the square root of (B^2-4AC). We could transcribe these formulas directly:

```
S := Sqrt(Sqr(B)-4*A*C);
WriteLn ('Roots are : ', (-B+S)/(2*A):12, ',', (-B-S)/(2*A):12)
```

But consider the case A=C=0.001, B=1.0; this gives S=0.999998 correct to 6 significant digits. Thus the first root will be computed as (−1.00000+ 0.999998)/0.002, that is −0.001 correct to only 1 significant digit. The problem here is *cancellation of significant digits*, caused by subtracting two nearly equal numbers 1.00000 and 0.999998. In general, addition and subtraction yield results which are accurate only to the same number of decimal places (not to the same number of significant digits) as their operands.

We can achieve greater accuracy by first computing the larger root (in magnitude), and then computing the other root using the fact that the product of the roots is C/A:

```
S := Sqrt(Sqr(B)−4*A*C);
if B > 0 then
   LargerRoot := (−B−S)/(2*A)
else
   LargerRoot := (−B+S)/(2*A);
WriteLn ('Roots are:   ',   C/A/LargerRoot:12,   ',', LargerRoot:12)
```

The following output was obtained by running each of the program fragments on one computer:

(1)
Roots are: −1.04308E−03, −9.99999E+02

(2)
Roots are: −1.00000E−03, −9.99999E+02

As you can see, the smaller root is very inaccurate in the first case.

EXERCISES 10

10.1. Express the following numbers in scientific notation, in such a way that each number's mantissa (the part on the left of E) lies between 0.1 and 1.0:

0.00000000001234   0.009   0.254   3.14159265   981.0   250000.0

10.2. Express the following numbers in ordinary fractional notation:

45.67E−10   981E−2   3.00E0   1.885E+1   2.82743E+3   93E6

10.3. Evaluate the following Real expressions, working throughout to three significant decimal digits:

(A+B)+C   (B+C)+A   X*Y/Y   Z+Z+Z+Z+Z+Z+Z+Z+Z+Z   10*Z

assuming that A=0.004, B=1.00, C=−1.00, X=3.88, Y=3.88 and Z=0.333. Comment on the results.

10.4. Write down Pascal expressions which will compute the following: (a) the volume of a sphere whose radius is R; (b) the surface area of a rectangular block whose sides have lengths A, B and C; (c) the polar coordinates of a point whose rectangular coordinates are X and Y; and (d) the power dissipated in an electrical component whose resistance is R and whose rated voltage is V.

10.5. Given the lengths A, B and C of the sides of a triangle, write a program fragment which outputs the area of the triangle. (If S is half the perimeter of the triangle, the area is equal to the square root of $S(S-A)(S-B)(S-C)$. No triangle with sides A, B and C exists if $S(S-A)(S-B)(S-C)$ is negative.)

PROGRAMMING EXERCISES 10

10.6. Write a program which reads real numbers Amount and Rate, and an integer N, and which outputs a table showing the simple interest and the compound interest which will have accrued after 1, 2, ..., N years to the sum of money Amount at the annual rate of interest Rate. Sums of money should be written in the conventional format for your national currency. (Simple interest is calculated on Amount only. Compound interest is calculated each year on Amount plus all the interest accumulated in previous years.)

10.7. A rough graph of a suitable function can be plotted on a line-printer, like this:

```
Graph of x*x*x - 6*x*x | 11*x      Scale factor = 2.0

0.0 *
0.5 |         *
1.0 |              *
1.5 |               *
2.0 |              *
2.5 |            *
3.0 |            *
3.5 |               *
4.0 |                    *
4.5 |                           *
5.0 |
```

The position of the plotted point in each line is obtained by multiplying the function value by a suitable scale factor (2.0 above) and then rounding to the nearest integer. Write a program which plots sin x for values of x from 0 to 180 *degrees,* in intervals of 5 degrees. Use a scale factor of 50.0. Then modify the program to handle negative function values, and extend the plot of sin x to 360 degrees.

10.8. Write a program which reads positive real numbers and computes their square roots, *without* using the standard function Sqrt. Use *Newton's method*: if E is an estimate of the square root of X, then a better estimate is $(E+X/E)/2$. Initialize E to 1, then repeatedly replace E by a better estimate using the formula above, stopping when two successive estimates are equal to within 4 significant digits.

Part III

Arrays and strings

11

Arrays

This chapter covers:

* applications for arrays
* array types in Pascal
* indexing, index types and component types
* typical array-processing algorithms

11.1 THE NEED FOR ARRAYS

So far we have met only *simple* variables. These are variables whose values are single numbers, truth values, characters or such like. Much of programming, however, is concerned with collections of data, such as *arrays,* which we now introduce by means of an example.

Example 11.1

Consider an election contested by four candidates. Let us write a program fragment to read the ballots and count the votes cast for each candidate. Assume that the candidates are numbered 1 to 4, and that each ballot is presented as a line of input containing one of these candidate numbers.
    The following is a skeleton solution:

initialize all vote-counts to 0;
while not all ballots have been read **do**

```
begin
    read a ballot;
    increment the chosen candidate's vote-count
    end;
write all vote-counts
```

To hold the vote-counts, we could use four Integer variables Count1, Count2, Count3, and Count4. If the candidate number on each ballot is read into an Integer variable Ballot, we could refine as follows:

```
(* increment the chosen candidate's vote-count *)
if Ballot = 1 then
    Count1 := Count1 + 1
else if Ballot = 2 then
    Count2 := Count2 + 1
else if Ballot = 3 then
    Count3 := Count3 + 1
else if Ballot = 4 then
    Count4 := Count4 + 1
```

You might feel that this solution is rather clumsy. Imagine how much worse it would be if the program were modified to handle ten or fifty candidates!

If we observe that the variables Count1, Count2, Count3 and Count4 are all used in exactly the same way, however, we have a clue to a better solution. Let us rename the variables Count[1], Count[2], Count[3], and Count[4]. The variables now form an *array*, with a single identifier Count. We distinguish the variables from one another by writing an *index* between square brackets after Count. {Indices in programming are in many respects similar to subscripts in mathematics. In conventional mathematical notation the subscripts are written below the line without brackets; Pascal uses brackets because of the limitations of most computer input devices.} Count[2] is one *component* of the array Count, namely the component whose index is 2.

We have made no real progress if we can use only constants as indices. The power of the index notation, however, is such that we can use any suitable *expression* as an index. For example, we can use Count [Ballot] to refer to the component of Count whose index is the value of Ballot. Thus we can recast our refinement as follows:

```
(* increment the chosen candidate's vote-count *)
Count[Ballot] := Count[Ballot] + 1
```

This is much more elegant and, moreover, requires no modification if the number of candidates is changed.

Arrays occur outside computer programming, in the guise of *tables*. For example:

(a) A table of the atomic weights of the chemical elements is an array. If we call the array AtomicWeight, we can for example denote the atomic weight of silicon by AtomicWeight[Si].

(b) A table of the number of days in each month is an array. If we call the array DaysInMonth, we can for example denote by DaysInMonth[May] the number of days in May.

(c) A substitution cipher is a table which maps each letter on to another letter. If we call the table Cipher, we can for example denote the encipherment of 'A' by Cipher['A'].

11.2 ARRAYS IN PASCAL

In Pascal an array is declared just like any other variable, but its type will be an *array type* which specifies:

(a) the range of indices of the array, and
(b) the type of its components.

It is an important property of an array that every component has the same type.

Example 11.1 (continued)

The array variable Count would be declared in Pascal as follows.

```
Count: array [1. .4] of 0. .MaxInt
```

This declaration specifies that the variable Count's type is an array:

(a) whose *index type* is 1. .4, i.e. its indices are 1, 2, 3 and 4; and
(b) whose *component type* is 0. .MaxInt, i.e. each component of the array is of type 0. .MaxInt.

We can picture Count as a row of 'boxes', or store locations, one for each index value, for example:

	1	2	3	4
Count	27	36	0	9

Here the current value of the component Count[1] is 27, the current value of Count[2] is 36, the current value of Count[3] is 0, and the current value of Count[4] is 9.

Count[Ballot] is an example of an *indexed variable*. The component of Count for which it stands depends on the *current* value of Ballot. It is most important that this value is indeed a value of the index type, 1. .4. Suppose that the value of Ballot is 0. Then Count[Ballot] in this case stands for Count[0], which does not exist. This is a common and serious programming error ('index out of range') which must always be avoided, since it will cause the program to fail.

In this example, it is quite possible that one of the numbers read may be outside the range 1 to 4, and our program, as it stands, might indeed fail. We should modify the program to avoid this possibility of failure. We might reasonably treat a number outside the range 1 to 4 as a 'spoilt ballot', and make the program count the spoilt ballots separately. Here is a complete program for the election problem which does this:

```
program Election (Input, Output);
const
   NrCandidates = 4;
var
   Count     : array [1. .NrCandidates] of 0. .MaxInt;
   Spoilt    : 0. .MaxInt;
   Candidate: 1. .NrCandidates;
   Ballot    : Integer;
begin
(* initialize all vote-counts to 0 *)
for Candidate := 1 to NrCandidates do
   Count[Candidate] := 0;
Spoilt := 0;
while not EOF(Input) do        (* not all ballots have been read *)
   begin
   (* read a ballot *)
   ReadLn (Ballot);
   (* increment the chosen candidate's vote-count,
             unless the ballot was spoilt *)
   if (Ballot >= 1) and (Ballot <= NrCandidates) then
      Count[Ballot] := Count[Ballot] + 1
   else
      Spoilt := Spoilt + 1
   end;
(* write all vote-counts *)
WriteLn ('Candidate': 10, 'Votes': 10);
for Candidate := 1 to NrCandidates do
   WriteLn (Candidate: 10, Count[Candidate]: 10);
WriteLn ('There were', Spoilt: 5, 'spoilt ballots.')
end.
```

The refinement of 'initialize all vote-counts to 0' includes a loop which assigns 0 to each component of Count in turn; and the refinement of 'write all vote-counts' includes a loop which writes the value of each component in turn.

As an exercise, devise some test data (including some 'spoilt ballots') and hand-test program Election.

The use of the constant identifier NrCandidates makes the program more flexible: if the program had to be modified to handle more candidates, then only the constant definition would need to be altered.

The syntax of array types is summarized in Figure 11.1. **array** and **of** are both reserved words. Array types may be used, like other types, in type definitions as well as in variable declarations.

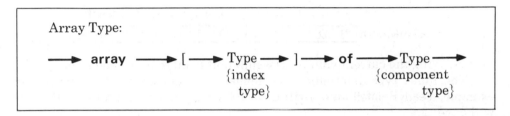

Figure 11.1. Syntax of Array Types (simplified)

The syntax of indexed variables is summarized in Figure 11.2. Any expression can be used as an index; we are not restricted to constants or simple variables. In every case, however, the index expression must yield a value of the array's index type. An indexed variable may be used anywhere a simple variable can, as illustrated by Example 11.1

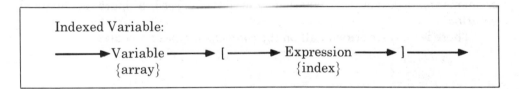

Figure 11.2. Syntax of Indexed Variables (simplified)

Within reason, any *ordinal* type may be chosen as the *index type* of an array: Boolean, Char, any enumeration type, or any subrange type.

Example 11.2

Assuming the type definition:

Months = (Jan,Feb,Mar,Apr,May,Jun,Jul,Aug,Sep,Oct,Nov,Dec)

the following are legitimate array variable declarations:

```
CharCount     : array [Char] of 0. .MaxInt;
LetterCount   : array ['A'. .'Z'] of 0. .MaxInt;
DaysInMonth   : array [Months] of 28. .31;
MonthlyRainfall: array [Months] of Real;
SummerRainfall: array [Jun. .Aug] of Real;
YearlyRainfall : array [1900. .1999] of Real
```

DaysInMonth might be used to store the number of days in each month. After initialization it might look like this:

Jan Feb Mar Apr May Jun Jul Aug Sep Oct Nov Dec

DaysInMonth | 31 | 28 | 31 | 30 | 31 | 30 | 31 | 31 | 30 | 31 | 30 | 31 |

here showing the current value of DaysInMonth[Jan] to be 31, and so on.

The index type determines the number of components of an array; for example, YearlyRainfall above will have 100 components, and MonthlyRainfall will have 12.

Although the stores of some computers are very large, they are not unlimited and a declaration of an array with index type 1. .100000 or Integer, for example:

```
Prime : array [Integer] of Boolean
```

is very unlikely to be acceptable to a compiler! Most programming problems, certainly those you will meet in this book, can be solved without using very large arrays; if you find yourself declaring an array with thousands of components, ask yourself whether you have missed a more economical solution.

There is no restriction at all on the *component type* of any array.

Example 11.3

The following is a legitimate array type definition:

```
Lines = array [1 . . 120] of Char
```

The following are legitimate array variable declarations:

```
WettestMonth: array [1990. .1999] of Months;
DaysInMonth : array [Months] of 28. .31;
PageImage    : array [1 . . 64] of Lines;
Prime        : array [1 . . N] of Boolean
```

provided N is a constant identifier. (N must not be a variable.)

Arrays of characters are of special interest because they can be used for storing and manipulating legible data, i.e. words and text. This important topic will be discussed in Chapter 12.

11.3 COMPONENT-BY-COMPONENT PROCESSING OF ARRAYS

The most common manipulation of arrays is component-by-component processing, whereby we perform similar operations on some or all components of the array, one component at a time. We have already seen some simple examples of component-by-component processing: the initialization of the vote-counts, and the writing of the vote-counts, in Example 11.1.

Since several components are to be processed, component-by-component processing is performed by a loop. We need a variable to index the array. If we know in advance which components are going to be processed, we can use a **for** statement whose control variable will range over the indices of these components. Otherwise we use a **while** (or **repeat**) statement; in this case the variable used for indexing the array must be explicitly initialized, and incremented or decremented inside the loop.

Example 11.4

Assuming the type identifier Months is defined as in Example 11.2, and given a table of monthly rainfall readings stored in the array:

```
Rainfall : array [Months] of Real
```

let us write a program fragment to determine the total rainfall for the whole year. We declare the following variables:

```
Month : Months;
Total : Real
```

and we use Month as the indexing variable. Here we can use a **for** statement:

```
(* Determine total rainfall for the whole year *)
Total := 0;
for Month := Jan to Dec do
   Total := Total + Rainfall[Month]
```

The solution can easily be adapted to process only some of the array components, for example:

```
(* Determine total rainfall from April to September *)
Total := 0;
for Month := Apr to Sep do
   Total := Total + Rainfall[Month]
```

Verify these solutions by hand-testing.

Example 11.5

Continuing Example 11.4, let us write a program fragment to determine the maximum rainfall in any one month of the year.

This problem amounts to finding the value of the largest of Rainfall[Jan], ..., Rainfall[Dec]. We need the variables:

```
Month      : Months;
MaxRainfall: Real
```

This problem can be solved by initializing MaxRainfall to the first component of the array, then comparing MaxRainfall in turn with each of the remaining components, updating MaxRainfall to any component which is found to be greater. This can be done with a **for** statement:

```
(* Determine maximum monthly rainfall *)
MaxRainfall := Rainfall[Jan];
for Month := Feb to Dec do
   if Rainfall[Month] > MaxRainfall then
      MaxRainfall := Rainfall[Month]
```

Example 11.6

We return to the election problem (Example 11.1). Let us modify program Election to determine the winner of the election, i.e. the candidate with the greatest number of votes (neglecting the possibility of a tie).

This amounts to finding the *index* of the maximum component of the array Count. Note the difference from Example 11.5, where the problem was to find the *value* of the maximum component.

We insert the variable declaration:

```
Winner: 1. .NrCandidates
```

and add the following at the end of the program:

```
(* determine the election winner, neglecting ties *)
Winner := 1;
for Candidate := 2 to NrCandidates do
   if Count[Candidate] > Count[Winner] then
      Winner := Candidate
```

Another common theme is *linear search*, whereby the components of an array are examined one by one to find which component, if any, satisfies some specified condition.

Example 11.7

Assume the variable declarations:

```
List   : array [1. .N] of integer;
Target: Integer
```

Let us develop a program fragment which will search List for a component which equals the value of Target. For example, in the following situation (assuming N = 10):

	1	2	3	4	5	6	7	8	9	10			
List	13	7	45	0	99	13	21	77	37	19		Target	99

we should find that List[5] matches Target. On the other hand, if the value of Target is 22, we should find that no component of List matches Target.

The program must examine List[1], List[2], etc., in turn until *either* it finds a component which matches Target *or* it has examined all the components without success. This observation leads to the following outline solution:

```
initialize the search;
while the search is incomplete do
    try to match Target to the next component of List;
if the search was successful then
    report which component of List matches Target
else
    report lack of success
```

We will need a variable, say Loc, to index the array. The outline also suggests introducing a Boolean variable, Matched, to use in the **while** and **if** conditions. Completing the refinement:

```
Loc := 0; Matched := False;
while not Matched and (Loc < N) do
    begin
    Loc := Succ(Loc);
    if List[Loc] = Target then
        Matched := True
    end;
if Matched then
    Write ('Target matched at index', Loc)
else
    Write ('Target not matched')
```

The comparison Loc < N is essential in the **while** condition, otherwise when Target is not matched by any component of List the program would fail by attempting to inspect List[N+1]. Check your understanding of the solution by hand-testing using the data cited above, with the value of Target being (a) 99, and (b) 22.

   This solution forces us to declare Loc with type 0. .N. It would be prefer-able to declare Loc with type 1. .N, since it is used to index List. In fact, there is an alternative solution which does allow Loc to be declared with type 1. .N. This is based on the observation that, during the search, there are *three* possible states: (a) a match has been found; (b) there is definitely no match; and (c) it is not yet known whether there is a match or not. We can represent these states by introducing the variable:

```
Match : (Unknown, Yes, No)
```

to replace Matched, and refining the outline solution as follows:

```
Loc := 1; Match := Unknown;
while Match = Unknown do
   if List[Loc] = Target then
      Match := Yes
   else if Loc = N then
      Match := No
   else
      Loc := Succ(Loc);
if Match = Yes then
   Write ('Target matched at index', Loc)
else
   Write ('Target not matched')
```

This time Loc is initialized to 1, but it never exceeds N because if Loc equals N and List[Loc] does not match Target then Match is set to No and Loc is *not* incremented. Verify this solution by hand-testing using the same data as before.

   It should be obvious to you that the **while** condition in the second solution will always be True the first time it is tested, so the loop must be repeated at least once. If you have read Section 6.5, improve this solution further using a **repeat** statement.

Example 11.8

Returning once more to the election problem, let us modify program Election to determine which candidate, if any, received a clear majority of the votes cast.

   First we must modify the program to accumulate the total number of unspoilt ballots, and hence the required majority. We add:

```
(* determine required majority *)
Votes := 0;
```

```
for Candidate := 1 to NrCandidates do
   Votes := Votes + Count[Candidate];
Majority := Votes div 2 + 1
```

together with the necessary variable declaration:

```
Votes, Majority : 0. .MaxInt
```

The rest of the solution is analogous to Example 11.7:

```
(* determine which candidate, if any,
             received at least Majority votes *)
Candidate := 1;
Clear := Unknown;
while Clear = Unknown do
   if Count[Candidate] >= Majority then
      Clear := Yes
   else if Candidate = NrCandidates then
      Clear := No
   else
      Candidate := Succ(Candidate);
if Clear = Yes then
   Write ('Clear majority for candidate', Candidate)
else
   Write ('No clear majority')
```

This assumes the variable declaration:

```
Clear: (Unknown, Yes, No)
```

Check this program fragment by hand-testing in the following three cases:

(a) Count

27	36	0	8

Majority

36

(b) Count

10	20	30	70

Majority

66

(c) Count

27	36	0	9

Majority

37

All the previous examples have illustrated problems where we know exactly the size of the array required to store the data. The following example illustrates a situation where this is not the case.

Example 11.9

Let us write a program which reads a single line of characters and outputs them in reverse order. (This might be the first step in constructing a rhyming dictionary.)

Clearly the program must read and store all the characters before writing them. A natural place to store all the characters is in an array, but we do not know how many characters will be supplied as input, so how big should the array be? In situations like this it is necessary to declare an array big enough to hold the largest number of characters likely ever to be supplied, and to use another variable to count the *actual* number of characters supplied as input. In this example, 80 would be a reasonable upper limit, since input data on cards and on many terminals is in fact limited to 80 characters per line. Here is a solution:

```
program ReverseLine (Input, Output);
const
   MaxLineLength = 80;
var
   Line   : array [1. .MaxLineLength] of Char;
   Count: 0. .MaxLineLength;
   Pos    : 1. .MaxLineLength;
begin
(* read and store a line of characters *)
Count := 0;
while not EOLn(Input) do
   begin
   Count := Count+1;
   Read (Line[Count])
   end;
(* write the line of characters in reverse *)
for Pos := Count downto 1 do
   Write (Line[Pos]);
WriteLn
end.
```

For example, given the following input data:

THE QUICK BROWN FOX JUMPED OVER THE LAZY DOG.

after reading all the characters up to the period we have:

Count [45]

1	2	3		42	43	44	45	46		80
Line 'T'	'H'	'E'	- - -	'D'	'O'	'G'	'.'	?	- - -	?

The components Line[46] to Line[80 remain undefined, but the rest of the program does not attempt to inspect them.

What will happen if a line of more than 80 characters is supplied after all? The program will fail when it attempts to increment Count to 81. Since the limit of 80 is arbitrary, it is good programming practice to allow for this limit being exceeded. Here we need only change the **while** condition to:

```
(Count < MaxLineLength) and not EOLn(Input)
```

to ensure that no more than MaxLineLength characters are read and stored in Line.

This program illustrates the use of **downto** in a **for** statement. The control variable Pos is made to take *decreasing* values Count, Count−1,..., 2, 1, so that the characters are written out in reverse order. Given the input data cited above, the output would be:

.GOD YZAL EHT REVO DEPMUJ XOF NWORB KCIUQ EHT

Check your understanding of program ReverseLine by hand-testing. (Hint: choose a smaller value for MaxLineLength, say 10. Include a test with more than 10 characters as input.)

11.4 MULTI-DIMENSIONAL ARRAYS

As we have seen, the components of an array may be of any type we choose. In particular, the components may themselves be arrays. An array whose components are simple (i.e. single numbers, truth values, characters or such like) is called a *one-dimensional array*. An array whose components are themselves one-dimensional arrays is called a *two-dimensional array*. Likewise, we can define three-dimensional arrays, and so on.

All the arrays in previous examples have been one-dimensional, except for PageImage in Example 11.3 which is a two-dimensional array of characters.

Example 11.10

Consider a table containing the marks scored by a class of students in each of several papers of an examination. Assume the number of papers and the number of students are given by the constant identifiers NrPapers and NrStudents respectively. The marks of one student could be stored in a one-dimensional array of type:

```
array [1..NrPapers] of 0..100
```

The whole marks table could be stored in an array of such arrays, i.e. a two-dimensional array:

```
Mark: array [1..NrStudents] of
           array [1..NrPapers] of 0..100
```

Assume the variable declarations:

> Student: 1..NrStudents;
> Paper   : 1..NrPapers

The indexed variable Mark[Student] selects one component of the array Mark. This component is itself an array with NrPapers components; in fact it is an array containing all the marks of the student numbered Student. Thus we can apply an index to it: Mark[Student][Paper] is the mark obtained by the same student in paper Paper.

We can think of a two-dimensional array as having rows and columns. The array Mark would have one row for each student and one column for each paper. Assuming NrStudents is 10 and NrPapers is 4, it might look like this:

Mark			
33	51	27	20
83	90	66	85
100	88	82	75
44	32	0	21
32	50	49	52
65	49	62	56
29	46	52	39
77	68	80	63
55	52	65	60
72	49	66	54

{Compare the mathematical notation for matrices.} Then Mark[2], the set of marks scored by student 2, is row 2 of Mark:

83	90	66	85

Finally, Mark[2][4], the mark scored by student 2 in paper 4, is component 4 of row 2. Here the value of Mark[2][4] is 85.

Multi-dimensional arrays are so common that Pascal allows multi-dimensional array types to be abbreviated. For example, the declaration of Mark in Example 11.10 could be abbreviated to:

> Mark: **array** [1..NrStudents, 1..NrPapers] **of** 0..100

Likewise, the indexed variable Mark[Student][Paper] may be abbreviated to Mark[Student,Paper].

The simplest examples of manipulation of multi-dimensional arrays are row and column processing.

Example 11.11

Given the array **Mark** of Example 11.10, let us write a program fragment to output the total mark of each student.

The best way to attack this problem is to consider it as an example of component-by-component processing of **Mark**, forgetting for the moment that the components of **Mark** are themselves arrays. We declare:

```
Student: 1. .NrStudents
```

and write:

```
for Student := 1 to NrStudents do
    calculate and write the total mark of student Student
```

Now the refinement of 'calculate and write the total mark of student **Student**' will itself be an example of component-by-component processing, this time of the array **Mark[Student]**. We further declare:

```
Paper: 1. .NrPapers;
Total : 0. .MaxInt
```

(We know that **Total** cannot exceed 100*NrPapers, but unfortunately 0. .100*NrPapers is not a legal subrange type in Pascal.) The refined solution is:

```
for Student := 1 to NrStudents do
    (* calculate and write the total mark of student Student *)
    begin
    Total := 0;
    for Paper := 1 to NrPapers do
        Total := Total + Mark[Student,Paper];
    WriteLn (Student, Total)
    end
```

Verify this solution by hand-testing.

This example illustrates a typical situation: a two-dimensional array being processed by two nested loops, using two indexing variables.

Example 11.12

Vectors in mathematics are one-dimensional arrays, and matrices are two-dimensional arrays. The follow declare V to hold an N-element vector, and A, B and S to hold $M \times N$ matrices (where M and N are suitably defined constants):

```
V      : array [1. .N] of Real;
A, B, S: array [1. .M, 1. .N] of Real
```

11.5 TYPE RULES FOR ARRAYS

INDEXING

An index expression must be assignment compatible with the array variable's index type.

ASSIGNMENT COMPATIBILITY

A complete array may be assigned to an array variable provided the two arrays are of *identical* type. This is the case only if both variables are declared at the same place, or are declared with the same type identifier. For example, if we declare:

```
Mark        : array [1. .NrStudents] of
                  array [1. .NrPapers] of 0. .100;
OneStudent: array [1. .NrPapers] of 0. .100
```

the assigning statement

```
OneStudent := Mark[Student]
```

would be illegal since the two array variables are declared separately. On the other hand, if we introduce the type definition:

```
StudentsMarks = array [1. .NrPapers] of 0. .100
```

and rewrite the variable declarations as follows:

```
Mark        : array [1. .NrStudents] of StudentsMarks;
OneStudent: StudentsMarks
```

then the above assignment statement *would* be allowed, since both arrays are now of type StudentsMarks. Its effect would be to copy a complete row of Mark into the array OneStudent.

EXERCISES 11

11.1. Assume the number of rooms in a hotel is given by a constant NrRooms. (a) Write a declaration of an array variable suitable for keeping track of which rooms are free. (b) Write a program fragment which counts how many hotel rooms are free, given that appropriate values have been stored in the array.

11.2. Write a program fragment which reverses the order of the integers in an array A of type **array** [1. .100] **of** Integer.

11.3. Write a program fragment which determines the *range* of the elements, i.e. the maximum difference between any two elements, of the array YearlyRainfall of Example 11.2.

11.4. Modify program Election (Example 11.1) so that it writes the vote counts in the form of a histogram with one asterisk for each vote, for example:

Candidate 1 **************************
Candidate 2 ***********************************
Candidate 3
Candidate 4 *********

11.5. Modify program Election (Example 11.1) so that it handles *any* number of candidates up to a *maximum* of 10. The actual number of candidates is provided as the first line of the input data.

11.6. Write a program fragment which normalizes the vector V of Example 11.12, i.e. divides each component by the maximum of the components' absolute values.

11.7. Write a program fragment, using the matrices A, B and S of Example 11.12, which sets S to the matrix sum of A and B.

11.8*. Given a square matrix:

Matrix: **array** [1. .N, 1. .N] **of** Integer

write program fragments which determine: (a) whether Matrix is symmetrical about the main diagonal; and (b) whether Matrix is lower-triangular, i.e. every element above the main diagonal is zero. (The main diagonal is the one which runs from Matrix[1,1] to Matrix[N,N].)

PROGRAMMING EXERCISES 11

11.9. Write a program which accumulates the frequency of occurrence of each of the letters of the alphabet in its input data, and which outputs the frequency of each letter as a percentage of the total number of letters read. Run the program with some text from a book as input data.

11.10. The heights of a group of people are provided as input, one per line. Write a program which computes and outputs the mean and standard deviation of these measurements, the number of measurements which are within one standard deviation of the mean, the number which are between one and two standard deviations from the mean, and the number outside this range. Note that it will be necessary to store all the measurements; you may assume that there are not more than (say) 100 of them.

The standard deviation of a group of N measurements is given by the formula Sqrt(SumOfSquares/N−Sqr(Mean)), where Mean is their mean and SumOfSquares is the sum of their squares.

11.11. *Pascal's triangle* is the following pattern:

$$
\begin{array}{c}
1 \\
1 \quad 1 \\
1 \quad 2 \quad 1 \\
1 \quad 3 \quad 3 \quad 1 \\
1 \quad 4 \quad 6 \quad 4 \quad 1 \\
1 \quad 5 \quad 10 \quad 10 \quad 5 \quad 1 \\
1 \quad 6 \quad 15 \quad 20 \quad 15 \quad 6 \quad 1
\end{array}
$$

etc.

in which each integer inside the triangle is the sum of the two integers above it. {Mathematicians should recognize that the integers in Pascal's triangle are the binomial coefficients. Both the triangle and the programming language are named after the great Frenchman Blaise Pascal (1623–1662).}

Write a program to generate the first ten rows (say) of Pascal's triangle.

11.12. Write a program which reads and writes a table Mark (declared as in Example 11.10). Assume that the table elements are supplied paper by paper, i.e. all the marks for paper 1, followed by all the marks for paper 2, and so on. The table is to be written with one row for each student and one column for each paper. On the right of each row write the student's total mark. At the foot of each column write the average mark (rounded to the nearest integer) for the paper. Also write the average total mark at the foot of the totals column.

11.13. Write a program which reads a representation of a bridge hand of 13 cards, and which outputs (a) the contents of the hand, with the cards arranged in descending order by rank within each suit, and (b) the points value of the hand (counting 4 for an Ace, 3 for a King, 2 for a Queen and 1 for a Jack), e.g.:

```
Clubs       K   10   9
Diamonds    J    9   4   3
Hearts      A    Q  10   8   2
Spades      7
```

Points Value = 10

On input, each card is to be represented by a pair of integers, the first representing its suit (1 for Clubs, 2 for Diamonds, 3 for Hearts, 4 for Spades), and the second representing its rank (14 for Ace, 13 for King, 12 for Queen, 11 for Jack, 2–10 for other ranks). The cards are supplied in random order. (Hint: use a two-dimensional Boolean array, with one element for every card of the pack.)

12

Packed arrays and strings

This chapter covers:

* packed data
* string types in Pascal
* input/output of strings
* string comparison and lexicographic ordering

12.1 PACKED ARRAYS

Up to now we have pictured simple items of data (e.g. numbers, characters and truth values) as occupying one 'box' or store location each. This is the natural or *unpacked* arrangement for storing such data.

When we are dealing with bulky arrays, however, it may be expedient to consider more economical use of storage. In certain circumstances, this can be achieved by squeezing several items of data into each store location. Since it is not the purpose of this book to explain exactly how numbers, characters and so on are represented in computer storage, we shall illustrate this idea by analogy.

Consider the example of an array of ten two-digit integers. Normally this would occupy ten store locations, e.g.:

| 51 | 27 | 20 | 44 | 32 | 0 | 21 | 4 | 99 | 18 |

If our computer can accommodate a four-digit integer in each store location, however, we can squeeze two components of this array into each store location, so the whole array will fit in only five store locations:

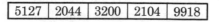

| 5127 | 2044 | 3200 | 2104 | 9918 |

155

If our computer can accommodate six-digit integers, we need only four store locations (with part of one location unoccupied):

512720	443200	210499	18????

In each case, we say that the array is *packed*. It is still possible to access the individual components of a packed array, but such access is more difficult since it will require the stored data to be broken down into its constituent digits. Thus the saving of space has been bought at the expense of slowing down access to individual components.

In Pascal, any array may be specified as packed simply by prefixing **array** by the reserved word **packed**.

Example 12.1

In a hotel room reservation system, it might be convenient to use a Boolean array Free, such that Free[Room] indicates whether room Room is free or not. If the number of rooms to be controlled is large, it would make sense to store this array in packed form:

```
Free: packed array [1 . . NrRooms] of Boolean
```

Typically, packing might reduce the storage required for this array by a factor between 4 and 32.

Notice that there is no way in Pascal to specify exactly how the data is to be packed. The Pascal compiler will *automatically* choose a suitable arrangement, which will depend on the size of the items to be packed and on the capacity of the computer's store locations.

Using the attribute **packed** generally makes no difference to the meaning of a program, in the sense that the program will produce the same results whether **packed** is present or absent. The main difference **packed** makes is to the efficiency of the program: less space will be required to store its data, but access to individual components may be slower and require a longer machine-code program.

Generally speaking, you should not concern yourself at this stage with the problems of balancing storage space against execution time. The main reason for mentioning the **packed** attribute here is to introduce the important topic of the next section.

12.2 STRINGS

A *string* is just a packed character array with a lower bound of 1. We have used strings already, as parameters in Write statements such as:

```
Write ('Total')
```

Here the string 'Total' is just a constant of the *string type*:

```
packed array [1 . . 5] of Char
```

5 being the *length* of the string, i.e. the number of characters in it. We can also define string constants, define string types, and declare string variables, as illustrated by Example 12.2.

Example 12.2

```
const
    ThisBook = 'Pascal        ';
    MaxTitleLength = 10;
type
    Names = packed array [1 . . 12] of Char;
var
    Title: packed array [1 . . MaxTitleLength] of Char;
    Author1, Author2: Names
```

Using these we may write statements like:

```
Title := ThisBook;
Author1 := 'B I LL  F I NDLAY'
Author2 := 'DAVID  WATT    '
```

Note that a string must always be *exactly* the same length as the string variable to which it is being assigned. For example, we may assign any 10-character string to Title, but not any shorter or longer string.

String variables are useful for storing and manipulating legible data, i.e. words and text. For example, given the declarations of Example 12.2, we can store in Author1 and Author2 names up to 12 characters long:

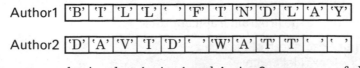

These diagrams emphasize that Author1 and Author2 are arrays of characters. Alternatively we may picture string variables like this:

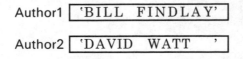

Note that Author2 has been assigned a name with fewer than 12 significant characters; the number of characters has been made up to 12 by adding blanks.

This common practice is known as *padding* or *filling out* with blanks. Notice also that the name itself has been placed as far to the left as possible; the extra blanks have been added on the right. We say that the name has been stored *left-justified*. Analogously, the name could be stored *right-justified* in the string, but left-justification is the more usual convention for words and text. (Right-justification is the convention for output of numbers to a text file, however: see Section 8.2.)

Example 12.3

Assume that a title has been stored, left-justified, in the string variable Title of Example 12.2, for example:

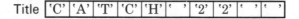

Let us write a program fragment to output the title centred on the line, assuming for this purpose that the line width is LineWidth=60 columns.

This can be done quite simply once we know the actual length of the title, i.e. excluding padding blanks:

```
determine the actual length of the title, Length;
write the title, preceded by ((LineWidth−Length) div 2) blanks
```

We can determine the length of the title by searching *backwards*, i.e. from right to left, to find the rightmost non-blank character. This is just an example of linear search. We define the constant:

```
Blank = '  '
```

and declare the variables:

```
Length: 0 . . MaxTitleLength;
Padding: Boolean
```

We can now refine the program fragment thus:

```
(* determine the length of the title *)
Length := MaxTitleLength;
Padding := True;
while Padding and (Length > 0) do
  if Title[Length] <> Blank then
     Padding := False
  else
     Length := Length−1;
(* write the title preceded by necessary blanks *)
WriteLn (Blank: (LineWidth−Length) div 2, Title)
```

Assuming the contents of Title shown above, the output from this program fragment would be:

CATCH 22

in which the title is indented by 26 spaces.

As Example 12.3 illustrates, a statement like Write(Title) may be used to write a complete string. On the other hand, Standard Pascal does *not* allow a statement like Read(Title) to be used to read a complete string, since it would be unclear how many characters were to be read. Instead we must program string input ourselves. The following example illustrates one way to do so.

Example 12.4

Write a program fragment to read characters into the string variable

```
String: packed array [1 . . L] of Char
```

Exactly L characters are to be read, unless the end of the current line of input is reached, in which case String is to be filled out with blanks.

Since every component of String is to be assigned a character—either a character read from input or a padding blank—this problem can be solved most neatly using a **for** statement:

```
for Pos := 1 to L do
  if EOLn(Input) then
    String[Pos] := Blank
  else
    Read (String[Pos])
```

which uses the variable Pos: 1 . . L.

Verify the following cases (with L=10) by hand-testing:

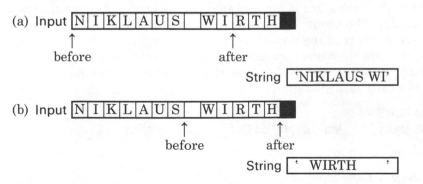

Example 12.4 illustrates why you must program string input yourself: you might wish to read L characters exactly; or in different circumstances you

might prefer to stop reading characters at an end-of-line, or at a blank, or at a non-alphabetic character. Moreover, you might wish to skip preceding blanks before storing any characters in the string (see Exercises 12).

You will be familiar with the ordinary *alphabetical ordering* of words. For example, names in a telephone directory would be ordered as follows:

    Dahl
    Dijkstra
    Hoare
    Knuth
    Wilkes
    Wirth

The names are ordered on their first letters; names which have the same first letters are ordered on their second letters; and so on. In computers an ordering is defined for all characters (not just letters) so we can generalize this to the *lexicographic ordering* of strings.

As you know already, individual characters may be compared using the comparison operators '=', '<>', '<', '<=', '>=' and '>'. We may also compare complete strings (of the same length) using these same operators. For example, if the value of Name is 'Wirth   ', then the expressions

Name = 'Wirth   '   Name <> 'Dijkstra'
Name > 'Wilkes   '   Name >= 'Dahl   '
Name < 'Wulf   '   Name <= 'Wirth   '

all have the value True.

Example 12.5

Let us develop a program which reads a sequence of names, one per line, and checks whether the names are in lexicographic order or not. Assume that no name is longer than MaxLength characters.

The program can read the names one at a time, and compare each name (except the first) with the name immediately before it in the sequence. Thus we need to declare two string variables, to hold the current name and the previous name. With the variable declaration:

```
ThisName, LastName:
    packed array [1 . . MaxLength] of Char
```

here is an outline solution:

```
read a name into LastName;
while more names remain to be read do
    begin
```

```
      read a name into ThisName;
      check that LastName precedes ThisName in lexicographic order;
      LastName := ThisName
   end
```

The commands 'read a name into ...' can be refined along the lines of Example 12.4, adding ReadLn in each case so that the condition 'more names remain to be read' can be refined simply to **not** EOF(Input). The remaining refinement is straightforward using a comparison operator on the two string variables:

```
   (* check that LastName precedes ThisName in lexicographic order *)
    if LastName > ThisName then
       WriteLn (LastName, 'should follow', ThisName)
```

Check the solution by hand-testing: (a) using the sequence of names cited above; and (b) having interchanged two of the names.

As a rule of thumb, character arrays should always be packed, to take advantage of the ability in Pascal to use string constants and to compare strings directly. Typically, packing compresses character arrays by a factor of 4, and assignment and comparison of strings are speeded up by a similar factor.

12.3 TYPE RULES FOR STRINGS

ASSIGNMENT COMPATIBILITY

A string must be exactly the same length as the string variable to which it is to be assigned. (This rule is slightly less restrictive than the assignment-compatibility rule for other arrays: see Section 11.5.)

COMPARISONS

Strings to be compared must be exactly the same length.

EXERCISES 12

12.1. Modify the program fragment of Example 12.3 so that it 'underlines' the title as well as centring it.

12.2. Assume that some text has been stored, but *not* left-justified, in the array String of Example 12.4. Write a program fragment which will left-justify this text within String.

12.3. (a) Rewrite Example 12.4 to read characters up to a blank or end-of-line. If fewer than L non-blank characters are read, String is to be padded with blanks. If more than L non-blanks are read, the excess characters are to be discarded. (b) Modify your solution to skip blanks before storing any characters in String.

12.4. Modify Example 11.7 so that List and Target contain 10-character strings rather than integers.

12.5. (a) A string variable TimeString contains the time of day in the format '17:14', i.e. the hours and minutes parts are each exactly two digits. Write a program fragment which uses TimeString to compute the number of minutes since midnight. (b) Write a program fragment which, given the number of minutes since midnight as an integer, reconstructs the time in the same string format.

PROGRAMMING EXERCISES 12

12.6. Write a program that reads an ordered sequence of names (as in Example 12.5), and writes out every name that occurs more than once.

12.7. A car dealer keeps a record of all his sales in the form of a text file, with each line having the fixed format:

    characters 1–8:   registration number;
    characters 9–17: make;
    characters 18–20: sale date.

Each item is left-justified within its character field. The sale date is coded as the last two digits of the year followed by a single letter for the month ('A' for January, 'B' for February, and so on). For example:

    T KY 123 P   D A T S U N   75A
    L DN 614 R   T R I UMP H   76H
    W D C 11N   C H E V R O L E T74L
    P R S 975 W R E N A U L T   80G
    B O N 919 V A U D I   79B

Write a program which will read such data and output the details of all Renaults sold from August 1977 (77H) to July 1978 (78G) inclusive. *Hint*: treat the dates as 3-character strings, and use string comparisons on them.

12.8. Each line of input data contains a person's full name, with the surname marked by an asterisk, for example:

ABU JA'FAR MOHAMMED IBN MUSA *AL-KHOWARIZMI
*HALAYUDHA
*CHU SHIH-CHIEH
BLAISE *PASCAL

Write a program which reads the names and outputs each person's name with the surname first, followed by a comma and all the other names, for example:

AL-KHOWARIZMI, ABU JA'FAR MOHAMMED IBN MUSA
HALAYUDHA
CHU, SHIH-CHIEH
PASCAL, BLAISE

12.9*. Sometimes it is useful to be able to output 'banner headlines', in larger than normal characters. For example, 'PASCAL' might be output as:

```
PPP     AA    SSS   CCC   AA   L
P   P   A   A S       C   A   A L
PPP     AAAA  SS    C     AAAA L
P       A   A   S C       A   A L
P       A   A SSS     CCC A   A LLLL
```

Design a complete set of letters for banner headlines, and write a program which outputs each line of input data as a banner headline. *Hint*: for each letter initialize and use an array of perhaps five four-character strings, for example:

' AA '
'A A'
'AAAA'
'A A'
'A A'

Part IV
Subprograms

13

Functions

This chapter covers:

* functions in Pascal
* formal and actual parameters
* local declarations
* functions and data structures

13.1 THE NEED FOR FUNCTIONS

Suppose we are writing a program in which we want to determine whether the
Integer variables CheckSum and Parity have odd values. We could include in
our program expressions such as (CheckSum **mod** 2 <> 0) and (Parity **mod**
2 <> 0). A better way to achieve the same effect, however, would be to use the
standard function Odd. The program would then contain the expressions
Odd(CheckSum) and Odd(Parity). These expressions are more readable, partly
because they are shorter, but more importantly because the identifier Odd
concentrates attention on the *meaning* of the expressions rather than the way
they are computed. They are also more pleasant to write. The tedium of
reworking similar expressions several times is avoided, and with it the risk of
making a mistake.

When we consider functions such as Sin and Exp which are defined by
complicated algorithms containing many statements, these advantages are
strongly emphasized.

Although programming languages like Pascal provide a fair selection of
such standard functions, this selection is necessarily limited. For example,
Pascal does not provide standard functions to compute the tangent of a given

angle, nor to determine whether a given number is prime, nor to determine whether a given character is a letter, although such functions might sometimes be just as useful as **Odd, Sin** and **Exp**. Since we cannot expect a programming language to anticipate every conceivable need for a function, we need a facility by which we ourselves can provide functions to our own specification. In Pascal this facility is called the *function declaration*.

13.2 FUNCTIONS IN PASCAL

Odd(CheckSum) and **Sin**(2*Pi*X) are examples of *function designators,* and in these examples **CheckSum** and **2*Pi*X** are called *actual parameters*. Each actual parameter is an expression of a type appropriate to the function.

The syntax of function designators is summarized in Figure 13.1. This shows that, in general, a function designator may have several actual parameters (although none of the standard functions has more than one).

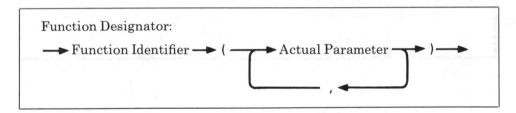

Function Designator:

Figure 13.1. Syntax of Function Designators (simplified)

To write our own function declaration, we must specify the identifier of the function, the type(s) of its parameter(s), and the type of the result to be computed. This information decides the way in which the function may be called. The function declaration must also contain statements which specify how the function result is computed from the values of the actual parameters.

A function may be called from several different places, possibly with different actual parameters. For example, if we declare a function **Tan** to compute the tangent of an angle, we might wish in different places to evaluate **Tan**(A) or **Tan**(B+C). This implies that the declaration of **Tan** cannot refer directly to any actual parameter. The problem is solved by introducing into the declaration of **Tan** an identifier, say **X**, which will stand for the value of the actual parameter. Thus **X** will stand for the value of **A** during the computation of **Tan**(A), and it will stand for the value of **B+C** during the computation of **Tan**(B+C). We call **X** a *formal parameter*, and it is available for use only *inside the declaration of* **Tan**. In general, each function declaration must specify an identifier for each of its formal parameters.

Example 13.1

We might declare the tangent function as follows:

```
function Tan ( X: Real) : Real;
  begin
  Tan := Sin(X) / Cos(X)
  end
```

This example illustrates the features of a function declaration.

(a) '**function** Tan' defines the function identifier to be Tan.
(b) '(X: Real)' is the function's *formal parameter part*. This says that the function has a single formal parameter whose identifier is X and whose type is Real.
(c) ': Real' following the formal parameter part defines the function's *result type* to be Real.
(d) **begin** and **end** enclose the *statement part* of the function declaration.
(e) Within the statement part, the special assignment statement Tan := Sin(X)/ Cos(X) assigns a value to the function itself. It is this value which is returned when the function is invoked.

Since Tan has a single Real formal parameter, it must be called by a function designator containing a single Real expression as actual parameter. This function designator is itself a Real operand (since the result type of Tan is Real), and as such it may be used in Real expressions, for example:

```
Height := Range * Tan(Elevation)
Write (Tan(Degrees*Pi/180))
```

In the first of these statements, the function designator Tan(Elevation) is evaluated as follows: first the current value of the actual parameter Elevation is assigned to the formal parameter X of Tan; then the statement part of Tan is executed, and the value assigned to Tan is treated as the value of the function designator. The value of the function designator in this statement is multiplied by Range and the product assigned to Height.

In the second statement, the function designator Tan(Degrees*Pi/180) is evaluated similarly, except that the value of the actual parameter Degrees*Pi/180 is assigned to X. The value of the function designator in this statement is written out.

The following complete program, incorporating the function Tan, writes a table of tangents of angles 0, 10, 20, ..., 360 degrees. Note that the function declaration is inserted between the program's variable declarations and statement part.

```
program TableOfTans ( Output );

const
  Pi = 3.1415926536;
var
  Degrees: 0. .360;
  Line    : 0. .36;

function Tan (X: Real) : Real;
  begin
  Tan := Sin(X)/Cos(X)
  end (*Tan*);

begin (*TableOfTans*)
WriteLn ('Angle':5, 'Tangent':15); WriteLn;
for Line := 0 to 36 do
  begin
  Degrees := 10*Line;
  Write (Degrees:5);
  if Degrees mod 180 = 90 then
    WriteLn ('Infinity':15)
  else
    WriteLn (Tan(Degrees*Pi/180):15)
  end
end (*TableOfTans*).
```

Example 13.2

Given the type definitions:

```
Years        = 1753. .9999;
Months       = (Jan,Feb,Mar,Apr,May,Jun,
                Jul,Aug,Sep,Oct,Nov,Dec);
MonthLengths = 28. .31
```

the following function determines whether a given year is a leap year:

```
function IsLeap ( Year: Years ) : Boolean;
  begin
  IsLeap := (Year mod 4 = 0) and (Year mod 100 <> 0)
            or (Year mod 400 = 0)
  end (*IsLeap*)
```

and the following function calls IsLeap to determine the number of days in a given month and year:

```
function NrDaysIn ( Month: Months; Year: Years ) : MonthLengths;
  begin
  case Month of
    Jan, Mar, May, Jul, Aug, Oct, Dec:
      NrDaysIn := 31;
    Apr, Jun, Sep, Nov:
      NrDaysIn := 30;
    Feb:
      if IsLeap(Year) then
        NrDaysIn := 29
      else
        NrDaysIn := 28
  end
end (*NrDaysIn*)
```

IsLeap has one formal parameter, of type Years, and its result type is Boolean. Therefore a function designator calling IsLeap must have a single actual parameter of type Years, and it is itself a Boolean operand. For example, see how the function designator IsLeap(Year) is used as an **if** condition within function NrDaysIn.

NrDaysIn has two formal parameters—the first of type Months and the second of type Years—and its result type is MonthLengths. Therefore a function designator calling NrDaysIn must have two actual parameters—the first an expression of type Months and the second an expression of type Years—and it is itself an operand of type MonthLengths. An example of such a function designator would be NrDaysIn(Feb,1984), which would yield the value 29.

A function designator must supply one actual parameter for each formal parameter of the function it calls. Whenever the function designator is to be evaluated, the value of each actual parameter is assigned to the corresponding formal parameter, as illustrated below.

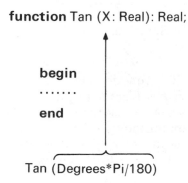

```
function Tan (X: Real): Real;

  begin
  .......
  end
```

Tan (Degrees*Pi/180)

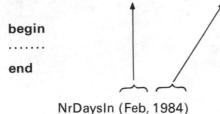

function NrDaysIn (Month: Months; Year: Years): MonthLengths;

> **begin**
> ....
> **end**

NrDaysIn (Feb, 1984)

The syntax of function declarations is summarized in Figures 13.2 and 13.3. **function** is a reserved word.

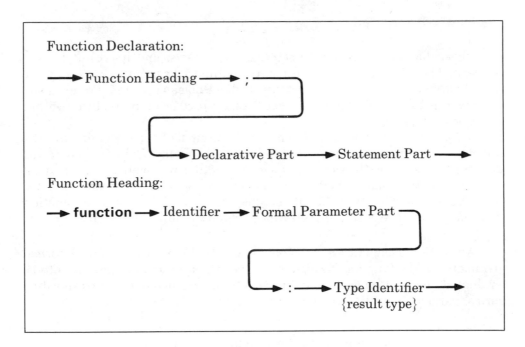

Figure 13.2. Syntax of Function Declarations

Note that the result type of a function, and the types of its formal parameters, must all be specified by *type identifiers*. These may be standard type identifiers, such as **Real** or **Boolean**; otherwise they must be defined outside the function, like **Years**, **Months** or **MonthLengths** above.

Every function must yield a result which is a single value. This means that the result type may be any ordinal type or **Real**, but not an array type nor a string type.

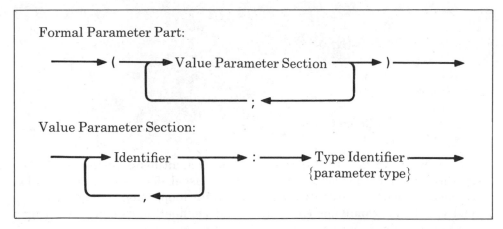

Figure 13.3. Syntax of Formal Parameter Parts (simplified)

13.3 DECLARATIONS WITHIN FUNCTIONS

The examples in the previous section illustrate functions whose results can be computed essentially by obeying a single statement involving the formal parameters. More usually, several statements are needed to work out the result and these statements may require variables of their own, variables which are of no concern to the rest of the program. Such variables could be declared in the program's declarative part, as *global variables*. However, doing this would make the working of the function dependent on something outside of itself; it would no longer be self-contained. To avoid this, Pascal allows a function to have its own internal declarative part, as we can see in Figure 13.2. As well as variables, we can declare constants, types, and even further functions, inside the function declaration, and these will be available for use only within the function. Thus the function resembles a complete program in miniature—it is an example of a *subprogram*.

Example 13.3

Pascal does not have an operator to compute powers of numbers. However, a function with this purpose is easy to write. Let us write the declaration of a function to calculate an Integer power of a Real number, giving a Real result.

```
function Power (X : Real; N : Integer) : Real;
   var
     Temp : Real;
     P     : 1 . . MaxInt;
```

```
begin
Temp := 1.0;
for P := 1 to Abs(N) do
   Temp := Temp * X;
if N >= 0 then
   Power := Temp
else
   Power := 1.0/Temp;
end (*Power*)
```

Here we have had to introduce two *local* identifiers, Temp and P. The variable P *must* be declared inside Power—Pascal does not allow a global variable to be used as the control variable of a **for** loop. Temp could be declared globally, but that would make the function dependent on its context, giving a much less modular program.

As an important aside, note that we do need a working variable such as Temp to accumulate the result in. Any attempt to do without it, such as follows:

```
Power := 1.0;
for P := 1 to Abs(N) do
   Power := Power * N;
```

is illegal, because Power is *not* a variable and cannot be used as such in an expression. Do not be confused by assignment statements such as:

```
Power := 1.0/Temp
```

that serve to define the value returned by a function. Within a function's statement part the function identifier normally may appear only in this manner.

The Power function can be used in a complete program as follows.

```
program RealPowers (Output);
var
   V      : Real;
   M, N, P: Integer;

   function Power (X: Real; N: Integer): Real;
      var
         Temp: Real;
         P     : 1 . . MaxInt;
      begin
      Temp := 1.0;
      for P := 1 to Abs(N) do
         Temp := Temp * X;
      if N >= 0 then
         Power := Temp
```

```
    else
       Power := 1.0/Temp;
    end (*Power*);

begin
Read (V, M, N);
for P := M to N do
   WriteLn (V, ' to the power ', P:1, ' is ', Power(V, P));
end (*RealPowers*).
```

Note the indentation of the internal declarative and statement parts of the function declaration. This helps to set them apart visually from the declarative and statement parts of the main program.

Note also that the *local variable* P, declared and used within **Power**, is quite separate from the *global variable* P declared and used in the main program.

Let us see exactly what happens when the function is called by the function designator **Power**(V, P) in the WriteLn statement. Before the function is called, each time round the loop, the store picture for the program might look like this:

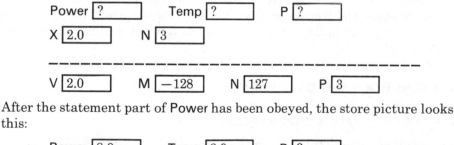

When we enter the function to evaluate **Power**(V, P), we need additional storage for the function result, for the formal parameters X and N, and for the local variables Temp and P. The formal parameters are assigned the values of the corresponding actual parameters. The function result and the local variables are initially undefined:

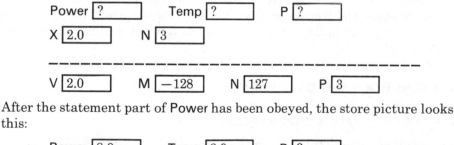

After the statement part of **Power** has been obeyed, the store picture looks like this:

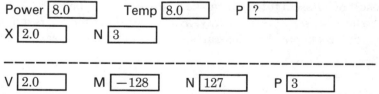

All the storage above the broken line is now discarded, since it was needed only for the evaluation of the function designator. And so we get back to the original picture:

V $\boxed{2.0}$ M $\boxed{-128}$ N $\boxed{127}$ P $\boxed{3}$

Although the location holding the function result (**Power**) has been discarded, its *value* is retained as the value of the function designator. In this example 8.0 is immediately output by the WriteLn statement.

As Example 13.3 illustrates, a subprogram is a very convenient way of gathering together in one place the declarations and statements needed to perform some routine task, isolating its details from the rest of the program. The subprogram is a powerful tool for achieving the ideals of localization and modularity recommended in Chapter 7.

Let us conclude by summarizing the manner in which a function designator is evaluated.

(1) A store location is created for the function result. Its initial value is undefined.
(2) The actual parameters of the function designator are paired off, from left to right, with the formal parameters of the function. (It follows that for each formal parameter exactly one actual parameter must be supplied.)
(3) A store location is created for each formal parameter of the function, to which is assigned the value of the corresponding actual parameter. (It follows that each actual parameter must be an expression assignment-compatible with the type of the corresponding formal parameter.)
(4) A store location is created for each local variable of the function. Its initial value is undefined.
(5) The function's statement part is obeyed.
(6) Finally, all store locations created for the function result, for the formal parameters and for the local variables are discarded. The *value* from the function result location is retained as the value of the function designator.

13.4 FUNCTIONS AND DATA STRUCTURES

{This section may be omitted on a first reading.}

The result of a Pascal function can be of any ordinal type, or Real. It cannot be a data structure, such as an array. However, there is no restriction on the parameters. Example 13.4 illustrates a function with an array parameter.

Example 13.4

Assuming the type definitions:

```
Months = (Jan,Feb,Mar,Apr,May,Jun,
            Jul,Aug,Sep,Oct,Nov,Dec);
MonthlyStats = array [Months] of Real
```

the following function returns the value of the largest component of a given array of type MonthlyStats.

```
function Maximum ( Stats : MonthlyStats ) : Real;
   var
      Max    : Real;
      Month : Months;
   begin
   Max := Stats[Jan];
   for Month := Feb to Dec do
      if Stats[Month] > Max then
         Max := Stats[Month];
   Maximum := Max
   end (*Maximum*)
```

The function could be incorporated into a complete program as follows:

```
program YearlyMaxima ( Input, Output );

type
   Months = (Jan,Feb,Mar,Apr,May,Jun,
              Jul,Aug,Sep,Oct,Nov,Dec);
   MonthlyStats = array [Months] of Real;

var
   Rainfall, Temperature : MonthlyStats;
   Month                 : Months;

function Maximum ( Stats : MonthlyStats ) : Real;
   var
      Max    : Real;
      Month : Months;
   begin
   Max := Stats[Jan];
   for Month := Feb to Dec do
      if Stats[Month] > Max then
         Max := Stats[Month];
   Maximum := Max
   end (*Maximum*);

begin (*YearlyMaxima*)
for Month := Jan to Dec do
```

```
    Read (Rainfall[Month], Temperature[Month]);
  WriteLn ('Maximum monthly rainfall:',
            Maximum(Rainfall):4:1);
  WriteLn ('Maximum mean temperature:',
            Maximum(Temperature):4:1)
end (*YearlyMaxima*).
```

EXERCISES 13

13.1. Given that today's month and year have been stored in variables ThisMonth and ThisYear, write a statement, using the function NrDaysIn (Example 13.2) to assign the number of days in this month next year to an Integer variable N.

13.2. (a) Write a function that returns the fourth power of a given Real value. Use the Sqr function. Write a second version using the Power function of Example 13.3. (b) Write a statement that outputs the fourth power of the sum of A and B.

13.3. Write a function that decides whether a given character is a letter or not, and a function that decides whether a given character is a digit or not. Use your functions to rewrite program CharacterCount of Example 8.3.

13.4. Write a function that determines whether a given integer is prime, i.e. has no factors other than itself and 1. (b) Write a program fragment that reads an integer and outputs it together with the appropriate message 'prime' or 'non-prime'.

The following exercises need arrays or strings.

13.5. Draw store pictures for Example 13.4, like those in Example 13.3.

13.6. Modify Example 12.3 by introducing a function that computes the actual length of a title supplied as a parameter.

13.7. Modify function Maximum (Example 13.4) by making it determine the maximum component of Stats over the months Month1 to Month2 (instead of the whole year). Month1 and Month2 are to be additional formal parameters.

13.8. Make your answers to Exercise 11.8 into functions, with Matrix as the formal parameter in each case.

13.9. Write a function which accepts a person's full name (one or more fore-names followed by a surname) supplied as a string parameter, and returns the initial letter of the surname.

PROGRAMMING EXERCISES 13

13.10. The integer logarithm of a positive integer N to the base B is the largest integer L such that the L-th power of B does not exceed N. Write a function which computes the integer logarithm of N to the base B. Write a prog. incorporating your function, which outputs a table of integer logarithms, i. the bases 2, 3 and 10, of all the integers from 1 to (say) 50.

13.11. The total interest payable on a bank loan is calculated as the product of the amount of the loan, the loan period in months, and the monthly interest rate. The capital and interest are paid off in equal monthly instalments over the period of the loan. Write a function which computes the monthly repayment, given as parameters the amount of the loan, the loan period and the monthly interest rate. Include your function in a program which reads the monthly interest rate, and outputs a table showing the monthly repayment for loans of £100, £200, . . ., £1000, and for loan periods of 3, 6, . . ., 24 months.

13.12*. (Needs strings.) Write a function which, given a Roman numeral stored left-justified in a string, returns its integer value. (Take into account combinations like IV, whose value is 4, not 6.) Make sure your function deals sensibly with incorrectly formed Roman numerals. Write a program which reads Roman numerals and outputs them together with their values.

14

Procedures

This chapter covers:

* procedure subprograms
* value parameters and variable parameters
* procedures and data structures
* the scope rules of Pascal

14.1 THE NEED FOR PROCEDURES

In Chapter 13 we have viewed a Pascal function as a self-contained piece of program, or subprogram. A function takes one or more values, supplied as parameters. On return it produces a single result. This result may be assigned to a variable, if we choose, or it may be used as an operand in a more complicated expression. In this view a Pascal function is quite similar to a mathematical function. (Indeed, some of the standard functions correspond to well-known mathematical functions, such as Sin and Sqrt.)

When we say 'self-contained', we mean that a subprogram may contain inside it many details that are of no concern to the user of the subprogram. Inside the subprogram we find statements that do its work. We might also find constant definitions, variable declarations and so on. These are for use by the statements of the subprogram. But when we write down a statement calling a subprogram, we do not concern ourselves with these internal details. We care only about what results the subprogram will produce. For example, when we call the Sin or Sqrt function, we never worry about its internal details.

Thus subprograms are very useful. But Pascal functions are rather restricted in having just one result. Sometimes we need a subprogram with several results, or no results at all, or a result that is an array or string. So Pascal provides a second kind of subprogram that avoids the restrictions of a function. This is the *procedure*.

A function is called by a function designator, which has a value. On the other hand, a procedure is called by a new form of statement, called a *procedure statement*. It is not an expression, so it has no value.

How, then, does a procedure produce results? The answer is, through its parameters. Now all our examples of functions have shown parameters being used in one way only: to pass values into the functions. But there is another, quite different, way of using parameters. This allows a procedure to pass results out, storing them in variables for later use. Thus we can make a procedure produce as many results as we want. The two different ways of using parameters are discussed in Section 14.3.

We have used some procedures already, namely the standard procedures such as Read and Write. In fact, Read and Write statements are just procedure statements. They are rather irregular, however, because the number and types of their parameters are not fixed. They are like the irregular verbs of English, exceptions to the general rule. An ordinary procedure, like a function, takes a fixed number of parameters, with fixed types.

14.2 PROCEDURES IN PASCAL

A procedure is unlike a function in that it does not itself have a value; therefore a procedure has no result type. Apart from this, and the replacement of **function** by the reserved word **procedure**, the syntax of a procedure declaration is similar to that of a function declaration; see Figure 14.1.

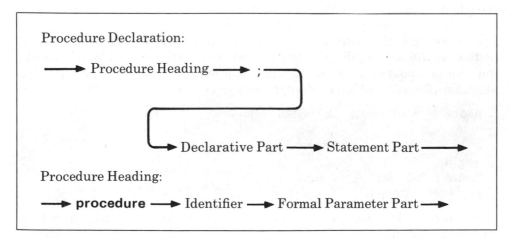

Figure 14.1. Syntax of Procedure Declarations

Procedure declarations, like function declarations, are inserted between the program's variable declarations and its statement part. For a complete summary of the positioning of constant definitions, type definitions, variable declarations and procedure and function declarations, see the Declarative Part syntax diagram in Appendix 1.2.

We call a procedure by means of a *procedure statement*. Like a function designator this specifies the identifier of the procedure to be invoked, together with any actual parameters; see Figure 14.2.

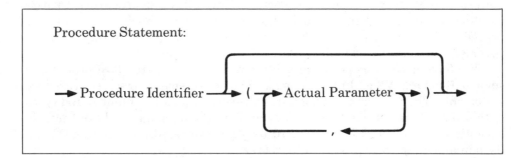

Figure 14.2. Syntax of Procedure Statements

Apart from the treatment of actual parameters (described in Section 14.3), the effect of obeying a procedure statement is simply to obey the procedure's statement part.

Example 14.1

The following little procedure writes out a date in the form 'day/month/year' (with only the last two digits of the year written), given the day of the month, the month and the year. We assume appropriate definitions of the type identifiers **DaysOfTheMonth**, **Months** and **Years** (see below).

```
procedure WriteDate ( D: DaysOfTheMonth;
                      M: Months;
                      Y: Years             );
begin
Write (D:2, '/', M:2, '/', (Y mod 100):2)
end (*WriteDate*)
```

This procedure will pass back no results when called; its only effect is to write some output.

Here is a complete program, incorporating procedure **WriteDate**, which simply reads in the three components of a date, writes that date, and writes the date exactly nine months thereafter:

```
program Dates ( Input, Output );

type
   DaysOfTheMonth = 1. .31;
   Months         = 1. .12;
   Years          = 0. .9999;
var
   Day    : DaysOfTheMonth;
   Month: Months;
   Year   : Years;

procedure WriteDate ( D : DaysOfTheMonth;
                      M : Months;
                      Y : Years            );
   begin
   Write (D:2, '/', M: 2, '/', (Y mod 100):2)
   end (*WriteDate*);

begin (*Dates*)
Read (Day, Month, Year);
WriteDate (Day, Month, Year);
WriteLn;
if Month > 3 then
   WriteDate (Day, Month−3, Year+1)
else
   WriteDate (Day, Month+9, Year);
WriteLn
end (*Dates*).
```

Given the input:

    5 10 1979

this program will output:

    5/10/79
    5/ 7/80

Here is an alternative version of procedure WriteDate, which writes the *name* of the month and also writes the year in full.

```
procedure WriteDate ( D : DaysOfTheMonth;
                      M : Months;
                      Y : Years            );
```

```
begin
Write (D:1, '   ');
case M of
    1: Write ('January');
    2: Write ('February');
    3: Write ('March');
    4: Write ('April');
    5: Write ('May');
    6: Write ('June');
    7: Write ('July');
    8: Write ('August');
    9: Write ('September');
   10: Write ('October');
   11: Write ('November');
   12: Write ('December')
   end;
Write (Y :5)
end (*WriteDate*)
```

This illustrates the flexibility of procedures: the new version of procedure WriteDate can easily be slotted into the program in place of the old version, and the procedure statements invoking it need not be changed at all, since the procedure's heading remains unchanged. Given the input cited above, the program with this modified procedure would output:

    5 October 1979
    5 July 1980

14.3 VALUE PARAMETERS AND VARIABLE PARAMETERS

So far we have seen formal parameters used only to supply *values* for use by a function or procedure. Such formal parameters are called *value parameters*, and they work very simply. On entry to the function or procedure, each value parameter is assigned the value of the corresponding actual parameter.

In Example 14.1, the formal parameters of procedure WriteDate—D, M and Y—were all value parameters. Thus the effect of the procedure statement WriteDate(Day,Month−3,Year+1) is to obey the statement part of WriteDate having assigned the value of Day to D, the value of Month−3 to M, and the value of Year+1 to Y. Once the value parameters have been assigned the values of the actual parameters, there is no further interaction between the actual parameters and the formal parameters. If a procedure assigns a new value to a value formal parameter, this assignment has no effect whatsoever on the corresponding actual parameter.

A procedure, therefore, cannot use value parameters to pass back any results. For this purpose a new kind of formal parameter is needed, one which allows a procedure to *change* the value of the corresponding actual parameter. Since the actual parameter must be capable of receiving a new value, it follows that the actual parameter must be a *variable*. Hence formal parameters of this kind are called *variable parameters*. A variable parameter merely represents the variable which is placed in the corresponding actual-parameter position.

A variable parameter is specified by placing the word **var** in front of it in the formal parameter part of the procedure declaration.

Example 14.2

The following procedure will determine the minimum of three given Integer values, and pass back this minimum through the variable parameter Min.

```
procedure FindMinimum ( A, B, C: Integer;
                              var Min: Integer );
  begin
  if A < B then
    Min := A
  else
    Min := B;
  if C < Min then
    Min := C
  end (*FindMinimum*)
```

Assuming the variable declaration:

```
Weeks, Contributions, Benefit: Integer
```

an example of a procedure statement invoking FindMinimum would be:

```
FindMinimum (600, 5*Contributions, 25*Weeks, Benefit)
```

which would have the effect of storing in Benefit the minimum of 600, 5*Contributions and 25*Weeks. Let us see exactly how this works. Immediately before obeying the procedure statement, suppose we have the following situation:

Weeks [4]   Contributions [150]   Benefit [?]

Now we enter procedure FindMinimum. A, B and C are value parameters, so we create store locations for them and assign them the values of the corresponding actual parameters, namely the values of 600, 5*Contributions and 25*Weeks respectively. On the other hand, Min is a variable parameter. Instead of receiving the current value of Benefit, Min will represent the variable Benefit itself. We illustrate this by drawing an arrow between Min and the location of Benefit:

A [600]   B [750]   C [100]   Min ◄─────────────────────────┐
───┼───
                                                                       ▼
Weeks [4   ]   Contributions [150]   Benefit [?]

Now we start to obey the statement part of procedure FindMinimum. The expression A < B evaluates to True, so we obey the statement Min:=A. Since Min is a variable parameter, we assign the value of A, not to Min itself, but to *the variable represented by* Min, i.e. Benefit:

A [600]   B [750]   C [100]   Min ◄─────────────────────────┐
───┼───
                                                                       ▼
Weeks [4   ]   Contributions [150]   Benefit [600]

Now to evaluate the expression C < Min, we compare the current value of C with the current value of *the variable represented by* Min, i.e. Benefit; thus the expression evaluates to True. We obey the statement Min:=C, whose effect is to assign the value of C to Benefit:

A [600]   B [750]   C [100]   Min ◄─────────────────────────┐
───┼───
                                                                       ▼
Weeks [4   ]   Contributions [150]   Benefit [100]

Finally we leave the procedure, and discard all the store locations above the broken line. Thus obeying the procedure statement has had the following nett effect:

Weeks [4   ]   Contributions [150]   Benefit [100]

Since procedure FindMinimum passes back only one result, of type Integer, we might prefer to replace it by an Integer function with only A, B and C as formal parameters:

```
function Minimum ( A, B, C: Integer ): Integer;
  var
    Min: Integer;
  begin
  if A < B then
    Min := A
  else
    Min := B;
  if C < Min then
    Min := C;
  Minimum := Min
  end (*Minimum*)
```

In this version, Min is an ordinary local variable. The same effect as our procedure statement could now be achieved by the assignment statement:

> Benefit := Minimum(600,5*Contributions,25*Weeks)

When a choice is available, a function is often more convenient to use than a procedure. In the following example, however, we require a subprogram with *two* results. For this purpose a procedure is the more appropriate choice.

Example 14.3

The following procedure takes a Real number, representing a distance in metres, and converts it to two Real numbers, representing a distance in feet and inches.

```
procedure FeetAndInches (Metres: Real;
                            var Feet, Inches: Real);
   const
      FeetPerMetre = 3.280839895;
   var
      Imperial: Real;
   begin
   Imperial := Metres * FeetPerMetre;
   Feet := Trunc(Imperial);
   Inches := (Imperial — Feet) * 12;
   end (* FeetAndInches *);
```

As an exercise, write a short program incorporating this procedure. Draw store diagrams for your program just before the procedure is called, just after, just before it returns, and just after it returns.

A variable parameter gives a procedure indirect access to a variable. By operating on the parameter, the procedure causes the same operation to take effect on the variable. We have seen how this can be used to pass results out of a procedure. Now we look at an example where a variable parameter is also used to pass data into a procedure, giving it access to the current value of the actual parameter.

Example 14.4

The following procedure calculates the mean (average) of a sample containing $N+1$ numbers, given (a) N, (b) the mean of the first N of the numbers, and (c) one further number. The revised mean replaces the given mean, and the sample size is updated from N to $N+1$.

```
procedure RunningMean ( X: Real;
                        var N: Integer;
                        var Mean: Real);
   begin
   Mean := (Mean * N + X) / (N + 1);
   N := N + 1;
   end (*RunningMean*)
```

This procedure could be used in a program to give a running average for a product's daily sales figures (for example):

```
program PrintMeanSales (Input, Output);
var
   Day: Integer;
   Sale, MeanSale: Real;

procedure RunningMean ( X: Real;
                        var N: Integer;
                        var Mean: Real);
   begin
   Mean := (Mean * N + X) / (N + 1);
   N := N + 1;
   end (*RunningMean*);

begin
Day := 0; MeanSale := 0.0;
while not EOF(Input) do
   begin
   ReadLn (Sale);
   RunningMean (Sale, Day, MeanSale);
   WriteLn ('Running mean of sales up to day:', Day :1,
            ' is ', MeanSale);
   end;
end (*Print MeanSales*).
```

As an exercise, draw store diagrams showing the behaviour of this procedure during a typical call.

The syntax of formal parameter parts, including value parameters and variable parameters, is summarized in Figure 14.3. A variable parameter section is distinguished from a value parameter section by the reserved word **var**.

Let us summarize the effect of obeying a procedure statement.

(1) The actual parameters of the procedure statement are paired off, from left to right, with the formal parameters of the named procedure. (It follows

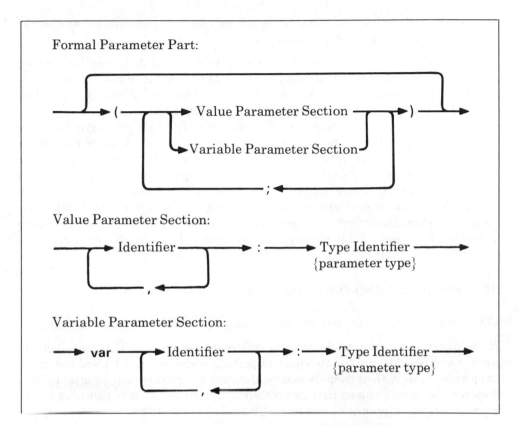

Figure 14.3. Syntax of Formal Parameter Parts (simplified)

that for each formal parameter exactly one actual parameter must be supplied.)

(2) For each *value parameter* of the procedure a store location is created, to which is assigned the value of the corresponding actual parameter. (It follows that the actual parameter must be an expression assignment-compatible with the type of the value parameter.)

(3) Each *variable parameter* of the procedure is made to represent the corresponding actual parameter (which must be a variable of identically the same type as the variable parameter).

(4) For each local variable of the procedure a store location is created whose initial value is undefined.

(5) The procedure's statement part is obeyed. At this stage value parameters behave exactly like ordinary local variables, but each reference to a variable parameter is effectively a reference to the actual parameter it represents. In particular, assigning a value to a variable parameter effectively changes the value of the actual parameter.

(6) Finally, all store locations created for formal parameters and local variables of the procedure are discarded.

Thus the effect of obeying a procedure statement is similar to the evaluation of a function designator, except for the absence of a function result. Compare the summary above with the summary at the end of Section 13.3. (The latter, however, took only value parameters into account.)

Although it is not illegal in Pascal for a function to have variable parameters, you will find no such examples in this book. It is more natural to use functions with only value parameters, since this corresponds more closely to the mathematical concept of functions. If a function, when called, changes the value of any non-local variable, either through a variable parameter or by any other means, or performs any input or output, this phenomenon is known as a *side-effect*. Side-effects are generally considered to be bad programming practice, since they tend to make programs more difficult to understand.

14.4 PROCEDURES AND DATA STRUCTURES

{This section may be omitted on a first reading.}

Subprograms (i.e. functions and procedures) and data structures (such as arrays and records) are the two most important ideas in Pascal. Used together, they provide us with extremely powerful means to organize our programs. The following example shows that components of data structures can be used as parameters to subprograms just as easily as simple variables.

Example 14.5

The following little procedure can be called with any Integer variable as actual parameter. The effect is to increment its value by one.

```
procedure Increment ( var Count: Integer );
  begin
  Count := Count+1
  end (*Increment*)
```

Suppose we wished to count the frequencies of individual upper-case letters, and the total frequency of all other characters, in a piece of text. Let us declare the variables:

```
LetterFreq: array ['A' . .'Z'] of Integer;
OtherFreq : Integer;
Character : Char
```

and initialize OtherFreq, and each component of LetterFreq, to 0. After storing a character in Character we can update the appropriate frequency by:

```
if ('A' <= Character) and (Character <= 'Z') then
   Increment (LetterFreq[Character])
else
   Increment (OtherFreq)
```

When the statement Increment(LetterFreq[Character]) is obeyed, the variable parameter Count represents the variable LetterFreq[Character], i.e. a *single* component of the array LetterFreq. For example, when Character has the value 'C', Count represents LetterFreq['C']:

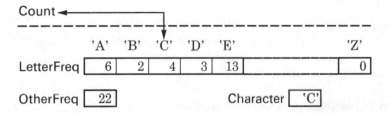

The effect of the procedure statement will then be to change the value of LetterFreq['C'] from 4 to 5; the remaining components of LetterFreq will not be disturbed.

Almost any realistic program using data structures will have subprograms to help process them. Often it is best if all references to a data structure are incorporated in subprograms. This makes the program, as a whole, much less dependent on the details of the data structure. As a consequence it is easier to understand and to modify. The generality of the parameter mechanisms of procedures makes them especially useful in this respect. (The only restriction applying to procedures is that files may not be value parameters. The same restriction applies to functions too.)

The following example shows an entire data structure (not just a component) as a parameter to a procedure.

Example 14.6

Suppose that we are supplied with input data in the form of natural-language text, which consists of 'words' separated by blanks (and end-of-lines). We are to treat any sequence of non-blank characters as a word, and assume that no word is longer than MaxWordLength characters.

When writing a program which processes such textual data, it is a good idea to include a procedure whose task is to read a single word and to pass back the word itself and its length.

The procedure must take into account the possibility that the next word in the input data may be preceded by several blanks, so two steps will be necessary, the first to scan (and ignore) blanks, the second to scan (and store) the non-blank characters which comprise the word itself. The procedure must also take into account the possibility that the unread input data consists entirely of blanks, implying that all the words have already been read.

At this stage it is unnecessary to commit ourselves on how to store the word. Let us agree that the word's spelling will be assigned to a variable parameter of type WordSpellings, and that its length will be assigned to a second variable parameter of type WordLengths; we shall define these types later. A third variable parameter, of type Boolean, is also needed to indicate whether a word is actually read.

```
procedure Readword ( var InWord: WordSpellings;
                      var InLength: WordLengths;
                      var Success: Boolean );
   local declarations;
   begin
   skip any blanks up to the next word or end of input data;
   Success := not end of input data;
   if Success then
      read a word into InWord , storing its length in InLength
   end (*ReadWord*)
```

'Skip any blanks ...' will be refined into a loop which continues until either a non-blank character is read or EOF becomes True. 'Read a word ...' will be refined into a loop which continues until a blank following the word is read. (Even the last word on the last line must be followed at least by an end-of-line marker, which is read as a blank.)

We must now commit ourselves to a definition of the types WordSpellings and WordLengths. Let us choose the type definitions:

```
WordSpellings = packed array [1. .MaxWordLength] of Char;
WordLengths  = 1. .MaxWordLength
```

which will allow us to store words up to MaxWordLength characters in length; and let us decide to store each word left-justified in InWord. After further refinements, we may arrive at the following solution:

```
procedure ReadWord ( var InWord: WordSpellings;
                      var InLength: WordLengths;
                      var Success: Boolean);
   const
      Blank = ' ';
```

```
   var
      Character: Char;
      I: 0. .MaxWordLength;
   begin
   (* skip any blanks up to the next word or end of input data *)
   Character := Blank;
   while not EOF(Input) and (Character = Blank) do
      Read (Character);
   Success := not EOF(Input);
   if Success then
      (* read a word into InWord, storing its length in InLength *)
      begin
      I := 0;
      while Character <> Blank do
        begin
        (* store Character unless InWord is already full *)
        if I < MaxWordLength then
          begin
          I := I+1;
          InWord[I] := Character
          end;
        Read (Character)
        end;
      InLength := I;
      (* fill out with blanks *)
      for I := InLength+1 to MaxWordLength do
        InWord[I] := Blank
      end
   end (*ReadWord*)
```

Here is a complete program, incorporating **ReadWord** and another procedure, which simply reads words and writes them one per line:

```
program CopyWords ( Input, Output );
const
   MaxWordLength = 16;
type
   WordSpellings = packed array [1. .MaxWordLength] of Char;
   WordLengths  = 1. .MaxWordLength;
var
   Word: WordSpellings;
   Length: WordLengths;
   WordFound: Boolean;
```

```
procedure ReadWord ( var InWord: WordSpellings;
                      var InLength: WordLengths;
                      var Success: Boolean);

   . . . . . . . . . . . . . . . . . .
   . . . . . . . . . . . . . . . . . .    (* as above *)
   . . . . . . . . . . . . . . . . . .
procedure WriteWord ( OutWord: WordSpellings;
                      OutLength: WordLengths);
   var
     I: WordLengths;
   begin
   for I := 1 to OutLength do
     Write (OutWord[I]);
   WriteLn
   end (*WriteWord*);

begin (*CopyWords*)
ReadWord (Word, Length, WordFound);
while WordFound do
   begin
   WriteWord (Word, Length);
   ReadWord (Word, Length, WordFound)
   end
end (*CopyWords*).
```

Suppose the input data is:

PARIS
IN THE
SPRING-TIME

When we obey the statement ReadWord(Word,Length,WordFound), the variable parameters InWord, InLength and Success represent the variables Word, Length and WordFound respectively; in particular, InWord represents the *whole* of the array Word. On the first entry to ReadWord we have:

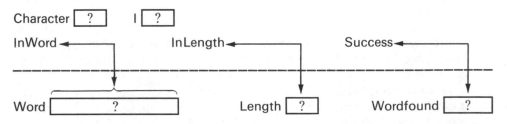

Assignment of characters to InWord[1], InWord[2] and so on, will actually result in these characters being stored in Word[1], Word[2] and so on. Thus after the first call of ReadWord we have:

Word `'PARIS           '`   Length `5`   WordFound `true`

and after the fourth call:

Word `'SPRING-TIME   '`   Length `11`   WordFound `true`

On the fifth call, WordFound is set to False but Word and Length are unaltered.

As an exercise, work through program CopyWords with the input data given above, verify the effects of procedure ReadWord, and show what output is produced.

As a general rule, if you intend that a procedure should not change a parameter P, it is best to make P a value parameter. The actual parameter is thus protected from any change the procedure makes to the formal parameter. However, safety is gained at the cost of copying the actual parameter on every call. When the parameter is a large data structure, such as an array, the storage space and processor time overheads of copying may be too great. Copying can be avoided by making P a variable parameter. A comment saying that the procedure, nevertheless, does not change the parameter greatly helps anyone who later reads the program.

14.5 THE SCOPE RULES OF PASCAL

{This section may be omitted on a first reading.}

When an identifier is declared inside a subprogram, the declaration has no effect outside the subprogram. The identifier is said to be *local* to the sub-program. On the other hand, an identifier declared at the head of the program might be used anywhere. Such an identifier is said to be *global*. In Example 14.3, Character is local to the procedure ReadWord, but MaxWordLength is global.

We now clarify these issues by stating the *scope rules* of Pascal. These rules define what identifiers may be used and where.

We shall use the program of Figure 14.4 to illustrate the scope rules. In this figure we have drawn a box round the declaration part and statement part of the program, and similar boxes round the declarative part and statement part of each subprogram. We call each box a *block*.

Blocks can be *nested*. In other words, one block may lie entirely within another. Blocks cannot, however, overlap in any other way. This is all a consequence of the syntax of Pascal. In Figure 14.4 there is only one level of nesting, but in larger programs blocks can be nested quite deeply.

In general, there will be one block for each function, one block for each procedure, and one block for the program as a whole. We include the formal parameters of a function or procedure inside the corresponding block.

Let us name each block after the corresponding function, procedure or program identifier. Thus in Figure 14.4 we have an outer block, Labels, and two inner blocks, ReadLabel and WriteLine.

Scope Rule 1. No identifier may be declared more than once in the same block.

The reason for this is obvious. Suppose we had two declarations of identifier X in the same block. Then every occurrence of X in a statement would be ambiguous.

   We may, however, declare the same identifier in different blocks. In Figure 14.4 L is declared as a constant in block Labels, and as a value parameter in block WriteLine. These are two distinct entities. Also, J is declared in two of the blocks. In both cases it is a variable, and by coincidence it has the same type. Nevertheless these are two distinct variables.

   When we use an identifier that has more than one declaration, how can we tell which declaration applies?

Scope Rule 2.   If an identifier X occurs in a statement, find the smallest block enclosing both this statement and a declaration of X. This is the declaration that applies.

Consider the identifier L in Figure 14.4.

(a) In block Labels, L is used in the statement WriteLine(51,L). Apply Scope Rule 2. The smallest block enclosing this statement and a declaration of L is, of course, Labels itself. This L is therefore the constant 80.

(b) In block ReadLabel, L appears in the **for** statement. But there is no declaration of L in this block. Consequently, the constant definition of L applies here too, since Labels is the smallest block enclosing both the **for** statement and a declaration of L.

(c) In block WriteLine, L also occurs in a **for** statement. But in this case there is a declaration of L as a value parameter of the procedure. Therefore this L is a value parameter. It takes its values from the corresponding actual parameters. On different occasions its value will be 1, 26 or 51.

   Now consider the identifier J. This is used as a control variable in each of the blocks ReadLabel and WriteLine. And in each block there is a declaration of J. In each case it is the local declaration that applies.

   To summarize, in Figure 14.4 we have drawn an arrow from each use of an identifier to the corresponding declaration.

   Note that if we apply Scope Rule 2 and cannot find a block enclosing both the statement and a declaration of the identifier X, then the program contains an error. Either the declaration has been omitted or it has been placed in the wrong block.

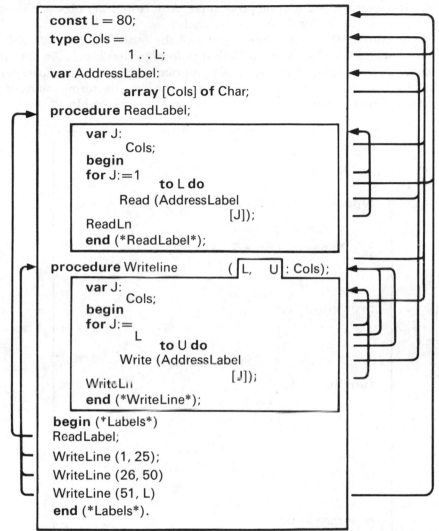

Figure 14.4. A Program with Nested Blocks

Scope Rule 3. No identifier may be used outside the block in which it is declared.

For example, the identifier U may not be used in block Labels nor in block ReadLabel. It is available for use only within block WriteLine.

The three scope rules apply to all identifiers: constants, types, variables, formal parameters, functions and procedures. Any violation of the scope rules is an error, and will be signalled by the compiler.

At the start of this section we mentioned the terms *local* and *global*. An identifier declared in a block are described as *local* to that block. An identifier declared in the outermost block (the main program) is described as *global*, since (potentially) it can be used anywhere. We also use the term *non-local*, to describe an identifier used in a block but declared in an outer block.

```
const
      MaxInt = . . . . .;

type
      Integer = . . . .;
      Boolean = (False, True);
      . . . . . . . . . . . . . . .


procedure Read . . . .;
      . . . . . . . . . . . . . . . .
      . . . . . . . . . . . . . . . .;


function EOF;
      . . . . . . . . . . . . . . . .
      . . . . . . . . . . . . . . . .;

      . . . . . . . . . . . . . . . . . . . . . . . . . . .

      . . . . . . . . . . . . . . . . . . . . . . . . . . .


program . . . .;
      ┌──────────────────────────────┐
      │  . . . . . . . . . . .        │
      │  begin                        │
      │  . . . . . . . . . .          │
      │  . . . . . . . . . .          │
      │  end.                         │
      └──────────────────────────────┘
```

Figure 14.5. The Invisible Outer Block

We can now clarify the status of the standard identifiers used for constants (such as MaxInt), types (such as Boolean and Integer), functions (such as EOF and Sin) and procedures (such as Read and Write). Imagine an invisible block enclosing the entire program: see Figure 14.5. The standard identifiers are declared in this invisible outer block. Thus we can see that the normal scope rules apply to the standard identifiers. They are not treated specially. Indeed, there is nothing to prevent us from redeclaring them to stand for something different. Occasionally this is useful (see Example 14.7). Normally, however, this would be unwise. Imagine redefining **type** Integer = Real—this would make the original definition of Integer inaccessible!

Some of our examples illustrate how the scope rules can be exploited in practical programming. In Example 14.6 there was a local declaration of I in each procedure. In Example 13.2 Year was declared as a formal parameter in two different functions. In Example 13.4, Month was declared both as a global variable and as a local variable within a function. The scope rules ensure that there is no ambiguity.

Imagine a programmer who is given a subprogram to write, without being told anything about the program in which it will be used. The programmer still has a free choice of identifiers for locally-declared constants, variables and so on. It does not matter if they happen to be the same as identifiers declared in outer blocks. The coincidence has no effect on the meaning of the subprogram.

The compiler is not confused by multiple declarations of the same identifier. Human readers are different, however. So do not use the same identifier indiscriminately for different purposes in different places. That would make the program difficult to understand.

We now turn to another example showing how we can exploit the scope rules.

Example 14.7

Suppose that someone has written a program which outputs a series of tables, one table per page (for example, tables of mathematical functions, or tables of students' examination marks grouped by subject). In skeleton form, the program might look like this:

```
program Tables ( Input, Output );
 . . . . . . . . .
 . . . . . . . . .
begin
Page;
write the first table;
Page;
```

```
write the second table;
. . . . . . . . . .
. . . . . . . . . .
end.
```

Page is a standard procedure, whose effect is to force subsequent output on to a fresh page.

Now suppose that most of the tables being written turn out to occupy only a few lines. Moreover computer paper is becoming very expensive; so, in order to economize on paper, we decide to separate the tables by lines across the page, instead of taking separate pages.

We could modify the program by replacing each invocation of **Page** by appropriate WriteLn statements. A much neater solution is to insert our own declaration of the procedure **Page**:

```
program Tables ( Input, Output );
. . . . . . . . . .
. . . . . . . . . .
procedure Page;
   begin (* paper-saving version *)
   WriteLn; WriteLn;
   WriteLn ('------------------------');
   WriteLn; WriteLn
   end (*Page*);

begin (*Tables*)
Page;
write the first table;
Page;
write the second table;
. . . . . . . . . .
. . . . . . . . . .
end (*Tables*).
```

The scope rules ensure that each procedure statement calling **Page** uses our own procedure and not the standard version in the invisible outer block.

This solution is very flexible; if desired, we could go back to writing one table per page simply by removing the procedure declaration. No change to the rest of the program is necessary.

Example 14.7 also illustrates the use of a parameterless procedure. Compare the declaration of **Page** with the syntax diagrams of Figures 14.1 and 14.3, and compare the procedure statements invoking it with the syntax diagram of Figure 14.2.

EXERCISES 14

14.1. Write a procedure which outputs N blank lines, where N is its formal parameter. Write a statement which calls your procedure to output four blank lines.

14.2. Write a procedure which interchanges the values of its two parameters (both of type Items, which you may assume to be defined elsewhere).

14.3. The Pascal Read statement cannot be used to read a Boolean value. Write a procedure which reads a Boolean value, represented in the input data by one of the characters 'F' or 'T', and passes it back through a parameter. The procedure should skip any blanks and end-of-lines preceding the 'F' or 'T'.

14.4. Make the program fragments of Examples 9.1 and 9.11 into procedures.

The following exercises need arrays and strings.

14.5. Write a procedure ReadLine which reads one line of characters and passes it back through a string parameter of type **packed array** [1. .L] **of** Char (see Example 12.4). You will find this procedure useful for many subsequent programming exercises.

14.6*. Assume the type definitions:

```
Centres    = (Frankfurt,London,NewYork,Paris,Tokyo,Zurich);
Profiles   = array [Centres] of Real;
Currencies = (Deutschmark,FrenchFranc,SwissFranc,Sterling,USDollar,Yen)
```

(a) Write a procedure which locates the maximum and minimum components of a parameter of type Profiles. The *indices* of the maximum and minimum components are to be passed back through parameters. (Assume that no two components are exactly equal.)

(b) Assume that each component of the two-dimensional array:

```
CurrencyValue: array [Currencies] of Profiles
```

contains the value (relative to gold, say) of one currency at one trading centre. Write a program fragment, invoking your procedure, to determine at which centres a dealer could most profitably buy Sterling and sell Sterling, and to compute his percentage profit on the deal.

PROGRAMMING EXERCISES 14

14.7. Modify procedure WriteWord of Example 14.6 so that OutWord is written on the same line as the previous word, unless that would make the output line longer than (say) 40 characters, in which case OutWord is to be written on a new line. Adjacent words are to be separated by a single blank.

Test program CopyWords with your amended procedure. Only minimal changes to the rest of the program should be necessary.

14.8. Assume the type definitions:

```
IndexRange = 1. .N;
Lists        = array [IndexRange] of Items
```

(a) Write a procedure Search which searches List (a parameter of type Lists) for a component which equals Target (a parameter of type Items). If the search is successful, the index of the matched component is to be assigned to Location (a parameter of type IndexRange). Found (a Boolean parameter) is to be set appropriately. (See Example 11.7.)

(b) Incorporate your procedure in a program which defines Items = Integer. The program should first read N integers into an array. Then it should read further integer targets, one per line. For each target it should call the procedure to search the array, and output a message indicating whether and where the target was located.

(c) Modify your program to handle 10-character names, rather than integers. You will need to change the type definition of Items, but your search procedure should not need to be changed at all. The only other change to your program should be to the statements which read the input data. Adapt procedure ReadLine (see Exercise 14.5) and use it in your program.

14.9. Write a program which reads the number of a year and the day of the week on which 1 January falls, and which outputs a complete calendar for that year. Include in your program a procedure which, given the name of a month, the number of days in that month, and the day of the week on which the first day of that month falls, outputs a calendar for that month, and passes back the day of the week on which the month ends.

15

Methodical programming with subprograms

This chapter reviews the benefits to be gained by using subprograms. These include:

* modularity
* readability
* reusability
* modifiability
* localization

15.1 THE VIRTUES OF SUBPROGRAMS

We cannot say that, for a program to work, it *must* contain functions and procedures. Every program given as an example in Chapters 13 and 14 could have been written as a single piece of code. Why, then, should we take the trouble to use functions and procedures? There are several very good reasons why this effort is worthwhile. The benefits might not be obvious when we look at a small program. But when we consider large programs, the benefits are striking.

(a) Using functions and procedures we can build a program from small self-contained pieces. Because they resemble programs in miniature, we call them subprograms. Each subprogram can be written and tested on its own, and this makes it easier to write and test a large program. Equally important, a subprogram can be read and understood on its own. This makes the program as a whole easier to understand.

(b) A subprogram has a name (identifier). If the name is chosen carefully, the purpose of the subprogram is clearly indicated, and a statement calling the subprogram can be read almost like a piece of prose.

(c) Once a subprogram is declared, it can be called wherever it is needed. This makes it unnecessary to duplicate code, a very tedious and error-prone task. The different calls can use different actual parameters. This gives the programmer additional flexibility.

(d) Since a subprogram is self-contained, it can easily be replaced by an alternative version. The reason for replacing it might be a change in specification (as in Example 14.1). Or it might simply be to substitute a more efficient version. Whatever the motivation, subprograms make programs easier to modify.

(e) Variables declared inside a subprogram occupy storage space only when the subprogram is being executed. After the subprogram has finished, the space is made available for other variables. On the other hand, global variables—those declared in the main program—occupy storage space permanently. Thus we can economize on storage space by using local variables whenever possible. This is important especially when storage space is limited.

To illustrate these points we now examine two versions of a program. The first version is monolithic (i.e. written as a single piece of code). The second version is conveniently broken into subprograms.

Example 15.1

Let us develop a program which reads two $N \times N$ integer matrices, computes and writes their matrix product.

The problem specification suggests the following program outline:

```
program MatrixProduct ( Input, Output );
   global declarations;
   begin
   read matrix A;
   read matrix B;
   make P the matrix product of A and B;
   write matrix P
   end.
```

Now we refine 'read matrix A', 'read matrix B', and so on. If we simply substitute these refinements into the program outline, we obtain a monolithic program like the following:

```
program MatrixProduct ( Input, Output ); (* version (a) *)
const
   N = 10;   (* say *)
type
   Matrix = array [1 . . N, 1 . . N] of Integer;
var
   A, B, P: Matrix;
   I, J, K: 1 . . N;
   ScalarProduct: Integer;
begin (MatrixProduct(a)*)
(* read matrix A *)
for I := 1 to N do
   for J := 1 to N do
      Read (A[I,J]);
(* read matrix B *)
for I := 1 to N do
   for J := 1 to N do
      Read (B[I,J]);
(* make P the matrix product of A and B *)
for I := 1 to N do
   for J := 1 to N do
      begin
      ScalarProduct := 0;
      for K := 1 to N do
         ScalarProduct := ScalarProduct + A[I,K]*B[K,J];
      P[I,J] := ScalarProduct
      end;
(* write matrix P *)
for I := 1 to N do
   begin
   Write ('[');
   for J := 1 to N do
      Write (P[I,J]);
   WriteLn ('   ]')
   end
end (*MatrixProduct(a)*).
```

In refining this program, we should observe that each refinement introduces details irrelevant to the rest of the program. Therefore it is a good idea to
package each refinement as a separate procedure, with the relevant matrix or
matrices as parameter(s). Indeed, 'read matrix A' and 'read matrix B' are
sufficiently similar to be refined into statements invoking the same procedure.
Each command in the program outline now becomes a single procedure statement.

```pascal
program MatrixProduct ( Input, Output ); (* version (b) *)
const
  N = 10;   (* say *)
type
  Matrix = array [1 . . N, 1 . . N] of Integer;
var
  A, B, P: Matrix;

procedure ReadMatrix ( var M: Matrix );
  var
    I, J: 1 . . N;
  begin
  for I := 1 to N do
    for J := 1 to N do
      Read (M[I,J]);
  end (*ReadMatrix*);

procedure WriteMatrix ( M: Matrix );
  var
    I, J: 1 . . N;
  begin
  for I := 1 to N do
    begin
    Write ('[');
    for J := 1 to N do
      Write (M[I,J]);
    WriteLn ('   ]')
    end
  end (*WriteMatrix*);

procedure Multiply Matrices (M1, M2: Matrix;
                                var Product: Matrix );
  var
    I, J, K: 1 . . N;
    ScalarProduct: Integer;
  begin
  for I := 1 to N do
    for J := 1 to N do
      begin
      ScalarProduct := 0;
      for K := 1 to N do
        ScalarProduct := ScalarProduct + M1[I,K]*M2[K,J];
      Product[I,J] := ScalarProduct
      end
  end (*MultiplyMatrices*);
```

```
begin (*MatrixProduct(b)*)
ReadMatrix (A);
ReadMatrix (B);
MultiplyMatrices (A, B, P);
WriteMatrix (P)
end (*MatrixProduct(b)*).
```

MatrixProduct(a) cannot be read without at once plunging into a morass of nested loops. Compare the statement part of program MatrixProduct(b), which is much easier to read and understand because of its brevity and its well-chosen procedure identifiers. It is simply a formalization in Pascal syntax of the original program outline. The messy details of matrix manipulation have been relegated to procedures, which can be read separately if desired.

Compare also the variable declarations in each program. In Matrix-Product(a) these declarations are rather cluttered, with the important Matrix variables placed on an equal footing with others which are merely auxiliary variables. In MatrixProduct(b) only the important Matrix variables are declared at the head of the program, where they stand out clearly; the declarations of auxiliary variables have been relegated to the procedures where they are needed.

MatrixProduct(a) contains two similar pieces of program, one for reading the matrix A, one for reading the matrix B. MatrixProduct(b) avoids this duplication by substituting two procedure statements invoking the same procedure, ReadMatrix, with actual parameters A and B respectively.

Although these two pieces of program are very short, it would be annoying if they had to be changed consistently (for example, if the matrix components were to be read in column by column, instead of row by row). In MatrixProduct(a) changes would be necessary in two places. In MatrixProduct(b) the change could be made in a single place, in the declaration of ReadMatrix; consequently the chance of error would be reduced.

The flexibility inherent in the use of procedures would become even more apparent if the programs were to be changed to write the matrices A and B as well as their product. The following would be inserted in the program outline:

```
write matrix A;
write matrix B
```

In MatrixProduct(a) these would be refined into yet more nested loops, making the program even less clear. In MatrixProduct(b) they would be refined immediately into the procedure statements:

```
WriteMatrix (A);
WriteMatrix (B)
```

which would not reduce the program's clarity at all.

A good, methodical approach to implementing a program such as Matrix-Product(b) would be to write and test the procedures one at a time.

(1) We could first write WriteMatrix and try it in a test program of the form:

```
begin (* test WriteMatrix *)
assign arbitrary values to the components of A;
WriteMatrix (A)
end.
```

(2) Then we could write ReadMatrix and test it using the following test program:

```
begin (* test ReadMatrix *)
ReadMatrix (A);
WriteMatrix (A);
end.
```

(3) Finally we could write MultiplyMatrices and test it in the completed program MatrixProduct.

This approach to testing is called 'bottom-up' testing, because we test the procedures on the bottom level of the program's structure diagram before testing the higher level(s) up to the main program (see Figure 15.1). Bottom-up testing uses temporary test programs which serve only to invoke the procedures under test.

An alternative approach is 'top-down' testing, whereby we write and test the top-level main program before writing and testing the lower-level subprograms. Top-down testing makes use of temporary, dummy versions of the subprograms.

(1) The main program of MatrixProduct is written *first*, in its final form.
(2) Then we write WriteMatrix, and test it using the main program and temporary versions of ReadMatrix and MultiplyMatrices. The temporary ReadMatrix could, for example, simply assign arbitrary values to the components of its formal parameter M. The temporary MultiplyMatrices could simply make Product a copy of M1.

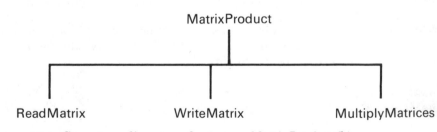

Figure 15.1. Structure diagram of program MatrixProduct(b)

(3) Then we replace the temporary ReadMatrix by its final version and repeat the test, still using the temporary MultiplyMatrices.

(4) Finally we replace the temporary MultiplyMatrices by its final version, and test what is now the complete program.

Observe that the same version of the main program is used at all stages of top-down testing.

We have stressed how subprograms can be exploited to structure even quite small programs written by a single programmer. In the development of large programs they are absolutely essential. Professional programmers often work in teams, collaborating in the construction of very large programs (100000 statements or more). A convenient method of splitting up such a task is to have each programmer independently write and test a single *module*—either a single subprogram or a related group of subprograms. This exploits the self-contained nature of subprograms. Later, the modules are combined to form a complete program.

Another common practice of experienced programmers is to write and test subprograms of general utility, and then to deposit them in 'libraries' where they become accessible to others. This avoids duplication of effort, and makes sophisticated algorithms available even to inexperienced programmers. The standard procedures and functions of Pascal form such a library, which is available to every Pascal programmer (see Appendix 3).

A programmer wishing to use subprograms written by another need not be concerned with *how* each subprogram performs its computation. The user needs to know only *what* each subprogram computes, and how it should be invoked (i.e. the number and types of its parameters, and its result type in the case of a function). The former information should be provided by an accurate abstract; the latter information is provided simply by the procedure or function heading.

15.2 CASE STUDY II: SORTING

PROBLEM SPECIFICATION

A list of names is supplied as input data, one name per line. The names are in no particular order. Write a program which will read all the names and output them in lexicographic order. Assume that there are no more than 100 names, and that each name is at most 20 characters in length.

SOLUTION

This is an example of *sorting*, a recurrent theme in computer programming. A bewildering variety of sorting techniques have been devised. Here we shall illustrate one of the simplest, called *insertion sorting*.

We can keep the names in a list. Let us arrange to read the names one at a time, and to insert each name immediately in its correct place in the list. For example, if the list already contains the names:

'Dijkstra', 'Knuth', 'Wirth'

and the next name is 'Hoare', this name will be inserted between 'Dijkstra' and 'Knuth', so now the list will consist of:

'Dijkstra', 'Hoare', 'Knuth', 'Wirth'.

In this way the names in the list will always be in correct order. This analysis leads to our level 1 outline.

Level 1 outline

```
program SortNames ( Input, Output );
global declarations;
begin
make the list empty;
while not end of input data do
   begin
   read a name;
   insert the new name in its correct position in the list
   end;
write all the names in listed order
end.
```

As an exercise, hand-test the Level 1 outline using suitable test data.

Refinements from Level 1

We must decide how to store the list. Since we are to assume that no more than 100 names will be input, we can store the list in an array with space for 100 names. We also need a variable to keep track of the actual number of names in the list. So we shall introduce the global declarations:

```
const
   MaxNames = 100;
   . . .
var
   Size: 0 . . MaxNames;
   List : array [1 . . MaxNames] of Names;
   . . .
```

where the type Names can be defined later. These decisions lead to the following refinements.

Refinement 1.1: make the list empty

```
Size := 0
```

Refinement 1.2: insert the new name in its correct position in the list

In general, the new name will be inserted in some intermediate position. This will require the names already stored in the array List in this and subsequent positions to be shifted along to make room for the new name. For example, in the following situation:

	1	2	3	4		
List	"Dijkstra"	"Knuth"	"Wirth"	?		Size 3

if the name to be inserted is 'Hoare', the names in positions 2–3 of List must be shifted into positions 3–4 before storing the new name in position 2:

	1	2	3	4		
List	"Dijkstra"	"Hoare"	"Knuth"	"Wirth"		Size 4

Since List has room for only MaxNames names, we ought to test whether List is already full before attempting to insert a new name. This leads to the following refinement:

```
if Size < MaxNames then
    begin
    find the position, NewPosition, where the new name will be inserted;
    shift up the names in positions NewPosition to Size inclusive;
    place the new name in position NewPosition;
    Size := Size+1
    end
else
    issue a warning that the new name cannot be sorted
```

Since this program fragment involves details, and variables such as NewPosition, which are of purely local interest, it is a good candidate for a procedure. The name to be inserted should be a parameter. Thus Refinement 1.2 becomes:

```
InsertName (name just read)
```

and we must introduce the global procedure declaration:

```
procedure InsertName ( NewName : Names );
var
    NewPosition : 1 . . MaxNames;
```

```
begin
if Size < MaxNames then
  begin
  find the position, NewPosition, where NewName will be inserted;
  shift up the names in positions NewPosition to Size inclusive;
  place NewName in position NewPosition;
  Size := Size + 1
  end
else
  issue a warning that NewName cannot be sorted
end (*InsertName*)
```

Refinement 1.3: write all the names in listed order

Using a variable, Position, this can easily be refined directly into Pascal:

```
for Position := 1 to Size do
  WriteLn (List[Position])
```

This is another candidate for a procedure, with Position as a local variable. So Refinement 1.3 becomes:

```
WriteAllNames
```

and we introduce the global procedure declaration:

```
procedure WriteAllNames;
  var
    Position: 1 .. MaxNames;
  begin
  for Position := 1 to Size do
    WriteLn (List[Position])
  end (*WriteAllNames*)
```

Nearly all the operations on the list (represented by the variables List and Size) have now been wrapped up tidily in the procedures InsertName and WriteAllNames. The only exception is Refinement 1.1. To be consistent we shall make that also into a procedure statement:

```
MakeListEmpty
```

and introduce the following global procedure declaration:

```
procedure MakeListEmpty;
  begin
  Size := 0
  end (*MakeListEmpty*)
```

The advantages of this way of using procedures are:

(a) The main program now contains no direct references to List and Size; all these references are collected together in three procedures which will be adjacent to one another. This improves the localization of the program.
(b) The main program is expressed largely in terms of procedure statements like MakeListEmpty and InsertNames (name just read), which concentrate attention on *what* is being done rather than *how* it is being done.
(c) It is fairly easy to modify the program to use a different representation of the list of names. (This will be done in Example 20.3.) Only the global declarations (including the procedures) need to be altered. If procedures are not used in this way, the whole program would have to be scanned for possible alterations.

Level 2 outline

```
program SortNames ( Input, Output );
global declarations;
begin (*SortNames*)
MakeListEmpty;
while not end of input data do
   begin
   read a name;
   InsertName (name just read)
   end;
WriteAllNames
end (*SortNames*).
```

Let us hand-test the outline of procedure InsertName with several test cases.

(1)

NewName ["Knuth"]   NewPosition [?]

- -

```
          1          2          3          4
List [    ?    |    ?    |    ?    |    ?    |      ]   Size [ 0 ]
```

In this situation, Size < MaxNames has the value True; 'find the position . . .' should set NewPosition to 1; 'shift up the names . . .' should do nothing, since there are no names in position 1 to 0 inclusive; 'place NewName . . .' should place 'Knuth' in List[1]; and Size:=Size+1 will increment Size to 1.

(2)

NewName | "Dijkstra" | NewPosition | ? |

- -

      1   2   3   4

List | "Knuth" | ? | ? | ? | | Size | 1 |

In this situation, Size < MaxNames has the value True; 'find the position . . .'
should set NewPosition to 1; 'shift up the names . . .' should shift 'Knuth' into
List[2]; 'place NewName . . .' should place 'Dijkstra' in List[1]; and
Size:=Size+1 will increment Size to 2.

(3)

NewName | "Wirth" | NewPosition | ? |

- -

      1   2   3   4

List | "Dijkstra" | "Knuth" | ? | ? | | Size | 2 |

In this situation, Size < MaxNames has the value True; 'find the position . . .'
should set NewPosition to 3; 'shift up the names . . .' should do nothing, since
there are no names in positions 3 to 2 inclusive; 'place NewName . . .' should
place 'Wirth' in List[3]; and Size:=Size+1 will increment Size to 3.

(4)

NewName | "Hoare" | NewPosition | ? |

- -

      1   2   3   4

List | "Dijkstra" | "Knuth" | "Wirth" | ? | | Size | 3 |

In this situation, Size < MaxNames has the value True; 'find the position . . .'
should set NewPosition to 2; 'shift up the names . . .' should shift 'Knuth' and
'Wirth' into List[3] and List[4]; 'place NewName . . .' should place 'Hoare' in
List[2]; and Size:=Size+1 will increment Size to 4. Thus we reach the situation
illustrated above (at Refinement 1.2).

(5) When the value of Size is 100, Size < MaxNames has the value False, so
InsertName will do nothing except issue a warning message.

    As an exercise, hand-test the Level 2 outline of the main program, and the
completed procedure WriteAllNames.

Refinements from Level 2

First we can complete the refinement of procedure InsertName.

Refinement 2.1: find the position, NewPosition, where NewName will be
inserted

This can be done by linear search, comparing NewName in turn with List[1],
List[2], and so on, until we find a name in the list which should *follow* NewName
in lexicographic order. We must set NewPosition to the position of this name in
the list. If no such name is found, we must set NewPosition to Succ(Size),
indicating that the new name will be inserted at the end of the list. The details
are shown below, in the completed program.

Refinement 2.2: shift up the names in positions NewPosition to Size inclusive

```
for Position := Size downto NewPosition do
   List[Succ(Position)] := List[Position]
```

If NewPosition equals Succ(Size), this loop shifts no names at all, which is
precisely what we want.

(Note the use of **downto** to ensure that the last name in the list is shifted
first. Can you see what will happen if we use:

```
for Position := NewPosition to Size do
   List[Succ(Position)] := List[Position]
```

instead?)

Refinement 2.3: place NewName in position NewPosition

```
List[NewPosition] := NewName
```

As an exercise, hand-test the completed procedure InsertName with the test
data used for testing its Level 2 outline. Alternatively, you could test Refinements 2.1–2.3 individually.

Refinement 2.4: read a name

We must now decide how to represent a name, that is how to define the type
Names. Given the assumption in the problem specification, we can introduce
the global declarations:

```
const
   NameLength = 20;
   . . .
type
   Names = packed array [1 . . NameLength] of Char;
   . . .
```

Now 'read a name' can be refined along the lines of Example 12.4. Again, this is a good candidate for a procedure, especially as it is the only part of this program which manipulates a name character by character. The details are shown below, in the completed program. The refinement includes a ReadLn to allow the following refinement.

Refinement 2.5: not end of input data

```
not EOF(Input)
```

Completed program

```
program SortNames ( Input, Output );
const
  MaxNames  = 100;
  NameLength =  20;
type
  Names = packed array [1 . . NameLength] of Char;
var
  Size        : 0 . . MaxNames;
  List        : array [1 . . MaxNames] of Names;
  CurrentName: Names;

procedure ReadName ( var Name: Names );
  var
    Col:1 . . NameLength;
  begin
  for Col := 1 to NameLength do
    if EOLn(Input) then
      Name[Col] := ' '
    else
      Read (Name[Col]);
  ReadLn
  end (*ReadName*);

procedure WriteAllNames;
  var
    Position:1 . . MaxNames;
  begin
  for Position := 1 to Size do
    WriteLn (List[Position])
  end (*WriteAllNames*);
```

```
    procedure MakeListEmpty;
      begin
P     Size := 0
      end (*MakeListEmpty*);

    procedure InsertName ( NewName: Names );
      var   NEXT    POINTER
        Position, NewPosition: 1 . . MaxNames;
        Located              : Boolean;
      begin
      if Size < MaxNames then
          begin
          (* find the position where NewName will be inserted *)
Pointer   NewPosition := 1;
          Located := False;                  Pointer          P
          while not Located and (NewPosition <= Size) do
            if NewName <= List[NewPosition] then
                Located := True              Pointer
            else               Succ ( Pointer )
                NewPosition := Succ(NewPosition);
          (* shift up the names in succeeding positions *)
          for Position := Size downto NewPosition do
            List[Succ(Position)] := List[Position];
          (* place NewName in position *)
          List[NewPosition] := NewName;
          Size := Size+1
          end
      else
          WriteLn (NewName, ' cannot be sorted: too many names.')
      end (*InsertName*);

  begin (*SortNames*)
  MakeListEmpty;
  while not EOF(Input) do
    begin
    ReadName (CurrentName);
    InsertName (CurrentName)
    end;
  WriteAllNames
  end (*SortNames*).
```

As an exercise, hand-test procedure ReadName, and the completed program.

Program SortNames has an interesting property. As it stands it serves to sort 20-character strings, but it can easily be adapted to sort single characters, integer numbers, real numbers, months, or any other items which can be ordered! It is necessary only to change the definition of the type identifier Names, the refinement of 'read a name', and possibly the WriteLn statement in procedure WriteAllNames. It can even be adapted to sort more complex items like dates or telephone directory entries, although that would force us to replace the simple comparison NewName <= List[Position] in procedure InsertName by something more complex (see Exercises 15 and 16).

EXERCISES 15

15.1. Systematically modify both versions of program MatrixProduct (Example 15.1) to compute and write the sum as well as the product of the two input matrices.

15.2. Systematically modify both versions of program MatrixProduct (Example 15.1) to handle *lower-triangular* matrices, i.e. matrices where every component above the main diagonal is zero, for example ($N=4$):

$$\begin{bmatrix} 9 & 0 & 0 & 0 \\ 1 & 3 & 0 & 0 \\ 2 & 5 & 1 & 0 \\ 8 & 5 & 7 & 4 \end{bmatrix}$$

The components above the diagonal are omitted from the input data, so each matrix is input as one component value for row 1, followed by two component values for row 2, and so on.

15.3. Systematically modify program SortNames so that it sorts integers rather than names.

15.4*. Surnames beginning with 'Mc' or 'Mac' are very common in Scotland (for example 'McKay' or 'MacKay'). It is conventional in directories to sort names beginning with 'Mc' as if they began with 'Mac'. Systematically modify program SortNames so that it sorts names beginning with 'Mc' in conventional directory order.

PROGRAMMING EXERCISES 15

15.5. Write a program which reads 12-character names, one per line, and outputs the names together with their Soundex codes. For an explanation of the Soundex system, see Example 9.12. The Soundex code is to be a 4-character string. If the code would be too long, it is to be truncated to four characters; if it would be too short, it is to be padded out with '0' characters (*not* blanks).

15.6*. Write a procedure which reads a molecular formula, enclosed in parentheses, such as (Na2SO4), and passes back the molecular weight of the compound it represents. Assume that the molecular formula itself contains no parentheses.

Write a program which uses your procedure to read a number of molecular formulas, one per line of input, and which writes their molecular weights. Your program should declare and initialize tables of atomic symbols and atomic weights to be used by your procedure:

```
type
   Elements = (Hydrogen,Helium,...);
var
   Symbol: array [Elements] of
                 packed array [1..2] of Char;
   AtomicWeight: array [Elements] of Real
```

For the purposes of this exercise, you need take only a few of the more common elements into account.

Part V

Further data structures

16

Records

This chapter covers:

*   records in Pascal
*   programming with records
*   the **with** statement
*   hierarchical data structures
*   variant records
*   packed records
*   type rules for records

16.1 THE NEED FOR RECORDS

The idea of a *record* is common in everyday life. Every time we fill out a form we are providing the data for a record. Examples are student records, vehicle records and stock records. Records must be stored somewhere. They might be held in a ledger, in a card box, in a filing cabinet, or in a computer.

A record, then, is a collection of data about a particular object. This idea is useful in programming, since we often need to identify collections of data in this way. We do not assume that every record will be held in long-term storage, though this is often the case as in everyday life.

An important property of a record is that we can refer either to the record as a whole or to the individual items of data within the record. These items are called the *fields* of the record. Each field has a name, which we use to refer to the field. Consider two examples.

Example 16.1

A *date* has three components: the day of the month, the month, and the year. Sometimes we are interested in the date as a whole, for answering queries like 'What is today's date?' or 'What is your date of birth?'. On other occasions we are interested in particular components of a date, for answering queries like 'What month is it?' or 'In what year will the next eclipse occur?'. A date may be considered as a record with three fields.

Example 16.2

A population registry office would be interested in the following information about each person in the area it covers: (a) surname, (b) forename, (c) date of birth, (d) sex, and (e) marital status. This information about one person may be considered to be a record with five fields. Notice that one of the fields is itself a record.

The idea of a record is most useful when we consider similar records relating to several objects. For example, the registry office will have similar records for many different persons. So we can refer to 'my record', to 'Susanne's record', and so on. Each of these records will contain the same fields. So we can refer to 'my surname', to 'my date of birth', to 'Susanne's date of birth', and so on. In each case we combine a possessive ('my' or 'Susanne's') with a field name ('surname' or 'date of birth'). The possessive indicates which record we are referring to, and the field name indicates which field of that record. Similarly we can refer to different dates, such as 'today' or 'the date of the next eclipse'. And we can refer to fields of these dates, such as 'this month' or 'the year of the next eclipse'.

You should never confuse arrays with records. Although each contains several components, they are different in every other way. A *record* is a collection of components (*fields*) which may be of differing types. Each field has its own name. An *array* is a collection of components (*elements*) which are all of the same type. An array element is not named individually. Instead it is identified by an index, which determines its position in the array. It is valid to refer to the *I*th component of an array. It is not valid to refer to the *I*th component of a record, since there would be no way of knowing its type.

16.2 RECORDS IN PASCAL

A *record type* in Pascal is specified by writing down the identifiers and types of its fields (using syntax similar to that of variable declarations), enclosed between the reserved words **record** and **end**. There is no restriction on the types of the fields.

To refer to an individual field of a record we use a *field designator*, in which the record variable is suffixed by a period and the field identifier.

Example 16.1 (continued)

The type definition:

```
Dates = record
          Day   : 1 . . 31;
          Month: 1 . . 12;
          Year  : 0 . . 9999
       end
```

could be used to declare variables whose values are dates:

```
Today, Manana, NextEclipse: Dates
```

Each of these record variables can be visualized as a box divided into three compartments, named Day, Month, and Year:

An example of a field designator is Today.Month, which designates the field Month of the record variable Today. In the diagram, the current value of the field Today.Day is 3, Today.Month is 8, and Today.Year is 1986.

The following statement updates one field of Manana:

```
Manana.Day := Today.Day + 1
```

In a field designator such as Today.Day, the field identifier Day is *qualified* by the record variable Today. A field identifier used in a statement must normally be qualified. For example, Write(Day) would be ambiguous. We do not know whether Day here designates Today.Day, or Manana.Day, or something else entirely.

Within each record type, every field must have a distinct identifier. However, field identifiers may be the same as identifiers given to constants, types, variables, functions, procedures, and even fields of other record types. The requirement to qualify field identifiers prevents ambiguity.

The syntax of record types is given in Figure 16.1.

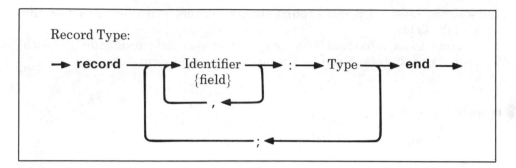

Figure 16.1. Syntax of Record Types (simplified)

The syntax of field designators is summarized in Figure 16.2. A field designator may be used anywhere an ordinary variable may be used.

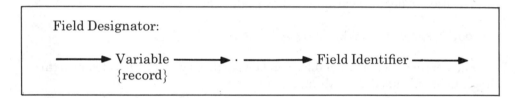

Figure 16.2. Syntax of Field Designators

We have seen that the individual fields of a record may be used just like ordinary variables. A major advantage of collecting data together in records, however, is that we may choose sometimes to treat a record as a whole, without regard to its individual fields. Thus we are interested in the operations that Pascal allows on complete records. The simplest is assignment, which copies one record into another.

Example 16.3

Assume the definition of types **Dates** from Example 16.1, and the variable declarations:

    Today, LetterDate: Dates

The single assignment statement:

    LetterDate := Today

copies the *whole* of the record Today into the variable LetterDate. It is equivalent to the three assignments of individual fields:

```
LetterDate.Day    := Today.Day;
LetterDate.Month := Today.Month;
LetterDate.Year   := Today.Year
```

but it is both clearer and more concise than the latter.

16.3 PROGRAMMING WITH RECORDS

{This section may be omitted on a first reading.}

The full generality of Pascal is available with records. In particular, records may have fields of any type—even arrays or records.

Example 16.2 (continued)

The structure of the records held by a registry office could be specified by the type definition:

```
PersonalDetails =
  record
     Surname,
       Forename  : packed array [1 . . 12] of Char;
     BirthDate    : Dates;
     Sex           : (Male, Female);
     MaritalStatus: (Single, Married, Divorced, Widowed)
  end
```

Whole records can be used as parameters of subprograms. Both value parameters and variable parameters are allowed.

Example 16.4

Let us write a procedure to inspect the registry office records of a man and a woman to determine whether they may legally marry, and if so to update their records accordingly. The procedure will take the two records as parameters. Since it may update these records, they must be variable parameters. {Marriage laws vary considerably from state to state. The following is based on the current law of Scotland.}

```
procedure Marry ( var Husband, Wife: PersonalDetails;
                  var Legal: Boolean );
begin
Legal := (Husband.Sex = Male) and
         (Wife.Sex = Female) and
         (Husband.MaritalStatus <> Married) and
         (Wife.MaritalStatus <> Married);
if Legal then
  (* update the records *)
  begin
  Husband.MaritalStatus := Married;
  Wife.MaritalStatus := Married
  end
end (* Marry *)
```

The actual parameters corresponding to Husband and Wife must be record variables of the same type as the formal parameters. For example, given the variable declarations:

```
Napoleon, Josephine: PersonalDetails;
Permis              : Boolean
```

we may use the procedure statement:

```
Marry (Napoleon, Josephine, Permis)
```

We can make procedure Marry more elaborate by checking that both partners have reached the age of majority. For this purpose it will be convenient to introduce a function which, given a person's details, computes that person's age in years. The PersonalDetails record will be a value parameter to this function. (Let us assume that today's date is available in a *global* variable Today.)

```
procedure Marry ( var Husband, Wife: PersonalDetails;
                  var Legal: Boolean );
const
  AgeOfMajority = 16;

function Age ( Person: PersonalDetails ): Integer;
  begin
  if (Today.Month > Person.BirthDate.Month) or
     (Today.Month = Person.BirthDate.Month) and
     (Today.Day >= Person.BirthDate.Day) then
    Age := Today.Year — Person.BirthDate.Year
  else
    Age := Today.Year — Person.BirthDate.Year — 1
  end (* Age *);
```

```
      begin (* Marry *)
   Legal := (Husband.Sex = Male) and
            (Wife.Sex = Female) and
            (Husband.MaritalStatus <> Married) and
            (Wife.MaritalStatus <> Married) and
            (Age(Husband) >= AgeOfMajority) and
            (Age(Wife) >= AgeOfMajority);
   if Legal then
      (* update the records *)
      begin
      Husband.MaritalStatus := Married;
      Wife.MaritalStatus := Married
      end
   end (* Marry *)
```

16.4 THE with STATEMENT

{This section may be omitted on a first reading.}

When writing statements to process a single record, we tend to find ourselves using the same record variable time and time again to qualify field identifiers. Since this can become rather tedious, Pascal provides a convenient shorthand, in the form of the *with statement*.

Example 16.5

Given the declaration (using the type from Example 16.2):

```
   YourDetails: PersonalDetails
```

the following program fragment:

```
Write (YourDetails.Forename, '   ',
       YourDetails.Surname, ' is ');
case YourDetails.Sex of
   Male: Write ('male');
   Female: Write ('female')
   end
```

can be abbreviated thus:

```
  with YourDetails do
     begin
     Write (Forename, '   ', Surname, ' is ');
```

```
case Sex of
   Male: Write ('male');
   Female: Write ('female')
   end (* case *)
end (* with *)
```

We simply write the name of the record variable (YourDetails) between **with** and **do**, and inside the **with** statement there is no need to qualify the field identifiers of that particular record.

The syntax of **with** statements is summarized in Figure 16.3. **with** and **do** are both reserved words.

With Statement:

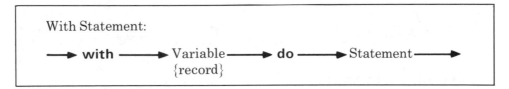

Figure 16.3. Syntax of With Statements (simplified)

Inside a **with** statement, any unqualified identifier which is a field identifier of the record variable actually designates that field. So, inside the **with** statement of Example 16.5, the unqualified identifier Surname, which is a field identifier of the record variable YourDetails, actually designates the field YourDetails.Surname.

A **with** statement is the only place where a field identifier may be used without qualification.

When we are processing more than one record of the same type, we can abbreviate the field designators of only one of these records.

Example 16.6

The function Age of Example 16.4 may be recast as follows:

```
function Age ( Person : PersonalDetails ) : Integer;
   begin
   with Person.BirthDate do
      if (Today.Month > Month) or
         (Today.Month = Month) and
            (Today.Day >= Day) then
         Age := Today.Year — Year
      else
         Age := Today.Year — Year — 1
   end (* Age *)
```

Here Day, Month and Year, where unqualified, refer to the fields of Person.BirthDate. There is no ambiguity, as the corresponding fields of Today are still qualified.

with statements play a part in the scope rules of Pascal (Section 14.5). The component statement of a **with** statement acts as a block in which the field identifiers of the record variable may be imagined to have been declared as ordinary variables. The behaviour of **with** statements can now be understood by applying the normal scope rules of Pascal.

16.5 DATA STRUCTURES

{This section may be omitted on a first reading.}

A *data structure* is just an organized collection of data. Arrays and records are different kinds of data structures, with their own particular properties. An array is a data structure whose components are homogeneous and are selected by (variable) indices. A record is a data structure whose components are non-homogeneous and are selected by (fixed) names. The fact that the components of arrays and records may themselves be structured allows us to build up data structures of some complexity.

Data structures form a subject of study in their own right, a subject whose proper treatment is well beyond the scope of this book. We shall confine ourselves here to examples illustrating some simple structures.

A record with fields which are themselves records is sometimes called a *hierarchical record*.

Example 16.7

The record type PersonalDetails of Example 16.2 contains a field, BirthDate, which is itself a record, of type Dates. Thus records of type PersonalDetails have a hierarchical structure, which can be pictured in a diagram such as Figure 16.4.

The field MyDetails.BirthDate is itself a record variable, so we may select a field from it, such as MyDetails.BirthDate.Year. The following statements are all equivalent:

```
Write (MyDetails.BirthDate.Year)

with MyDetails do
   Write (BirthDate.Year)

with MyDetails.BirthDate do
   Write (Year)
```

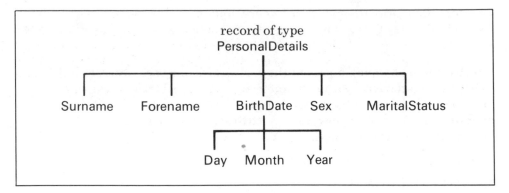

Figure 16.4. Hierarchical Structure of Type PersonalDetails

Hierarchical records are often processed by nested **with** statements, for example:

```
with MyDetails do
  begin
  Sex := Male;
  MaritalStatus := Single;
  with BirthDate do
    begin
    Day := 24; Month := 11; Year := 1947
    end
  end
```

Tables are very useful data structures, of which we have already seen some rather simple examples (Chapter 11). In general, a table may have several items of data in each entry; that is, each table entry may itself be a record.

Example 16.8

A table of the names and populations of a number of cities might be defined as follows:

```
City: array [1 . . MaxCities] of
          record
              Name: packed array [1 . . 10] of Char;
              Population: Integer
          end
```

The population of the N-th city would be designated:

```
City[N].Population
```

Example 16.9

A personal telephone directory might be stored as an array of records, each holding a name, trunk dialling code and (local) number. The array would have to be big enough for the maximum number of directory entries. We would also need to know how many were actually being used. Using the type definitions:

```
Names   = packed array [1 . . 16] of Char;
Codes   = packed array [1 . . 4] of Char;
Numbers = packed array [1 . . 8] of Char
```

we can represent the directory as follows:

```
Directory: record
              NrEntries: 0 . . MaxEntries;
              Entry: array [1 . . MaxEntries] of
                          record
                              Name   : Names;
                              Code   : Codes;
                              Number: Numbers
                          end
           end
```

(Code has been defined as a string rather than an integer because it is necessary to represent leading zeros. Number has been defined as a string because many computers would not be able to cope with seven-digit integers.)

Directory might be visualized as follows, assuming that MaxEntries is 8.

Directory

NrEntries	6		
Entry	'Addyman, A. '	' 061'	'273 7121'
	'Elder, J. '	'0232'	' 4 5133'
	'Findlay, W. '	' 041'	'339 8855'
	'Watt, D. '	' 041'	'339 8855'
	'Welsh, J. '	' 061'	'236 3311'
	'Wilson, I. '	' 061'	'273 7121'
	?	?	?
	?	?	?

Name   Code   Number

Let us write a procedure which outputs the number and dialling code of a person whose name is given, or a suitable message if there is no such name in Directory. This is an example of linear search.

```
procedure WriteTelephoneNumber ( GivenName: Names );
  var
    Index: 1 . . MaxEntries;
    Status: (Unknown, Present, Absent);
  begin
  with Directory do
    if NrEntries = 0 then
      WriteLn ('The directory is empty')
    else
      begin
      Status := Unknown;
      Index := 1;
      while Status=Unknown do
        with Entry[Index] do
          if Name = GivenName then
            begin
            Status := Present;
            WriteLn (GivenName, ' (', Code, ')', Number)
            end
          else
          if Index=NrEntries then
            Status := Absent
          else
            Index := Succ(Index);
      if Status=Absent then
        WriteLn ('There is no entry for ', GivenName)
      end
  end (* WriteTelephoneNumber *)
```

Inside the outer **with** statement we have access to the fields of Directory, for example NrEntries, without qualification. Inside the loop we examine one directory entry, namely Entry[Index]. Since each entry is itself a record variable, we conveniently make use of a further **with** statement to access its component fields without qualification. Thus, for example:

```
WriteLn (GivenName, ' (', Code, ')', Number)
```

is equivalent to the much less concise:

```
WriteLn (GivenName,
         ' (', Directory.Entry[Index].Code, ')',
         Directory.Entry[Index].Number)
```

The directory could alternatively have been stored in four separate variables:

```
NrEntries : 0 . . MaxEntries;
Name      : array [1 . . MaxEntries] of Names;
Code      : array [1 . . MaxEntries] of Codes;
Number    : array [1 . . MaxEntries] of Numbers
```

But these declarations do not reflect the logical structure of the directory. They are more cumbersome than the original declaration, and so too would be the procedure which searches the directory. (Convince yourself of this by rewriting it accordingly.)

16.6 VARIANT RECORDS

{This section may be omitted on a first reading.}

All the records we have seen so far have been completely rigid in their structure, in that all records of one type have had the same number of fields, with the same names and the same types.

Sometimes it is convenient to use records with a more flexible structure. Pascal allows for *variant records*, in which the number and types of the fields may vary to some extent.

Example 16.10

A lending library might keep the following information in its catalogue about each item in stock:

(a) reference number,
(b) title,
(c) number of author/composer,
(d) name of publisher,
(e) class of item—book or recording,
(f) number of edition (books only),
(g) year of publication (books only),
(h) name of performer (recordings only).

We could represent this information by a record with eight fields, but that would be wasteful, since only six or seven fields will be used in any one case.

With a variant record, the class of the library item determines the fields that actually are present in each record:

```
ItemClasses = (Book,Recording);

LibraryItems =
  record
    Ref      : 0 . . 999999;
    Title    : packed array [1 . . 30] of Char;
    Author   : packed array [1 . . 16] of Char;
    Publisher: packed array [1 . . 20] of Char;
    case Class: ItemClasses of
      Book:
        ( Edition: 1 . . 50;
          Year   : −2000 . . 1999 );
      Recording:
        ( Performer: packed array [1 . . 20] of Char )
  end
```

Up to **case** the fields are defined normally. The clause 'case Class: ItemClasses of' defines a special field, called a *tag field,* of type ItemClasses. This gives each record of type LibraryItems the following special property: the number and types of the fields *following* the tag field will depend upon the tag field's *current value.* Specifically, when the tag field's current value is Book, the tag field is assumed to be followed by two fields, Edition and Year; when its current value is Recording, on the other hand, it is assumed to be followed by a single field, Performer. Thus the internal structure of the record variable:

```
Item: LibraryItems
```

will depend upon the current value of Item.Class:

	Ref	Title	Author	Publisher	Class	Edition	Year
Item					Book		

or:

	Ref	Title	Author	Publisher	Class	Performer
Item					Recording	

Suppose the library catalogue has been stored as a table as follows:

```
Catalogue:
      record
        NrItems: 0 . . MaxItems;
        Accession: array [1 . . MaxItems] of LibraryItems
      end
```

where the number of items actually held is kept in the NrItems field. The following procedure will output the contents of Catalogue:

```
procedure WriteCatalogue;
  var
    Index: 1 . . MaxItems;
  begin
  WriteLn ('Ref.':6, 'Title':34, 'Author':20, 'Publisher':24,
           '   ':4, 'Other details');
  WriteLn;
  with Catalogue do
    for Index := 1 to NrItems do
      with Accession [Index] do
        begin
        Write (Ref:6, Title:34, Author:20, Publisher:24, '   ':4);
        case Class of
          Book:
            WriteLn ('edition ', Edition:2, Year:8);
          Recording:
            WriteLn ('performed by ', Performer)
          end (*case*)
        end
  end (* WriteCatalogue *)
```

It would be a serious error to attempt to access the field **Performer** when the tag field's value is not **Recording**, for then the field **Performer** does not exist. Similarly, it would be wrong to attempt to access the fields **Edition** and **Publisher** when the tag field's value is not **Book** (see the diagram above). That is why the procedure inspects the tag field of each record (using a **case** statement), in order to deduce which further fields are available for examination.

The complete syntax of record types (including variant records) is given in Appendix 1.7. A tag field may be of any *ordinal* type, but note that its type must be specified by a type *identifier*.

A variant must be specified for *every* value of the tag field's type, if necessary using empty variants for values that have no additional fields associated with them.

Example 16.11

Given that the input data consists of English-language text, let us write a procedure to read and store a single 'token', where a token is a word, a period, a comma, a semicolon, a colon, or an end-of-data indication. Assume that a word is a sequence of consecutive letters. All other characters are to be ignored.

On reading a token the procedure should note what kind of token it is. When the token is a word, the procedure should in addition store its spelling. In the other cases, however, no further information is needed. The natural way to represent a token, therefore, is by a variant record:

```
TokenKinds = (Word,Period,Comma,Semicolon,Colon,EndMarker);
Tokens =
  record
    case Kind: TokenKinds of
      Word:
        ( Spelling: packed array [1 . . MaxLength] of Char);
      Period, Comma, Semicolon, Colon, EndMarker:
        (  )
  end
```

This illustrates three points:

(a) the tag field may be the first field of a record;
(b) the tag field may be the last field of the record for some values of the tag field—this is specified simply by putting nothing between the parentheses, thus defining an empty variant;
(c) several values of the tag field may share the same variant.

  Given this definition of type Tokens, we can write the procedure as follows:

```
procedure ReadToken ( var Token: Tokens );
  var
    Length: 0 . . MaxLength;
    Fill: 1 . . MaxLength;

  function IsLetter ( Ch: Char ): Boolean;
    begin
    IsLetter := ('A' <= Ch) and (Ch <= 'Z')
    end (* IsLetter *);

  begin (* ReadToken *)
    (* skip characters up to the beginning of a token,
       or end of input, whichever comes sooner . . . *)
    while not ( EOF(Input) or IsLetter(CurrentChar) or
                (CurrentChar='.') or (CurrentChar=',') or
                (CurrentChar=';') or (CurrentChar=':') ) do
      Read (CurrentChar);
    with Token do
      if EOF(Input) then
        Kind := EndMarker
      else
      if IsLetter (CurrentChar) then
        begin
```

```
        Kind := Word;
        (* store the spelling of the word *)
        Length := 0;
        repeat
          if Length < MaxLength then
            begin
            Length := Length + 1;
            Spelling[Length] := CurrentChar;
            end;
          Read (CurrentChar)
          until not IsLetter(CurrentChar);
        (* pad out the spelling with blanks *)
        for Fill := Length+1 to MaxLength do
          Spelling[Fill] := ' '
        end
      else
        begin
        case CurrentChar of
          '.': Kind := Period;
          ',': Kind := Comma;
          ';': Kind := Semicolon;
          ':': Kind := Colon
          end (*case*);
        Read (CurrentChar)
        end
  end (* ReadToken*)
```

Assignment of the value Word to the tag field Token.Kind brings the field Token. Spelling into existence. Only thereafter is assignment to (components of) Token.Spelling legitimate.

This procedure assumes the existence of a *non-local* variable CurrentChar which has been suitably initialized, either to the first character of the input or (harmlessly) to a blank. The procedure would not work properly if CurrentChar were a local variable. For example, if the input starts:

I, CLAUDIUS

then on the first invocation of ReadToken, after the word 'I' has been read and stored, the value of CurrentChar is ','. On the next invocation of ReadToken, however, the value of CurrentChar would be *undefined* (since local variables are always initially undefined on entry to a subprogram), so the comma would have been lost. Therefore, CurrentChar must be a non-local variable to ensure that it preserves its value between successive invocations of ReadToken. {This paragraph has no connection with variant records, but it is important nevertheless!}

There is a facility in Pascal to omit the tag field from a variant record type. (See the syntax of Variant Part in Appendix 1.7.) This is useful when the context tells us what variant is active in each record of the type. Unfortunately, omitting the tag field makes it impossible to check accesses to fields in the variant part. Tagless variant records therefore detract from the completeness of Pascal's type checking. They should be used with great care, and only when necessary.

16.7 PACKED RECORDS

{This section may be omitted on a first reading.}

A record type may be prefixed with the reserved word **packed**. This asks the compiler to economize on storage space for records of that type, even if access to the fields is thereby made more difficult for the computer (recall Section 12.1).

Example 16.12

Variables of the type Dates, defined in Example 16.1, normally would occupy three store locations, thus:

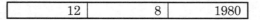

Observe, however, that the day and the month each need only two (decimal) digits, and that the year needs only four digits. Thus it may be desirable to amend the definition of Dates as follows:

```
Dates = packed record
            Day   : 1 . . 31;
            Month : 1 . . 12;
            Year  : 0 . . 9999
        end
```

If our computer is able to accommodate eight-digit integers, all three components of the date can be combined into one eight-digit integer which needs just one store location:

12081980

Even if our computer can accommodate only six-digit integers (say), space can be saved by combining the day and the month:

In any event, the degree of packing used (if any) is determined by the compiler and not by the programmer.

A field of a packed record is not allowed as an actual parameter corresponding to a variable formal parameter.

16.8 TYPE RULES FOR RECORDS

ASSIGNMENT COMPATIBILITY

A record may be assigned only to a record variable of the same type.

Example 16.13

Consider the variable declarations:

```
ComplexNumber: record
                    RealPart, ImagPart: Real
              end;
Root1, Root2: record
                    RealPart, ImagPart: Real
              end
```

Root1 and Root2 are considered to be of the same type, because they are declared together. ComplexNumber is considered to be of a different type, because it is declared separately. Thus the assignment statements:

```
Root1 := Root2
Root2 := Root1
```

are both valid; but the statements:

```
ComplexNumber := Root1
Root1 := ComplexNumber
Root2 := ComplexNumber
ComplexNumber := Root2
```

are all invalid.

EXERCISES 16

These exercises need arrays and subprograms.

16.1. (a) Write a definition of a record variable suitable for storing payroll details of an employee, namely the employee's name, number, grade (manual, skilled, clerical or managerial) and rate of pay. (b) Write a procedure which outputs these details in a suitable format.

16.2. (a) Rewrite procedure WriteDate of Example 14.1 to accept a single parameter of type Dates (see Example 16.1), rather than three separate parameters. (b) Rewrite program Dates of Example 14.1 correspondingly.

16.3. (a) Write a definition of a record type suitable for describing the position (latitude and longitude, in degrees) of a place on the Earth's surface. (b) Write a function which returns the solar time difference between two given places on the Earth's surface (1 hour for each 15 degrees difference in longitude). (c) Write a procedure which reads the position of a place, presented as two signed real numbers. (d) Write a procedure which outputs the position of a given place in degrees and minutes, using conventional notation (e.g. the latitudes +45.5 and −45.5 should be written as 45:30N and 45:30S respectively). (e) Write a program fragment which reads the positions of two places, and which outputs these positions together with the solar time difference between them.

16.4. Modify program SortNames of Section 15.2 to read, sort by name and output the personal telephone directory of Example 16.9.

Attempt the following exercise only after reading Section 16.6.

16.5. (a) Write a definition of a record type suitable for describing a plane figure, namely its shape plus the following: (i) for a circle, its radius, (ii) for a rectangle, the two lengths of its sides, or (iii) for a triangle, the lengths of all its sides. (b) Write a function which returns the area of a given plane figure.

PROGRAMMING EXERCISES 16

16.6. Write a procedure which outputs a single line containing the personal details from a record parameter of type PersonalDetails (Example 16.2). Write a procedure which reads personal details from a single line of input data in the same format and stores them in a parameter of type PersonalDetails. Assume that a person's sex is represented externally by a single character 'm' or 'f', and marital status by a single character 'S', 'M', 'D' or 'W'. Write a program to test these procedures and procedure Marry (Example 16.4).

16.7. Write a program which reads the x- and y-coordinates of the vertices of a polygon (given in clockwise order) and outputs the number of sides and the perimeter of the figure. (Hint: use a record to represent the position of a vertex.)

16.8. An entry in a city telephone directory consists of a name, an address and a telephone number. A name is a string of at most 20 characters and an address is a string of at most 30 characters. A telephone number consists of a three-digit exchange code and a four-digit line number. Write a program which reads directory entries (supplied in any format you choose) and outputs them in two columns on each page. You may assume that the entries are supplied in alphabetical order. On output, the entries must be arranged in order *down* the columns and under suitable column headings. On the last page the two columns should be as equal as possible.

17

Files

17.1 FILES AND FILE STRUCTURES

Each program that we have seen so far has had a single source of input data and a single destination for output results. These are, respectively, the sets of data Input and Output, which are listed in the program heading. However, programs with only Input and Output are rather untypical. Many programs are required to read several sets of data and to write several sets of data. These sets of data are called *files,* and are the subject of this chapter.

Many files read and written by computer programs are never seen by the human user. Instead, a file written by one program is often stored on a magnetic medium (such as a disk or tape). Later it can be read by another program, or perhaps even by the same program. Since the data is not examined by a human user, there is no point in converting it to text. So the data can be stored in its internal (binary) representation. (This saves much storage space, since the internal representation is often more compact than text. It also saves much computer time, since conversions of data to and from text are quite slow.)

It is useful to use the term *file* to mean any set of data read or written by a program. It can be a set of data held on a disk or tape, a stream of characters

243

entered on a keyboard, the contents of a display screen, or results printed on paper. The data can be text or binary. We shall treat all these as files.

Clearly there might be restrictions on the way a program can operate on a particular file. A magnetic file can be both written and read. On the other hand, a display screen is restricted to output only, and a keyboard to input only.

We illustrate these points by looking at two typical applications of files.

Example 17.1

Consider a bank that keeps on a magnetic file details of the customer accounts. For each customer there will be a name, address, account details and current balance.

At the end of each day, this file will be processed to update the balances as a result of the day's transactions. At the same time the program can produce statements to be mailed to those customers who are scheduled to receive them. The program to do this will therefore operate upon four files. The two input files are:

(a) a file of transactions (containing details of each debit and credit), entered through a keyboard;
(b) the file containing details of the customer accounts, as they stood at the start of the day.

The two output files are:

(c) a file of printed statements;
(d) an updated accounts file with the altered balances. (This file will be used as an input file to the same program on the following day.)

Note that other programs will use the same accounts file. There will be programs to open and close accounts, change addresses, and so on. Another program will send gentle reminders to customers who have absent-mindedly run into overdraft. Auditing programs will determine totals for the bank's accounts. Statistical programs will extract data for planning and forecasting.

Example 17.2

A reference library might keep on file details about its stock of books. The library user might be provided with terminals at which they can type queries such as 'List all books about computer programming'. This is called *information retrieval*. The information retrieval program would use three files. The two input files are:

(a) a file of queries, entered one at a time through the keyboard;
(b) the book file, permanently held on a disk.

The output file is:

(c) answers to the queries, perhaps displayed on the screen, or printed on paper to be taken away.

As in Example 17.1, other programs will access the same book file, for adding details of new books, producing statistics, and so on.

It is important to realize that data exists independently of the programs that use it. Do not imagine that data is generated only for the benefit of a specific program. In fact, new programs are often written to process data that exists already!

Files have many possible structures. The simplest of these is the *serial file*. This consists of a sequence of *components*, which are all of the same type. The accounts file of Example 17.1 would be a serial file whose components are records. (Each record in the file would have fields for the customer's name, address, current balance and so on.) In fact, in commercial data processing the components of all files are called records. We shall use the term *components*, however, because in Pascal they are not restricted to record types. For example, Input and Output are serial files whose components are characters.

Let us examine in detail the characteristics of a serial file. As the name implies, the components of a serial file can be read only in serial order. A program cannot read the 100th component until it has read the previous 99 components. Also, if the program wants to go back to an earlier component, it must restart reading from the beginning of the file. Similarly, a serial file can be written only by writing the first component first and the last component last.

A serial file would be suitable for the bank's account file of Example 17.1. The order in which the customers' accounts are processed does not matter. So the programs can process them in the order in which they happen to be filed.

For the reference library's information retrieval system, Example 17.2, a serial file would be totally unsuitable. To answer any query, the system would have to read through the whole file. This would be very inefficient: the users would get a very slow response to their queries. A different file structure is needed here, to allow the program *direct* access to specific components of the file. However, the topic of direct-access files is outside the scope of this book.

We shall use pictures to illustrate what happens when a serial file is read or written. In particular, we want to indicate the position of the next component to be read or written.

First consider reading a serial file. We picture this as follows:

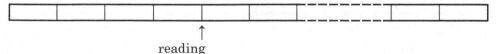

reading

In this example four components have already been read and the fifth component is due to be read next. Initially, the reading position is at the very beginning of the file (since no components have yet been read). After reading the last component, the reading position is at *end-of-file*.

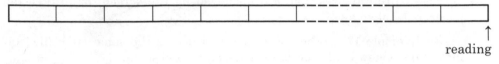

↑
reading

If the program attempts to read a further component at end-of-file, it will fail.

When writing a serial file, the writing position is *always* at end-of-file, since that is the only place where components can be written:

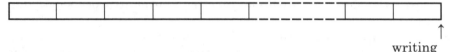

↑
writing

So writing a new component to this file makes it longer. The new component is appended at the end:

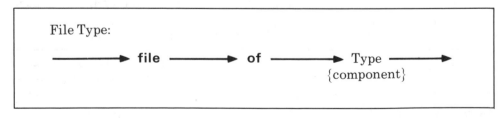

↑
writing

Files can be compared with other data structures. A serial file is similar to an array in one respect: its components are all of the same type. There the similarity ends. An array has a fixed size, whereas a serial file can be extended by writing new components. The elements of an array can be accessed at random, whereas the components of a serial file can be accessed only in serial order, one at a time. It is very important to remember these differences.

Pascal concerns itself only with serial files, so henceforth we shall use the terms 'file' and 'serial file' synonymously.

17.2 PASCAL FILES IN GENERAL

As it appears to a Pascal program, a file is an ordinary variable: it has an identifier and it is declared in a variable declaration. Its type specifies that it is a file, and also specifies the type of its components.

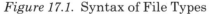

Figure 17.1. Syntax of File Types

The component type may be any Pascal type, except for a file type or a type containing a file type. Thus files cannot be components of files. This restriction is imposed to allow Pascal to be implemented on as many computers as possible, even those with very simple operating systems. (Most other restrictions on files are for the same reason.)

Example 17.3

A computer program to control the traffic lights at a junction represents the various signals by the enumeration type:

Signals = (Red, RedAndAmber, Green, Amber)

Each set of lights is associated with a file, and the program changes the lights by writing a value of type Signals to the file. The type of the file is:

Lights = **file of** Signals

and the four sets of lights are declared as file variables, thus:

North, South, East, West: Lights

The syntax of file types is summarized in Figure 17.1. **file** and **of** are both reserved words.

A file is generated by writing components to it, one at a time. This is achieved using the following standard procedures:

Rewrite(F)   makes the file F ready for writing, by emptying it of all components and establishing the initial writing position.

Write(F,*x*)   appends to the file F a component whose value is that of the expression *x* and moves the writing position to the new end-of-file. The expression *x* must be assignment compatible with the component type of F.

The effect of Write(F,*x*) is illustrated below:

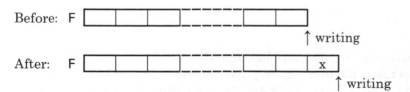

It is not possible to write to any file until it has been prepared for writing by Rewrite. The only exception to this rule is the file Output: the statement Rewrite(Output) is performed automatically at the start of any program which has Output among its program parameters.

Once a file has been generated it may be read by the program which wrote it, or by some other program. This is achieved using the following standard procedures:

Reset(F)   makes the file F ready for reading, by moving the reading position to the start of the file.

Read(F,V)   copies the next component of the file F into the variable V, then advances the reading position past this component. The components of F must be assignment compatible with the type of V.

After obeying Reset(F), F looks like this:

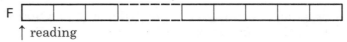

↑ reading

The effect of Read(F,V) is illustrated below:

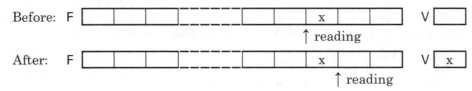

It is not possible to read from any file until it has been prepared for reading by Reset. The only exception to this rule is the file Input: the statement Reset(Input) is performed automatically at the start of any program which has Input among its program parameters.

Read(F,V) will fail if F is already at end-of-file. In order to prevent this we must be able to test the end-of-file condition, and for this purpose the Boolean standard function EOF(F) is provided. In the last diagram, EOF(F) is False, but it will become True after a further two components have been read.

File variables can be used as actual parameters to these, and other, standard procedures. We can also pass files as variable parameters to subprograms we have written ourselves. Pascal does not, however, allow whole file variables to be used in any other way. In particular, assignment of files is forbidden and files cannot be used as value parameters.

Example 17.4

A piece of music can be recorded *digitally*. This is done by measuring the strength of the signal from a microphone and representing it as a number in the range 0 to 65535. By taking many such measurements every second, it is possible to store and reproduce hi-fi sound. For studio processing of the digitized sound, audio engineers find it useful to have twice as many measurements per second. The following program takes a file of digitized audio and doubles the number of measurements, by fitting an average value between each two data values. It also reports how many pairs of data values were equal to

65535. (Too many such pairs would indicate that the recording level was excessive, and may cause distortion.)

```pascal
program DoubleSamples (SampleData, DoubleData, Output);

const
    MaxSample = 65535;

type
    Samples = 0 . . MaxSample;

var
    SampleData, DoubleData: file of Samples;
    PrevSample, ThisSample, AvSample: Samples;
    NrOfMaxPairs: 0 . . MaxInt;

begin
Reset (SampleData);
Rewrite (DoubleData);

NrOfMaxPairs := 0;
Read (SampleData, PrevSample);
Write (DoubleData, PrevSample);

while not EOF(SampleData) do
  begin
  Read (SampleData, ThisSample);
  AvSample := (PrevSample + ThisSample) div 2;
  if AvSample = MaxSample then
    NrOfMaxPairs := NrOfMaxPairs + 1;
  Write (DoubleData, AvSample);
  Write (Double Data, ThisSample);
  PrevSample := ThisSample;
  end;

WriteLn ('The number of maximum sample pairs was ',
        NrOfMaxPairs:1);

end (* DoubleSamples *).
```

This example illustrates the purpose of the program parameters: they are the identifiers of files used by the program. However, only files which are assumed to exist before the program is run (such as **SampleData**), or which are to be kept after the program is run (such as **DoubleData**), should be listed as program parameters. Some programs use files for *temporary* storage of large quantities of data, taking advantage of the (virtually) unlimited size of files. These files should not be listed as program parameters. This applies particularly to files declared inside subprograms.

Program parameters may stand for different files in different runs of the program. Consider program DoubleSample, for example: the actual file represented by SampleData in one run would not be the same file as that represented by SampleData in the following run.

All file variables, whether program parameters or not, must be declared in the usual way. Again, Input and Output are exceptions to this rule: they must *not* be declared even if they are used.

The syntax of program parameters is summarized in Appendix 1.1.

17.3 TEXT FILES

Text files, that is, files whose components are characters and end-of-line markers, are of special interest because they are the normal means of communication between humans and computers. Pascal provides a standard file type, Text, which is used to declare text files. The standard file variables Input and Output are of type Text.

Everything said in Section 17.2 applies to text files in particular, as well as to files of other types. Recall, however, that Input and Output must not be initialized by Reset or Rewrite and must not be declared.

The standard procedures we have used with Input and Output may be used with any text file by giving the name of the file as the (optional) first parameter. Furthermore:

(a) Read, ReadLn, EOF and EOLn may be invoked without a text file parameter, in which case they operate on Input. Similarly, Write, WriteLn and Page may be invoked without a text file parameter, in which case they operate on Output.

(b) Read, ReadLn, Write and WriteLn may be invoked with parameters of various types, in addition to the optional text file parameter. This is because, for many purposes, reading and writing one character at a time is too primitive. For example, we want to be able to read and write numbers, with automatic transformations between their internal and external forms. Here is a list of all the allowable parameter types:

Read, ReadLn	*Write, WriteLn*
Char	Char
Integer	Integer
Real	Real
	Boolean
	string

(c) Read, ReadLn, Write and WriteLn may be invoked with *several* parameters of these types.

(d) ReadLn and WriteLn may be invoked with just a text file parameter, if only the effect on the end-of-line marker is required.

Example 17.5

The following program makes an exact copy of a text file, without using the standard files Input and Output. Compare it with Example 8.5.

```
program Copy (Original, Duplicate);
var
   Original, Duplicate: Text;
   Character: Char;
begin
Reset (Original);
Rewrite (Duplicate);
while not EOF(Original) do
   begin
   while not EOLn(Original) do
      begin
      Read (Original, Character);
      Write (Duplicate, Character)
      end;
   WriteLn (Duplicate);
   ReadLn (Original)
   end
end (* Copy *).
```

17.4 FILE BUFFERS

{This section may be omitted on a first reading.}

We have seen, in Section 17.2, that the statement Read(F,V) has *two* effects: it copies the next component of F into the variable V, then it advances the reading position of F. In certain applications it is convenient to be able to separate the second step from the first. For such purposes, the concept of the *file buffer* is useful.

Consider a file F which is being read; the file buffer of F, which is designated F↑, is a copy of the component of F at the current reading position:

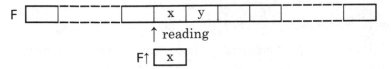

The file buffer can be used like any variable. In particular its value may be inspected directly without having to copy it into another variable.

The reading position may be advanced, *automatically* updating the file buffer, by means of the standard procedure Get(F), whose effect on F (above) is as follows:

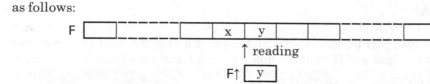

It may now be seen that the statement Read(F,V) is equivalent to:

begin V := F ↑; Get(F) **end**

Reset(F) copies the *first* component of F into F ↑:

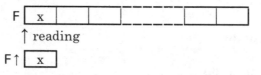

Example 17.6

A company keeps a payroll file containing the following details for each of its employees: name, employee number, grade (manual, skilled, clerical, or managerial), pay rate, tax allowance, and number of weeks (or months) of service. This file is used for printing payslips, for supplying data to the tax authorities, for calculating pension entitlements, and so on.

It is required to update the payroll file to include details of new employees. To this end a second file has been generated, consisting of records of the same type as those of the payroll file, and containing details of the new employees. All employees are assumed to have distinct employee numbers, and in both files the records are assumed to be arranged in ascending order by employee number. Write a program to generate an updated payroll file, also ordered by employee number.

For example, if the employee numbers in the two input files are as follows:

Old payroll: 3, 7, 8, 9, 11, 12, 15, 19
New employees: 1, 2, 5, 6, 10, 14

then the new payroll file should contain records for the following employees, in order:

New payroll: 1, 2, 3, 5, 6, 7, 8, 9, 10, 11, 12, 14, 15, 19

This is an example of *merging*, an important operation in commercial data processing.

At each step of the merge, we wish to compare the next record of the updates file, Updates, with the next record of the old payroll file, OldPayroll. The record which contains the smaller employee number is to be appended to the new employee file, and only the file from which that record was fetched is to have its reading position advanced. The records to be compared are available in the file buffers Updates↑ and OldPayroll↑, which can be inspected without advancing the reading position of either Updates or OldPayroll. If we find that Updates↑ contains the smaller employee number, for example, we append Updates↑ to the new payroll file and then obey Get(Updates), leaving OldPayroll↑ undisturbed for comparison with the following record of Updates.

```pascal
program Merge ( Updates, OldPayroll, NewPayroll );

type
   Grades = (Manual,Skilled,Clerical,Managerial);
   Money = Integer;
   Employees =
      record
         Name: packed array [1 . . 16] of Char;
         Number: 0 . . 9999;
         Grade: Grades;
         PayRate: Money;
         TaxAllowance: Money;
         Service: 0 . . MaxInt
      end;
var
   Updates, OldPayroll, NewPayroll: file of Employees;

begin
Reset (Updates);
Reset (OldPayroll);
Rewrite (NewPayroll);

(* merge until one file is exhausted *)
while not (EOF(Updates) or EOF(OldPayroll)) do
   if Updates↑. Number < OldPayroll↑. Number then
      begin
      Write (NewPayroll, Updates↑);
      Get (Updates)
      end
   else
      begin
      Write (NewPayroll, OldPayroll↑);
      Get (OldPayroll)
      end;

(* copy any records left in either file *)
while not EOF(OldPayroll) do
   begin
   Write (NewPayroll, OldPayroll↑);
```

```
      Get (OldPayroll)
    end;
  while not EOF(Updates) do
    begin
    Write (NewPayroll, Updates↑ );
    Get (Updates)
    end
  end (* Merge *).
```

This program serves to illustrate the use of file buffers and Get. It must be admitted, however, that it would *not* be acceptable in the real world of commercial data processing, since it depends on all the assumptions about the two input files. In practice, files are generated by programs which may be incorrect, they are recorded on media which are not completely reliable, and they are read and written by peripheral devices which sometimes fail. A realistic file-processing program must, therefore, check that the assumptions about its input files do indeed hold, taking appropriate action if they do not (see Exercises 17).

A file which is being written also has associated with it a file buffer, in which the value of each new component is stored until the writing position is advanced:

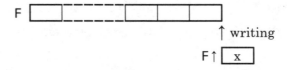

The file buffer may be used like any variable, so we may store a value in it, then examine or update it later if we wish.

The writing position is advanced by means of the standard procedure Put(F). This appends the contents of the file buffer to the file itself, and leaves the file buffer *undefined*:

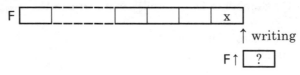

It may now be seen that the statement Write(F, x) is equivalent to:

```
  begin F↑ := x; Put(F) end
```

17.5 INTERACTIVE PROGRAMS

{Section 17.4 must be read before this section.}

All of the programs we have seen so far have been *batch* programs. In other words, all their input data is prepared in advance. The program is started, reads its input data and writes its output results, and finally stops. There is no involvement of the user while the program is running.

There is another possibility that will be familiar to anyone who has used a personal computer or time-sharing system. That is where the user 'converses' with the program as it runs, supplying input data or queries at appropriate moments. Such a program is called *interactive*. It differs from a batch program in that it must write prompts, to tell the user what input is expected next. Many interactive programs use 'menus'. A menu is a list of alternatives, and the user must select one of them.

Interactive programs tend to be more convenient to use, so the trend is towards interactiveness. Computer games, word processors, spreadsheets, airline reservation systems and information retrieval systems are all examples of interactive programs.

Let us take a very simple example—a program to read integer numbers, one per line of input, and output their squares. A typical conversation with this program might look as follows, where the material in italics is typed by the program and the rest by the user:

Number? **19**
  The square of 19 is 361
Number? **7**
  The square of 7 is 49
Number? ********

To end the conversation, the user types something to indicate the end of the input. This will depend on the operating system being used; we have given **** above as an example.

A program to this specification follows:

```
program Squares (Keyboard, Display);
const
   Prompt = 'Number? ';
var
   Keyboard, Display: Text;
   Number: Integer;
begin
Rewrite (Display);
Write (Display, Prompt);
Reset (Keyboard);
while not EOF(Keyboard) do
   begin
   Read (Keyboard, Number);
   WriteLn (Display, '   The square of ', Number:1, ' is ', Sqr(Number):1);
   Write (Display, Prompt);
```

```
    ReadLn (Keyboard)
    end
end (* Squares *).
```

When this program is run with the data shown above, the following sequence of events takes place:

(1) The program prepares the file variable Display for writing and outputs the *prompt*, a message inviting the user to type the first number. It then prepares the file variable Keyboard for reading. Recall that Reset(Keyboard) places the first character of the text file Keyboard in Keyboard↑, the buffer variable. Accordingly, the system sets up an input operation to read data from Keyboard, *even though the Pascal program has not yet obeyed any Read statement*. The program waits for the user to finish typing.
(2) The user sees the prompt and responds by typing '19' and some end-of-line indication, the details of which depend on the operating system.
(3) The program resumes execution. Keyboard↑ is equal to '1' and EOF(Keyboard) is False. The loop is entered, the Read statement scans the data line, converts the integer number to internal form, and assigns it to Number. The WriteLn statement then outputs the result (which appears on a fresh line because of the end-of-line marker just typed by the user) and takes a new line. The Write statement outputs the next prompt. Finally, to ensure that EOF(Keyboard) will have a useful value, the loop performs a ReadLn statement. This skips past the end-of-line marker which the user typed after the '19' and places the first character of the next line in Keyboard↑. Again the system sets up an input operation and the program waits for the user.
(4) The user now types '7' and an end-of-line marker.
(5) The program continues as in step (3), until it once more waits at the ReadLn statement.
(6) This time the user types an end-of-file indication.
(7) The program resumes. EOF(Keyboard) is now True and Keyboard↑ is undefined. The loop terminates, and so does the program.

Observe that we have to be very careful about the relative positions of the input and output statements in this program. If the Reset(Keyboard) statement had been any earlier, the program would have waited for input *before* giving the user the first prompt. Similarly, if the ReadLn(Keyboard) statement had been placed before any of the other statements in the body of the loop, reading the next datum and writing the results or the prompt would have gone out of sequence.

As an exercise, work out exactly what would happen, from the user's point of view: (a) if the ReadLn were placed before the second Write; (b) if the ReadLn were placed before the WriteLn; and (c) if the Reset were placed before the first Write.

So far so good. Now, however, a problem arises. Some operating systems require that data typed by an interactive user must be read from the standard file Input and that results for the terminal must be written to the standard file Output. Let us amend the program in accordance with these requirements. We get the following:

```
program Squares (* second version *) (Input, Output);
const
  Prompt = 'Number? ';
var
  Number: Integer;
begin
(* implicit Rewrite(Output) and Reset(Input) here *)
Write (Output, Prompt);
while not EOF(Input) do
  begin
  Read (Input, Number);
  WriteLn (OutPut, ' The square of ', Number:1,
                   ' is ', Sqr(Number):1);
  Write (Output, Prompt);
  ReadLn (Input)
  end
ond (* Squaroo *).
```

Trace through this version of the program with the data used above. The problem should quickly become apparent. Although the loop would work well enough, the initialization goes wrong. Before the program can output the first prompt, an *automatic* Reset(Input) is performed, and the program waits for the user to type a line of data. Unfortunately, the user will also be waiting—for a prompt which will never appear! Thus the prompts and responses are forced out of sequence from the start.

In reaching this conclusion however, we have assumed that the statement Reset(Input) causes an input transfer to be set up *immediately*. In practice this is not necessary. No transfer need be performed until: (a) Input↑ is inspected (either explicitly, or implicitly by means of Read or ReadLn); or (b) EOLn(Input) is tested; or (c) EOF(Input) is tested. By delaying the transfer to one of these points, the difficulty with Reset disappears and an interactive program can use Input as its interactive input file. The input transfer set up by ReadLn can be delayed similarly. This removes the constraints on the order of the statements inside the loop. If an implementation has these features (which are in complete conformity with Standard Pascal), then writing interactive programs need differ from writing non-interactive programs only in the use of prompts.

EXERCISES 17

17.1. Write a procedure which counts the components in a given file, a parameter of type **file of** Items. (The definition of type Items is irrelevant here.)

17.2. (a) Write a procedure which copies a given file, of type **file of** Items, to a second file of the same type. Assume that the second file has already been prepared for writing. (b) Using this procedure, write a program which copies to a file of type **file of** Items the concatenation of two other files of the same type.

17.3. Write a procedure, with a parameter of type **file of** Integer, which searches this file for a component equal to a given target value, setting a Boolean parameter accordingly.

The following exercises should not be attempted until Section 17.4 has been read.

17.4. Modify program Merge (Example 17.6) so that it writes an error message every time it finds an employee record out of sequence in either input file.

17.5*. Modify the procedure ReadToken of Example 16.11 so that it uses Input ↑ instead of the non-local variable CurrentChar to look ahead in the data.

17.6*. The Drinkers' Club maintains a file containing the names and other details of all its members, ordered by name. The Temperance Society maintains a similar file containing details of *its* members. Write a program which reads both files and outputs details of everyone who is a member of both groups.

17.7. Write a program to calculate the week's pay of all weekly-paid employees (i.e. all except managers) in the company of Example 17.6. Tax is to be deducted automatically according to the formula:

$$(pay\ rate-tax\ allowance)\times 33\%$$

The program is to output a table showing the name, number, gross pay, tax deduction and nett pay of each employee. It should also generate an updated file taking account of the past week's service.

PROGRAMMING EXERCISES 17

To run the following programs, you will have to find out how to create and access files on the computer you use.

17.8. Write a program with three text file parameters: Input, OldText and NewText. NewText is to be made a copy of OldText, except for certain one-to-one character transliterations. Each line of Input contains exactly two characters, xy, specifying that all occurrences of x in OldText are to be converted to y in NewText.

17.9. The personal telephone directory of Example 16.9 may be stored as a file of entries, say DirectoryFile, rather than as an array of entries. (a) Write a program which reads names, dialling codes and numbers from Input and writes them as records to DirectoryFile. (b) Write a program which reads names from Input and searches DirectoryFile to determine the corresponding telephone numbers (where known).

17.10*. (a) A bank accounts file is to be created from scratch. The first NameLength characters of each line of Input contain a customer's name (left-justified), the next AddressLength characters contain the customer's address, and the remainder of the line contains the customer's account number. Every customer starts with a balance of zero. Write a program which reads this data and generates the bank accounts file. (b) Write a program to update a bank accounts file and produce printed bank statements, as described in Example 17.1. Details of each transaction are supplied as a single line of Input containing the customer's account number followed by the amount of the transaction (positive for a credit transaction, negative for a debit transaction). Each bank statement must contain the customer's name, address and account number, original balance, list of transactions, and updated balance. A bank statement is to be printed for every customer, even where there are no transactions. Both the accounts file and the set of transactions are supposed to be ordered on the customer's account number; your program must print an error message every time an account number is found to be out of sequence, and take some appropriate recovery action.

17.11. If you have read Section 17.5, modify the program of Exercise 8.7 to work as an interactive calculator facility.

18

Methodical programming with data structures

> This chapter covers stepwise refinement with data structures, illustrating the topic in two major case studies. It concludes with a section stressing the importance of good program documentation.

18.1 PROGRAMMING BY STEPWISE REFINEMENT: A REVIEW

The purpose of this book is to explain methodical programming. As early as Chapter 7 we stressed the benefits of developing a program methodically from its specification. The resulting program is likely to be readable and relatively error-free.

In Chapter 15 we brought subprograms into the picture. When each subproblem is solved by writing a subprogram, the structure of the program shows clearly how it was developed.

Our example programs have all been developed using these methods. In most chapters, however, our primary objective was to demonstrate the features of Pascal. Demonstrating the process of program development was secondary. The example programs have been rather small.

By now you have met the main features of Pascal. With these at our disposal, we can now tackle more realistic programming problems.

First let us review the principles of stepwise refinement. We start by devising and writing down an outline solution, a mixture of instructions in English and Pascal. This is the Level 1 outline. We then refine each English instruction, by breaking it down in turn into simpler instructions. (They must be simpler, so that we have made a step towards a complete solution.) We now substitute these refinements into the Level 1 outline, to obtain the Level 2 outline. We continue in this way, filling in more and more detail, until all the English instructions have been refined. Then we have a program expressed entirely in Pascal.

Why do we choose English to express an unrefined instruction? The reason is that at first we are interested only in *what* the instruction is required to do. Only at a later stage should we decide *how* the instruction is to be done. By then our task will be smaller and easier. In this way stepwise refinement allows a large problem to be solved as a series of small ones. Actually, the choice of English is not essential. Any way of expressing *what* is to be done is suitable. For example, mathematical notation, decision tables and diagrams are all sometimes useful. The important thing is to be as precise as possible. If English is used, therefore, take care over the wording of the instructions.

Stepwise refinement also simplifies the task of testing the program. Each refinement can be hand-tested individually. Any errors can then be corrected immediately. This will save a lot of debugging effort later. If the tested refinements are put together carefully, the resulting program will be relatively error-free.

Perhaps you have attempted to develop your programs without being methodical. In that case you probably ran into unnecessary difficulties. Your programs probably contained lots of logical errors, discovered only after the programs were completely written. The errors were probably difficult to track down and difficult to correct. You might even have been forced to rewrite large parts of your programs.

Perhaps, on the other hand, you are especially talented at programming, and you can successfully develop small programs without being particularly methodical. But even you will find that large programs just cannot be tackled without a methodical approach. The best programmers in the world understand this well.

We now discuss two case studies. Each problem is complicated enough to illustrate the practical difficulties of developing substantial programs. We shall see that the choice of data structures is as important as the choice of control structures. We must aim to select our data structures methodically too.

To derive maximum benefit from each case study, you should put yourself in the place of the programmer. First read and make sure you understand the problem specification. Then attempt to solve the problem yourself. Only then read the text, and compare your experience with ours. The text does not simply present 'model' solutions. They are fully worked out, and they illustrate the mistakes and indecisions that are always a part of program development.

The lessons to be learned from the case studies are summarized and generalized in Section 18.4. Finally, in Section 18.5 we place programming in its proper context, as part of the software life cycle, and stress the importance of documentation.

18.2 CASE STUDY III: TEXT FORMATTING

PROBLEM SPECIFICATION

Write a program which will read natural language from a text file, **RawText**, and write it to the standard text file **Output** in paragraphs, with each line justified on both the left and the right margins. The text is supplied in free format, with successive words being separated by one or more blanks and/or end-of-lines. Each punctuation mark, such as a period or a comma, may be assumed to follow the preceding word *immediately,* that is without intervening blanks. A new paragraph is indicated by the special 'word' /PAR/, but the text does not necessarily start with a new paragraph.

The number of characters to be written on each line of output is to be read from the standard text file **Input**.

On output, as many words as possible are to be written on each line, with successive words on the same line separated by one or more blanks. Each punctuation mark must follow the preceding word immediately and must be on the same line. Each line is to be right-adjusted, if necessary, by writing extra blanks between words, the extra blanks being distributed as evenly as possible. No word may be split between two lines. The first line of each paragraph must be indented six spaces on the left, and must be preceded by a blank line. The last line of each paragraph, and the last line of the whole text, are *not* to be right-adjusted.

Assume that no word is longer than twenty characters. The program should ensure that the specified line width is sufficient to accommodate the longest possible word.

For example, if the input text is:

THE PRINCIPLES OF NEWSPEAK
/PAR/
NEWSPEAK WAS THE OFFICIAL LANGUAGE OF OCEANIA
AND HAD BEEN DESIGNED TO MEET THE IDEOLOGICAL NEEDS
OF INGSOC.
/PAR/
IN THE YEAR 1984
THERE WAS NOT AS YET ANYONE
WHO USED NEWSPEAK AS HIS SOLE MEANS
OF COMMUNICATION,
EITHER IN SPEECH OR IN WRITING.
IT WAS EXPECTED THAT NEWSPEAK WOULD HAVE FINALLY
SUPERSEDED OLDSPEAK
(OR STANDARD ENGLISH, AS WE SHOULD CALL IT)
BY ABOUT THE YEAR 2050.

then the written text on lines of 30 spaces should look like this:

THE PRINCIPLES OF NEWSPEAK

    NEWSPEAK   WAS   THE OFFICIAL   LANGUAGE   OF   OCEANIA AND HAD BEEN DESIGNED TO MEET THE   IDEOLOGICAL   NEEDS   OF INGSOC.
    IN   THE   YEAR   1984   THERE WAS NOT AS YET ANYONE WHO USED NEWSPEAK AS HIS SOLE MEANS OF COMMUNICATION,   EITHER   IN SPEECH OR IN WRITING. IT WAS EXPECTED THAT NEWSPEAK WOULD HAVE   FINALLY   SUPERSEDED OLDSPEAK (OR STANDARD ENGLISH, AS WE SHOULD CALL IT) BY ABOUT THE YEAR 2050.

SOLUTION

This is one of those problems in which close inspection of the specification reveals possibilities for simplification. A little thought should convince you that there is nothing special about the treatment of punctuation. If we combine each punctuation mark with the preceding word as a single string, then our program will meet the output specification without taking any special account of punctuation. Therefore, we shall treat any sequence of non blank characters in the input text as a single 'word'.

    The nature of the problem suggests that the heart of Level 1 will be some sort of loop. As always, the first question we must answer is 'What should be done during each repetition of the loop?' A number of answers are possible:

(a) deal with a single character;
(b) deal with a single word;
(c) generate a complete line of output;
(d) deal with a complete paragraph.

    Surely option (a) can be rejected immediately, since the action to be taken on each character read will vary wildly according to circumstances, such as whether the character is blank or non-blank.

    Option (b) is quite attractive. The input text can be viewed as a sequence of words (treating/PAR/ as a word), so it is natural to use a loop which processes one word per repetition.

    Option (c) is less attractive. Although the output text may be viewed as a sequence of lines, this sub-division is not at all apparent in the input text.

Option (d) is also quite attractive, for both the input and the output texts may equally naturally be viewed as sequences of paragraphs. As each paragraph in turn contains a number of words, a nested loop will be necessary to deal with individual words.

A good guiding principle in such circumstances is to opt for the solution which most accurately reflects the structure of both the input and the output data. Here it is not immediately clear whether option (b) or option (d) is better.

An experienced programmer might be able to choose between the alternatives by thinking ahead, mentally making one or two further refinements in each case, and judging which alternative will lead to the better solution. {This is much the same mental process as that adopted by a chess player, who must choose between alternative moves by thinking ahead a few moves and judging which alternative will lead to the better position.} Until we learn such foresight, we are forced to try both alternatives in turn and compare the results. {This, at least, is a strategy denied to chess players!}

In both versions it seems better to view the raw text as a sequence of 'tokens', rather than as a sequence of words, a token being either a word, or a paragraph mark, or an end-of-data mark. Both versions may need to initialize the processing of these tokens. Version (b) will need to initialize the processing of lines, at the least to read and validate the requested line width. Version (d) may additionally need to initialize the processing of paragraphs. These thoughts lead to the following Level 1 outlines.

Level 1b outline

```
program TextFormatter (* version b *)
                      ( Input, RawText, Output );
global declarations;
begin
prepare the processing of lines;
prepare the processing of tokens;
read a token;
while there is data to process do
   begin
   if the token is a word then
      append the word followed by a blank to the current line, right-adjust the
         line and start a new line if necessary
   else (* the token is a paragraph mark *)
      start a new paragraph;
   read a token
   end
end.
```

Level 1d outline

```
program TextFormatter (* version d *)
                       ( Input, RawText, Output );
global declarations;
begin
prepare the processing of paragraphs;
prepare the processing of lines;
prepare the processing of tokens;
read a token;
while there is data to process do
  begin
  if the token is a paragraph mark then
    begin
    start a new paragraph;
    read a token
    end;
  process a paragraph
  end
end.
```

Since 'process a paragraph' in Level 1d is more complex than anything in Level 1b, we shall refine it first.

Refinement 1d.1: process a paragraph

This involves processing a number of words (possibly none) up to the end of the raw text or the start of the next paragraph, whichever comes sooner.

```
while the token is a word do
  begin
  append the word followed by a blank to the current line,
    right-adjust the line and start a new line if necessary;
  read a token
  end
```

Level 2d outline

This is obtained by substituting Refinement 1d.1 into Level 1d:

```
program TextFormatter (* version d *)
                       ( Input, RawText, Output );
global declarations;
begin
preparing the processing of paragraphs;
```

```
prepare the processing of lines;
prepare the processing of tokens;
read a token;
while there is data to process do
  begin
  if the token is a paragraph mark then
    begin
    start a new paragraph;
    read a token
    end;
  (* process a paragraph *)
  while the token is a word do
    begin
    append the word followed by a blank to the current line.
      right-adjust the line and start a new line if necessary;
    read a token
    end
  end
end.
```

The elements in Level 2d which remain to be refined are similar to those in Level 1b, but it is clear that the latter is a more concise solution, and it is Level 1b (henceforth labelled simply Level 1) which we shall adopt.

Testing Level 1

Let us hand-test Level 1 with the example data. Assume a line width of 30 columns. The following table shows each token read, followed by the current line of output after dealing with that token. We use ♭ to represent a single blank.

Token	*Current line of output*
THE	THE♭
PRINCIPLES	THE♭PRINCIPLES♭
OF	THE♭PRINCIPLES♭OF♭
NEWSPEAK	THE♭PRINCIPLES♭OF♭NEWSPEAK♭
/PAR/	♭♭♭♭♭♭

{This is the start of a new paragraph.}

NEWSPEAK	♭♭♭♭♭♭NEWSPEAK♭
WAS	♭♭♭♭♭♭NEWSPEAK♭WAS♭
THE	♭♭♭♭♭♭NEWSPEAK♭WAS♭THE♭
OFFICIAL	OFFICIAL♭

{The previous line, already 23 characters long, cannot accommodate the

word 'OFFICIAL', so it will have been right-adjusted in some way, and a
new line started.}

LANGUAGE   OFFICIAL♭LANGUAGE♭

. . .

. . .

. . .

YEAR   THE♭YEAR♭

2050.   THE♭YEAR♭2050.♭

(end-of-date)   THE♭YEAR♭2050.♭

{The program terminates.}

Refinements from Level 1

Refinement 1.1:   append the word followed by a blank to the current line,
right-adjust the line and start a new line if necessary

```
begin
if the word will not fit into the current line then
    right-adjust and output the current line;
append the word to the current line;
if a blank will fit into the current line then
    append a blank to the current line
end
```

Notice that there is no need to take immediate action if there is no room for
the blank: the next word (if there is one) will certainly start a new line.

Testing refinement 1.1

Assume that the line width is 30 and that the current line contains 24
characters. The following table shows the contents of the current line after
dealing with each of several words of varying size.

Word	Current line of output	Size
THE	????????????????????????THE♭	28
MEANS	??????????????????????MEANS♭	30

{The next word, if any, will force this line to be right-adjusted.}

ANYONE	????????????????????ANYONE	30

{There was no room for the blank. Again, the next word, if any, will force
this line out.}

WRITING	WRITING♭	8

{The word is too long to fit into the current line. The current line is right-
adjusted, and a new line is started before appending the word.}

Level 2 outline

This is obtained by substituting Refinement 1.1 into Level 1:

```
program TextFormatter ( Input, RawText, Output );
   global declarations;
begin
prepare the processing of lines;
prepare the processing of tokens;
read a token;
while there is data to process do
   begin
   if the token is a word then
      (* append the word followed by a blank to the current line,
         right-adjust the line and start a new line if necessary *)
      begin
      if the word will not fit into the current line then
         right-adjust and output the current line;
      append the word to the current line;
      if a blank will fit into the current line then
         append a blank to the current line
      end
   else (* the token is a paragraph mark *)
      start a new paragraph;
   read a token
   end
end.
```

Refinements from Level 2

A noteworthy characteristic of the Level 2 outline is the frequent recurrence of
'line' and 'token'. This strongly suggests that a data structure to represent a
line, and another to represent a token, will be central to the development of
TextFormatter. We could proceed by designing these data structures and then
refining the component steps of Level 2 accordingly.

   For example, we might decide to represent a token by a string variable, say
S, to hold its spelling, and an Integer variable, say W, to hold its width. The
refinement of 'read a token' would place the characters of the word left-justified
in S and padded on the right with blanks, setting W appropriately. If there were
no words left in the input data, W would be set to zero and S to all blanks. We
could then make refinements such as the following.

Refinement 2.1': there is data to process

```
W > 0
```

Refinement 2.2': the token is a word

```
S <> '/PAR/
```

Going on in this way, and making similar refinements for the 'line' data structure, we might develop a workable program.

But this would be to ignore one of the main criteria guiding our choice of refinements: the importance of delaying decisions as long as possible, including those relating to data structures. By fixing on a representation for tokens and lines too early, we force the rest of the development to fit into that mould. If we have made a poor choice it will prove very difficult to change, as the entire program will be dependent on the details of the structure we have chosen. In short, the program will have very little modularity.

Let us decide, then, *not* to fix on detailed representations of 'line' and 'token' at the moment. Instead we will assume that each can be represented by a record variable of appropriate type, say Line of type Lines and Token of type Tokens.

We can, however, make some declarations which are independent of the details of Lines and Tokens and which we can anticipate being useful.

```
const
  Blank = '  ';
  . . .
type
  Styles = (Adjusted, Unadjusted);
  . . .
```

Further progress can be made by refining the steps of Level 2 in terms of two clusters of subprograms, one cluster concerned with Line and another concerned with Token. Since there is only one variable of type Tokens and only one of type Lines it will be sufficient for these subprograms to access their data structures as non-local variables. The variable and its associated subprograms form a module, which 'packages' the details of the representation. Should it later turn out that several variables of type Tokens or type Lines are needed, it will be a simple matter to amend the subprograms to use parameters instead.

We will declare a procedure, ReadToken, to read the next word or paragraph mark or end-of-data mark and place it in Token.

Refinement 2.1: read a token

```
ReadToken
```

Refinement 2.2: there is data to process

Token is not an end-of-data mark

Refinement 2.3: the token is a word

Token is a word

We will declare a **Boolean** function, **LineHasRoomFor**, which will return **True** if there is enough room on the current line for as many more characters as are specified by its parameter.

Refinement 2.4: the word will not fit into the current line

not LineHasRoomFor (the size of the word)

We will declare a procedure, **WriteLine**, which will output the current line, leaving **Line** clear to accept the first word of a new line. **WriteLine** will have a parameter of type **Styles** which specifies whether the line is to be right-adjusted or not.

Refinement 2.5: right-adjust and output the current line

WriteLine (Adjusted)

We will declare a procedure, **AppendWordToLine**, to add a word at the end of the current line. At the moment it is not clear whether this procedure is best considered as part of the **Token** cluster, as part of the **Line** cluster, or as a separate cluster on its own.

Refinement 2.6: append the word to the current line

AppendWordToLine

Refinement 2.7: a blank will fit into the current line

LineHasRoomFor (1)

We will declare a procedure, **AppendBlankToLine**, to add a blank to the end of the current line. This will only be called if there is in fact room for the blank.

Refinement 2.8: append a blank to the current line

AppendBlankToLine

To start a new paragraph it is necessary to output the current line, unadjusted, output an extra blank line, and start a new line with an indentation. We will declare a procedure, **IndentLine**, to do the latter.

Refinement 2.9: start a new paragraph

```
begin
WriteLine (Unadjusted);
WriteLn;
IndentLine
end
```

We will declare procedures, SetupLine and SetupToken, to initialize the Line and Token clusters respectively.

Refinement 2.10: prepare the processing of lines

```
SetupLine
```

Refinement 2.11: prepare the processing of tokens

```
SetupToken
```

Inserting these refinements in Level 2 gives us Level 3.

Level 3 outline

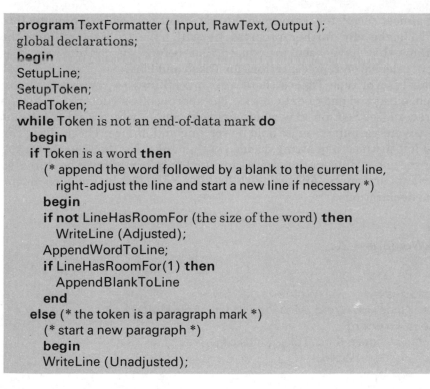

```
program TextFormatter ( Input, RawText, Output );
global declarations;
begin
SetupLine;
SetupToken;
ReadToken;
while Token is not an end-of-data mark do
  begin
  if Token is a word then
    (* append the word followed by a blank to the current line,
       right-adjust the line and start a new line if necessary *)
    begin
    if not LineHasRoomFor (the size of the word) then
      WriteLine (Adjusted);
    AppendWordToLine;
    if LineHasRoomFor(1) then
      AppendBlankToLine
    end
  else (* the token is a paragraph mark *)
    (* start a new paragraph *)
    begin
    WriteLine (Unadjusted);
```

```
      WriteLn;
      IndentLine
    end;
  ReadToken
  end
end.
```

Testing Level 3

Refinements 2.1 to 2.11 being so short, there is little point in testing them individually. Instead we should test the whole of Level 3. Do that now as an exercise.

   If you tested Level 3 thoroughly, then you will have discovered an error. The very last line of the output text is not written! Go back and make appropriate changes to Levels 1, 2 and 3, and add the new refinement step needed.

Refinements from Level 3

We have almost completely converted the statement part of TextFormatter into Pascal. To make any further progress we will have to start refining the subprograms that have been introduced, but before we can do that it is necessary to decide on representations for Token and Line.

   In the case of type Tokens there are three things to represent: words, paragraph marks and end-of-data marks. The appropriate structure for this is a variant record (see Section 16.6) whose tag field defines which kind of token it is. For the word variant we must hold its spelling and its size. The spelling can be stored left-justified in a string, padded with blanks. Neither the paragraph mark nor the end-of-data mark requires any further information to be stored, so these variants are empty. Accordingly, the following must be included among the global declarations.

```
const
  MaxWordSize = 20;
  . . .
type
  WordSizes = 1 . . MaxWordSize;
  TokenKinds = (AWord, AParagraphMark, AnEndMark);
  Tokens = record
              case Kind: TokenKinds of
              AWord:
```

```
                    ( Spelling: packed array [WordSizes] of Char;
                      Size: WordSizes );
                  AParagraphMark, AnEndMark:
                      (   )
          end;
  . . .
var
  Token: Tokens;
  . . .
```

We can now make the following trivial refinements which complete the statement part of TextFormatter.

Refinement 3.1: Token is not an end-of-data mark

```
Token.Kind <> AnEndMark
```

Refinement 3.2: Token is a word

```
Token.Kind = AWord
```

Refinement 3.3: the size of the word

```
Token.Size
```

Refinement of ReadToken

We have already seen a similar procedure in Example 14.6. Using that as a source of ideas, we can write down the present version directly. Test this refinement yourself.

```
procedure ReadToken;
  var
    Character: Char;
    I: 0 . . MaxWordSize;
  begin
  Character := Blank;
  while not EOF(RawText) and (Character = Blank) do
    Read (RawText, Character);
  with Token do
    begin
    if EOF(RawText) then
      Kind := AnEndMark
```

```
      else
        begin
        I := 0;
        Kind := AWord;
        while Character <> Blank do
          begin
          if I < MaxWordSize then
            begin
            I := I + 1;
            Spelling[I] := Character
            end;
          Read (RawText, Character)
          end;
        Size := I;
        for I := Size+1 to MaxWordSize do
          Spelling[I] := Blank;
        if Spelling = '/PAR/                    ' then
          Kind := AParagraphMark
        end
      end
  end (* ReadToken *)
```

We now decide how to represent the current line. The most important point to observe is that we must *not* write out individual words immediately they are appended to the line, because that would make it impossible to go back and insert extra blanks between them when it is necessary to right-adjust the line. Therefore, we must keep the current line in store until we are ready to right-adjust it. The most natural representation for a line, as for a word, is a string. This forces us to choose an upper limit on the line width, but the paper on which we are writing will have a limited width anyway. We need a field, Width, to hold the line width specified by the user. The width chosen must be great enough for the widest possible word, preceded by an indentation. Finally, we must be able to tell whether a word will fit into the current line, so we need a field, Size, to keep track of the number of characters already placed in the line. The following must therefore be added to the global declarations.

```
const
  Indent = 6;
  MinLineWidth = 26; (* = Indent + MaxWordSize *)
  MaxLineWidth = 80; (* assumed width of the paper *)
  . . .
type
  LinePositions = 1 . . MaxLineWidth;
  LineSizes = 0 . . MaxLineWidth;
```

```
Lines = record
              Width: MinLineWidth . . MaxLineWidth;
              Size: LineSizes;
              Column: packed array [LinePositions] of Char
        end;
    . . .
var
  Line: Lines;
    . . .
```

We now refine the remaining subprograms. Test each of these refinements yourself.

Refinement of LineHasRoomFor

This is straightforward.

```
function LineHasRoomFor (SpaceNeeded: WordSizes): Boolean;
    begin
    with Line do
       LineHasRoomFor := SpaceNeeded <= (Width—Size)
    end (* LineHasRoomFor *)
```

Refinement of WriteLine

WriteLine must output the line which has just been built up, either right-adjusted or otherwise, according to its parameter. It must also start a fresh line of output and make the Line data structure empty, ready for the first word of the next line.

Level 1 outline of WriteLine

```
procedure WriteLine (Style: Styles);
    local declarations;
    begin
    with Line do
      begin
      case Style of
        Adjusted:
          write Line with right-adjustment;
```

```
        Unadjusted:
            write Line verbatim
        end;
    WriteLn;
    make Line empty
    end
  end (* WriteLine *)
```

The following two refinements are dependent on their position inside the **with** statement.

Refinement 1.1 of WriteLine: make Line empty

```
Size := 0
```

Refinement 1.2 of WriteLine: write Line verbatim

```
for I := 1 to Size do
    Write (Column[I])
```

Writing adjusted lines seems quite complicated, so we introduce a local procedure, WriteAdjustedLine, to package up the details.

Refinement 1.3 of WriteLine: write Line with right-adjustment

```
WriteAdjustedLine
```

Refinement 1.4 of WriteLine: local declarations

```
var
    I: LinePositions;
declaration of WriteAdjustedLine
```

Level 2 of WriteLine is obtained by incorporating these refinements in Level 1. Only the declaration of WriteAdjustedLine remains to be refined.

Refinement of AppendBlankToLine

This is simple.

```
procedure AppendBlankToLine;
    begin
    with Line do
        begin
        Size := Size + 1;
        Column[Size] := Blank
        end
    end (* AppendBlankToLine *)
```

Refinement of IndentLine

There are two requirements here: (a) Line.Column[1] through Line. Column [Indent] must be made blank; (b) Line.Size must be left equal to Indent. We can assume that Line.Size initially has the value 0, as assigned to it by WriteLine. Therefore, all that is needed is to append a blank to the line, Indent times. The Pascal code follows directly from this.

```
procedure IndentLine;
  var
    I : 1 . . Indent;
  begin
  for I := 1 to Indent do
    AppendBlankToLine
  end (* Indentline *)
```

Refinement of AppendWordToLine

The issue here is whether AppendWordToLine is best considered as an operation on Token, on Line, or on both. At stake are the modularity and efficiency of the program. The most efficient approach, but the least modular, is for AppendWordToLine to have full access to the details of both data structures and to manipulate them directly (as do ReadToken and AppendBlankToLine). This we reject, as it would bind together two otherwise separate clusters.

The least efficient approach, but the most modular, is for AppendWordToLine to form a separate cluster of its own. It would access Token and Line entirely by means of subprograms in those clusters. Since that would require two procedure calls for every character copied from the word to the line, it might be too slow. Moreover, it seems difficult to give a natural definition of a subprogram that obtains successive characters of a word, at any rate with the present definition of type Tokens.

A third alternative is to consider AppendWordToLine as part of the Line cluster. This also requires an operation to fetch successive characters of a word. Another difficulty is that it seems somewhat artificial to hide the details of just one data structure from a subprogram which uses both of them equally.

The same remark applies to the idea of placing AppendWordToLine in the Token cluster. However, in this case it would need to use a procedure, AppendCharToLine of the Line cluster, which is very similar to AppendBlankToLine and implements a natural operation on lines. We will therefore take this approach as a compromise.

```
procedure AppendWordToLine;
  var
    I : WordSizes;
```

```
begin
with Token do
  for I := 1 to Size do
    AppendCharToLine (Spelling[I])
end (* AppendWordToLine *)
```

We could make AppendCharToLine a local subprogram of AppendWordToLine. Alternatively, if we make it global, we can alter AppendBlankToLine so that it simply does AppendCharToLine(Blank). This costs one more procedure call for each blank appended to the line—a negligible penalty. A more important effect is to confine to a single subprogram the details of appending characters to lines—a very significant increase in modularity. This is much the better choice: go back and alter the refinement of AppendBlankToLine accordingly. (It turns out to be even simpler than we thought!)

Refinement of AppendCharToLine

This is analogous to our original version of AppendBlankToLine.

```
procedure AppendCharToLine (Character: Char);
  begin
  with Line do
    begin
    Size := Size + 1;
    Column[Size] := Character
    end
  end (* AppendCharToLine *)
```

Refinement of SetupToken

The Token data structure needs no initialization, but we must Reset the RawText file before reading any tokens from it.

```
procedure SetupToken;
  begin
  Reset (RawText)
  end (* SetupToken *)
```

Refinement of SetupLine

The Width and Size fields of Line must be initialized.

```
procedure SetupLine;
  var
    WidthWanted: Integer;
```

```
begin
Read (Input, WidthWanted);
with Line do
  begin
  if WidthWanted < MinLineWidth then
    Width := MinLineWidth
  else
  if WidthWanted > MaxLineWidth then
    Width := MaxLineWidth
  else
    Width := WidthWanted;
  Size := 0
  end
end (* SetupLine *)
```

Refinement of WriteAdjustedLine

We have a line of characters which is to be expanded to a width of Line.Width characters exactly. This is achieved by distributing extra blanks as evenly as possible among the inter-word gaps on the line. The specification is vague about this distribution, so we are free to choose a strategy which is easy to implement.

Let us consider each gap in turn: if NrGaps is the number of gaps not yet widened, and ExtraBlanks is the number of blanks remaining to be distributed, then we can widen the gap under consideration by (ExtraBlanks **div** NrGaps) blanks and then decrease ExtraBlanks accordingly. It is easy to prove that this distribution expands the line to exactly Line.Width characters.

If, moreover, we scan the line (and its gaps) from left to right, then we can write the words and the widened gaps as we deal with them, so there is no need to shift characters within Line itself.

There will be a blank at the end of the current line if AppendBlank was obeyed more recently than AppendWord. If so, this blank is to be discarded. There will also be some blanks at the beginning of the current line if the line is the first of a paragraph. If so, these blanks are *not* to be considered as a gap to be widened. We shall find it convenient to introduce two variables, Leftmost and Rightmost, and make them indicate the first and last non-blank characters of the line.

Level 1 outline of WriteAdjustedLine

```
procedure WriteAdjustedLine;
  var
    ExtraBlanks, NrGaps, Widening: LineSizes;
```

```
        Leftmost, Rightmost, Pos: LinePositions;
begin
with Line do
  begin
  make Leftmost the position of the leftmost non-blank;
  make Rightmost the position of the rightmost non-blank;
  make NrGaps the number of inter-word gaps;
  ExtraBlanks := Width — Rightmost;
  for Pos := 1 to Rightmost do
     if there is an inter-word gap at position Pos then
       begin
       Widening := ExtraBlanks div NrGaps;
       Write (Blank: (Widening+1));
       ExtraBlanks := ExtraBlanks — Widening;
       NrGaps := NrGaps — 1
       end
     else
       Write (Column[Pos])
  end
end (* WriteAdjustedLine *)
```

Testing Level 1 of WriteAdjustedLine

The test cases to be considered are:

(a) a line which is the first line of a paragraph;
(b) a line which is not the first of a paragraph;
(c) a line which is already completely filled;
(d) a line which requires extra blanks between words;
(e) a line with only one word.

    Test case (a) is considered here. The rest are left to you as an exercise. Test case (e) is of particular interest; does WriteAdjustedLine deal with this case satisfactorily?

    Suppose that Width has the value 30, that Size has the value 29, and that the first 29 characters of Column are:

        ϸϸϸϸϸϸINϸTHEϸYEARϸ1984ϸTHEREϸ

Then Leftmost should be set to 7 and Rightmost to 28. Thus ExtraBlanks is set to 2. Counting the inter-word gaps should set NrGaps to 4 (since the leading blanks do not count as a gap). As we go round the loop, we write 'ϸϸϸϸϸIN' before coming to the first gap. We calculate Widening=0, so we write 1 blank, ExtraBlanks remains at 2, and NrGaps is decremented to 3. After further writing

'THE' we come to the second gap. We calculate Widening=0, so we write 1 blank, ExtraBlanks remains at 2, and NrGaps is decremented to 2. After further writing 'YEAR' we come to the third gap. This time we calculate Widening=1, so we write 2 blanks, ExtraBlanks is reduced to 1, and NrGaps is decremented to 1. After further writing '1984' we come to the fourth gap. We calculate Widening=1, so we write 2 blanks, and ExtraBlanks and NrGaps are reduced to 0. After further writing 'THERE' the loop terminates. So the written line is:

þþþþþþINþTHEþYEARþþ1984þþTHERE

Refinement 1.1 of WriteAdjustedLine:
   make Leftmost the position of the leftmost non-blank

```
Leftmost := 1;
while Column[Leftmost] = Blank do
    Leftmost := Succ(Leftmost)
```

Refinement 1.2 of WriteAdjustedLine:
   make Rightmost the position of the rightmost non-blank

```
Rightmost := Size;
while Column[Rightmost] = Blank do
    Rightmost := Pred(Rightmost)
```

Refinement 1.3 of WriteAdjustedLine:
   make NrGaps the number of inter-word gaps

Since exactly one blank has been placed between consecutive words in Column, this can be done simply by counting the blank characters between the first and last words:

```
NrGaps := 0;
for Pos := Leftmost to Rightmost do
    if Column[Pos] = Blank then
        NrGaps := NrGaps + 1
```

Refinement 1.4 of WriteAdjustedLine:
   there is an inter-word gap at position Pos

```
(Pos > Leftmost) and (Column[Pos] = Blank)
```

The latter part of this condition is based on the same observation as Refinement 1.3. The first part ensures that we are looking at an *inter-word* gap rather than a blank introduced at the start of a paragraph.

Testing Refinements 1.1 to 1.4 of WriteAdjustedLine

Test these refinements as an exercise.

Level 4 of TextFormatter

Putting together all these refinements, we have the final program. Test it yourself with some text from a book.

```
program TextFormatter ( Input, RawText, Output );

const
   Blank = '  ';
   MaxWordSize = 20;
   Indent = 6;
   MinLineWidth = 26; (* = Indent + MaxWordSize *)
   MaxLineWidth = 80; (* assumed width of the paper *)

type

   (* - - - - Types for the Line data structure - - - - *)

   Styles = (Adjusted, Unadjusted);
   LineSizes = 0 . . MaxLineWidth;
   LinePositions = 1 . . MaxLineWidth;
   Lines = record
               Width: MinLineWidth . . MaxLineWidth;
               Size: LineSizes;
               Column: packed array [LinePositions] of Char
           end;

   (* - - - - Types for the Token data structure - - - - *)

   WordSizes = 1 . . MaxWordSize;
   TokenKinds = (AWord, AParagraphMark, AnEndMark);
   Tokens = record
               case Kind: TokenKinds of
                  AWord:
                     ( Spelling: packed array [WordSizes] of Char;
                       Size: WordSizes );
                  AParagraphMark, AnEndMark:
                     ( )
           end;
var
   Token: Tokens;
   Line: Lines;
   RawText: Text;

(* - - - - The Line cluster of subprograms - - - - *)
```

```
procedure SetupLine;
  var
    WidthWanted: Integer;
  begin
  Read (Input, WidthWanted);
  with Line do
    begin
    if WidthWanted < MinLineWidth then
      Width := MaxLineWidth
    else
    if WidthWanted > MaxLineWidth then
      Width := MaxLineWidth
    else
      Width := WidthWanted;
    Size := 0
    end
  end (* SetupLine *);

procedure AppendCharToLine (Character: Char);
  begin
  with Line do
    begin
    Size := Size + 1;
    Column[Size] := Character
    end
  end (* AppendCharToLine *);

procedure AppendBlankToLine;
  begin
  AppendCharToLine (Blank)
  end (* AppendBlankToLine *);

procedure IndentLine;
  var
    I: 1 . . Indent;
  begin
  for I := 1 to Indent do
    AppendBlankToLine
  end (* IndentLine *);

function LineHasRoomFor ( SpaceNeeded: WordSizes): Boolean;
  begin
  with Line do
```

```
          LineHasRoomFor := SpaceNeeded <= (Width — Size)
     end (* LineHasRoomFor *);

procedure WriteLine (Style: Styles);

   var
      I: LinePositions;

   procedure WriteAdjustedLine;
      var
         ExtraBlanks, NrGaps, Widening: LineSizes;
         Leftmost, Rightmost, Pos: LinePositions;
      begin
      with Line do
         begin
         Leftmost := 1;
         while Column[Leftmost] = Blank do
            Leftmost := Succ(Leftmost);
         Rightmost := Size;
         while Column[Rightmost] = Blank do
            Rightmost := Pred(Rightmost);
         NrGaps := 0;
         for Pos := Leftmost to Rightmost do
            if Column[Pos] = Blank then
               NrGaps := NrGaps + 1;
         ExtraBlanks := Width — Rightmost;
         for Pos := 1 to Rightmost do
            if (Pos > Leftmost) and
                  (Column[Pos] = Blank) then
               begin
               Widening := ExtraBlanks div NrGaps;
               Write (Blank: (Widening+1));
               ExtraBlanks := ExtraBlanks — Widening;
               NrGaps := NrGaps — 1
               end
            else
               Write (Column[Pos])
         end
      end (* WriteAdjustedLine *);

   begin (* WriteLine *)
   with Line do
      begin
      case Style of
         Adjusted:
            WriteAdjustedLine;
```

```
      Unadjusted:
        for I := 1 to Size do
            Write(Column[I])
      end;
    WriteLn;
    Size := 0
    end
  end (* WriteLine *);

(* - - - - End of the Line cluster - - - - *)

(* - - - - The Token cluster of subprograms - - - - *)

procedure SetupToken;
  begin
  Reset (RawText)
  end (* SetupToken *);

procedure ReadToken;
  var
    Character: Char;
    I : 0 . . MaxWordSize;
  begin
  Character := Blank;
  while not EOF(RawText) and (Character = Blank) do
    Read (RawText, Character);
  with Token do
    begin
    if EOF(RawText) then
      Kind := AnEndMark
    else
      begin
      I := 0;
      Kind := AWord;
      while Character <> Blank do
        begin
        if I < MaxWordSize then
          begin
          I := I + 1;
          Spelling[I] := Character
          end;
        Read (RawText, Character)
        end;
      Size := I;
      for I := Size+1 to MaxWordSize do
        Spelling[I] := Blank;
```

```
            if Spelling = '/PAR/              ' then
                Kind := AParagraphMark
            end
        end;
    end (* ReadToken *);

procedure AppendWordToLine;
    var
        I: WordSizes;
    begin
    with Token do
        for I := 1 to Size do
            AppendCharToLine (Spelling[I])
    end (* AppendWordToLine *);

(* - - - - End of the Token cluster - - - - *)

begin (* TextFormatter *)
(* prepare the processing of lines *)
SetupLine;
(* prepare the processing of tokens *)
SetupToken;
(* read a token *)
ReadToken;
while Token.Kind <> AnEndMark do
    begin
    if Token.Kind = AWord then
        (* append the word followed by a blank to the current line,
            right-adjust the line and start a new line if necessary *)
        begin
        if not LineHasRoomFor(Token.Size) then
            WriteLine (Adjusted);
        AppendWordToLine;
        if LineHasRoomFor(1) then
            AppendBlankToLine
        end
    else (* the token is a paragraph mark *)
        (* start a new paragraph *)
        begin
        WriteLine (Unadjusted);
        WriteLn;
        IndentLine
        end;
    (* read a token *)
    ReadToken
    end;
```

```
WriteLine (Unadjusted)
end (* TextFormatter *).
```

By clustering all the subprograms concerned with Line, and likewise all the subprograms concerned with Token, we improve the localization of the final program. (Note that the Line cluster must come first, because AppendCharToLine in this cluster is invoked by AppendWordToLine in the Token cluster and Pascal requires each subprogram to be declared before it is used.) Similarly, the types of the Line cluster appear together, as do those of the Token cluster.

Ideally, all the constants, types, variables and subprograms of each cluster would be collected together with no intervening material, further improving the localization of the program. Unfortunately this is precluded by Pascal's strict order of declarations within the declarative part of a block.

18.3 CASE STUDY IV: TRANSFERABLE VOTE ELECTIONS

PROBLEM SPECIFICATION

The transferable vote system is a method of conducting an election in such a way that the successful candidate requires the support of an absolute majority of the voters, even when there are more than two candidates. Instead of voting for just one candidate, each voter is required to complete a ballot placing *all* the candidates in order of preference. In the first count of votes, only the first choice of each voter is considered. If no candidate obtains an overall majority in this count, then the candidate with the *fewest* votes is eliminated, and a recount is carried out in which votes cast for the eliminated candidate are ignored, that is the second choice of those voters who voted first for the eliminated candidate are now counted. Eliminations and recounts are continued in this way until one candidate has obtained an overall majority (or until all candidates still in contention have exactly equal votes, in which case a tie is declared).

For example, suppose the votes cast in a three-candidate election are as follows:

	1st choice	2nd choice	3rd choice
Voter A	3	1	2
Voter B	2	3	1
Voter C	2	1	3
Voter D	1	3	2
Voter E	2	1	3
Voter F	3	2	1
Voter G	1	3	2
Voter H	3	1	2
Voter I	2	3	1

in which the candidates have been numbered 1, 2 and 3. Then in the first count candidate 1 gets 2 votes, candidate 2 gets 4 votes, and candidate 3 gets 3 votes. There is no overall majority, so candidate 1 is eliminated. Both the voters (D and G) whose first choice was this candidate gave candidate 3 as their second choices, so in the recount candidate 2 gets 4 votes and candidate 3 gets 5 votes. Therefore candidate 3 is the winner.

If after any count several candidates have the same, smallest, number of votes, then any one of them may be eliminated.

Write a program to determine the winner, if any, of a transferable vote election. Assume that each ballot is presented as a single line of input, with the candidate numbers arranged in order of preference as above. Assume that these lines are preceded by a line containing the number of candidates. The program must reject invalid ballots, a valid ballot being one on which every candidate has been placed in exactly one position. (For example, with three candidates, 2 2 1 and 3 1 4 are invalid ballots.)

SOLUTION

The problem specification implies that the ballots are liable to be examined repeatedly, once on each count. Our very first deduction, therefore, is that it will not be sufficient to examine the ballots one by one when reading them, unlike the simpler vote-counting problem of Example 11.1. Instead we must first store all the valid ballots.

The heart of the solution will be a loop in which a candidate is eliminated and the votes are recounted as often as necessary. This leads us to Level 1:

Level 1 outline

```
program TransferableVotes ( Input, Output );
global declarations;
begin
prepare to count votes;
read all the ballots, storing the valid ones;
count the votes;
while  a recount is needed do
   begin
   eliminate the candidate with fewest votes;
   recount the votes, ignoring eliminated candidates
   end;
report the outcome of the election
end .
```

Testing Level 1

Let us check the logic of Level 1 in all possible cases.

(a) All the candidates have equal votes. In this case we skip the loop; then, since there is no overall majority, we should report a tie.
(b) One candidate has an overall majority. In this case also, we skip the loop; this time we should declare the winner.
(c) Neither (a) nor (b) applies. Then there must be more than two candidates still in contention. In this case, we enter the loop, eliminate one of the candidates, and recount; this must reduce to case (a) or (b), or to (c) with fewer candidates.

When only two candidates are left, either (a) or (b) must apply. Since we eliminate one candidate on each repetition, therefore, the loop must eventually terminate.

Refinements from Level 1

Now we may proceed to refine Level 1. Sooner or later, we shall have to decide how to store the ballots, but we can postpone this decision until we see how to organize the vote counting and recounting.

To count the votes we simply consider each ballot in turn, and credit a vote to the candidate who is the first choice on that ballot. Before rushing ahead with this refinement, we should examine the refinement of 'recount the votes, ignoring eliminated candidates' to see if we can profit from its similarity. Recounting is similar to counting, except that instead of the first-choice candidate every time, we credit the most favoured candidate who has not yet been eliminated.

In fact, counting is just a special case of recounting, since initially no candidates will have been eliminated, so we can use the same piece of program. This will use variables (such as those for accumulating the vote-counts) that will be irrelevant elsewhere, so we should package it as a procedure, CountVotes.

Examining the logic of Level 1, we can see that the following information must be extracted from the vote counting to be used by the rest of the program: (a) the most and least successful candidates still in contention, (b) whether the former obtained an overall majority, and (c) whether all candidates still in contention are tied. This information can be returned from CountVotes through variable parameters.

There are just three possible outcomes of a count or recount: a tie, an overall majority, or a recount. This suggests the use of an enumeration type.

We also need a type to represent vote-counts. With these considerations in mind, we see that the global declarations should include the following:

```
type
   VoteCounts = 0 . . MaxInt;
   Outcomes = (AllTied, OverallMajority, RecountNeeded);
var
   Leader, Trailer: Candidates;
   Outcome: Outcomes;
   . . .
```

The type Candidates will presumably reflect the specified numbering of the candidates; however, at this state it is unclear exactly how it should be defined.

We can now refine the counting steps in terms of CountVotes.

Refinement 1.1: count the votes

```
CountVotes (Leader, Trailer, Outcome)
```

Initially, we must consider all candidates as still in contention; this must be arranged by 'prepare to count votes'.

Refinement 1.2: recount the votes, ignoring eliminated candidates

```
CountVotes (Leader, Trailer, Outcome)
```

Refinement 1.3: a recount is needed

```
Outcome = RecountNeeded
```

We will introduce a procedure, Report, to report the result of the election.

Refinement 1.4: report the outcome of the election

```
Report (Outcome, Leader)
```

We will introduce a procedure, StoreValidBallots, to read and store the valid ballots.

Refinement 1.5: read all the ballots, storing the valid ones

```
StoreValidBallots
```

We can also make a start on the refinement of CountVotes. This can assume that all the stored ballots are valid ones, because invalid ballots will have been discarded previously.

Level 1 of CountVotes

```
procedure CountVotes
                    (var Leader, Trailer: Candidates;
                     var Outcome: Outcomes);
    local declarations;
    begin
    initialize all vote-counts to 0;
    prepare to scan valid ballots;
    while not at end of ballots do
      begin
      access the next ballot;
      determine the most favoured candidate on this
          ballot, apart from eliminated candidates;
      add 1 to this candidate's vote-count
      end;
    determine which of the candidates still in contention
        received most votes (Leader) and least votes (Trailer);
    if Leader and Trailer have equal votes then
        Outcome := AllTied
    else
    if Leader has more than half the votes then
        Outcome := OverallMajority
    else
        Outcome := RecountNeeded
    end (* CountVotes *)
```

Level 2 of TransferableVotes is obtained by substituting these refinements into Level 1. The complete Level 2 program is omitted to save space. Write it out yourself unless you can visualize it clearly. As an exercise, test the complete Level 2 outline using the sample data.

Refinements from Level 2

We cannot proceed any further without deciding how to store the ballots. The most obvious solution, perhaps, is an array each of whose components contains a single ballot. This solution has the disadvantage that, since an array is fixed in size, it would be necessary to fix some arbitrary upper limit on the number of ballots to be accepted, in order that we can declare an array with that number of components. But it would be difficult to choose a suitable limit: 1000 would be too small for many elections; even 100000 might not be large enough for some purposes, but it would be grossly wasteful of space when the actual number of ballots is much smaller.

A little thought suggests a much better solution: a serial file. A file has the decisive advantage of being (virtually) unlimited in size. If we store the ballots in a file, we will be restricted to examining them one by one in a fixed order, but that is perfectly adequate here: examining the logic of procedure CountVotes, we can see that each ballot is examined once only per count, and that the order of examination of the ballots is irrelevant. Having generated the file, we may scan it from beginning to end as often as required. So we include among the global declarations:

```
var
    BallotFile: file of Ballots;
    . . .
```

Each component, of type Ballots, will represent a single ballot. At this stage there is still no need to decide how to represent individual ballots, so we need not define the type Ballots just yet. Since the file will be generated by the program for its own use, and will not be retained afterwards, BallotFile will *not* be a program parameter. BallotFile is generated by the procedure StoreValidBallots.

Level 1 of StoreValidBallots

```
procedure StoreValidBallots;
    local declarations;
    begin
    Rewrite (BallotFile);
    while not EOF(Input) do
        begin
        read and check one Ballot;
        if Ballot is valid then
            Write (BallotFile, Ballot)
        end
    end (* StoreValidBallots *)
```

The local declarations of StoreValidBallots must include:

```
var
    Ballot: Ballots;
    . . .
```

Refinements from Level 1 of CountVotes

While scanning BallotFile, CountVotes must note the total number of valid ballots in order to be able to compute the number of votes needed for an overall majority.

Refinement 1.1 of CountVotes: not at end of ballots

```
not EOF(BallotFile)
```

Refinement 1.2 of CountVotes: access the next ballot

```
Read (BallotFile, Ballot);
NrValidBallots := NrValidBallots + 1
```

Refinement 1.3 of CountVotes: prepare to scan valid ballots

```
Reset (BallotFile);
NrValidBallots := 0
```

The local declarations of **CountVotes** must include:

```
var
   Ballot: Ballots;
   NrValidBallots: VoteCounts
```

Level 3 of TransferableVotes is obtained by substituting these refinements into Level 2. Again, test the complete Level 3 outline with your own data.

Refinements from Level 3

Now we must decide how to represent an individual ballot, that is how to define the type **Ballots**. Each ballot is a sequence of exactly **NrCandidates** candidate numbers, where **NrCandidates** is a variable of type **Candidates** containing the number read from the start of the input data. The ideal type definition would be:

```
Ballots = array [1 . . NrCandidates] of Candidates
```

but unfortunately Pascal does not allow this, since **NrCandidates** is a variable. {Some programming languages, such as Ada, Algol and PL/I, do allow arrays to have their size determined by variables. Such arrays are called *dynamic arrays*.} If, however, we agree on a fixed limit to the number of candidates, say 10, we can include the following among the global declarations:

```
const
   MaxCandidates = 10;
   . . .
type
   Candidates = 1 . . MaxCandidates;
   Placings   = 1 . . MaxCandidates;
   Ballots    = array [Placings] of Candidates;
   . . .
var
   NrCandidates: Candidates;
   . . .
```

Only the first NrCandidates components of each array of type Ballots will actually be used.

Refinements from Level 1 of Store ValidBallots

A ballot is valid if (a) it contains no numbers outside the range 1 to NrCandidates, and (b) each candidate number occurs just once. The latter can be checked easily by declaring:

```
var
    AlreadyChosen: array [Candidates] of Boolean;
    ...
```

and initializing all components to False. For each candidate number Choice on the ballot, we first check that AlreadyChosen[Choice] is still False, then we set it to True. Since this piece of program contains details and variables (notably AlreadyChosen) of no interest elsewhere, it should be packaged as a procedure, ReadAndCheckOneBallot. This will have two variable parameters, one to return the ballot and one to indicate its validity.

Refinement 1.1 of Store ValidBallots: read and check one Ballot

```
ReadAndCheckOneBallot (Ballot, Valid)
```

Refinement of ReadAndCheckOneBallot

We can write this down directly.

```
procedure ReadAndCheckOneBallot
                (var Ballot: Ballots;
                    var Valid: Boolean);
    var
      Choice: Integer;
      Place: Placings;
      AlreadyChosen: array [Candidates] of Boolean;
    begin
    Valid := True;
    for Choice := 1 to NrCandidates do
      AlreadyChosen[Choice] := False;
    for Place := 1 to NrCandidates do
      begin
      Read (Choice);
      if (Choice < 1) or (Choice > NrCandidates) then
        Valid := False
```

```
     else
     if AlreadyChosen[Choice] then
        Valid := False
     else
        begin
        Ballot[Place] := Choice;
        AlreadyChosen[Choice] := True
        end
     end;
   ReadLn
   end (* ReadAndCheckOneBallot *)
```

Refinement 1.2 of Store ValidBallots: Ballot is valid

```
Valid
```

Refinements from Level 2 of CountVotes

Refinement 2.1 of CountVotes: determine the most favoured candidate on Ballot, ignoring eliminated candidates

If we make the local declarations:

```
var
   Ballot: Ballots;
   Place: Placings;
   MostFavoured: Candidates;
   . . .
```

we can refine as follows:

```
Place := 1;
while the candidate placed in Ballot[Place]
      is one who has already been eliminated do
   Place := Succ(Place);
MostFavoured := Ballot[Place]
```

This is an example of linear search. Notice that the loop does not contain the usual check: Place <= NrCandidates. This is unnecessary here because at least two of Ballot[1], . . ., Ballot[NrCandidates] will be candidates who have not been eliminated, provided that the ballot is valid. Examination of the program logic shows that only valid ballots are considered by procedure CountVotes.

Level 4 of TransferableVotes is obtained by substituting these refinements into Level 3. As an exercise, hand-test Level 4 using suitable test data.

Refinements from Level 4

The remaining refinements are fairly straightforward. We can keep track of
which candidates have been eliminated using the global array:

```
var
    InContention: array [Candidates] of Boolean;
    . . .
```

This will be initialized as part of 'prepare to count votes', and updated by
'eliminate the candidates with fewest votes'.

Refinements from Level 3 of Count Votes

Refinement 3.1 of Count Votes: initialize all vote-counts to 0

Refinement 3.2 of Count Votes: add 1 to this candidate's vote-count

Both these refinements can be borrowed directly from Example 11.1. We
introduce the local declaration:

```
var
    Count: array [Candidates] of VoteCounts;
    . . .
```

Refinement 3.3 of Count Votes: determine which of the candidates still in contention received most votes (Leader) and least votes (Trailer)

This amounts to locating the maximum and minimum of Count[1], ..., Count
[NrCandidates], ignoring candidates who have been eliminated.

```
LeadersCount := 0;
TrailersCount := NrValidBallots+1;
for Contender := 1 to NrCandidates do
  if InContention[Contender] then
    begin
    if Count[Contender] > LeadersCount then
      begin
      Leader := Contender;
      LeadersCount := Count[Leader]
      end;
    if Count[Contender] < TrailersCount then
      begin
      Trailer := Contender;
      TrailersCount := Count[Trailer]
      end
    end
```

LeadersCount and TrailersCount will be local VoteCounts variables. Their initial values have been chosen so that they are certain to be altered, and so that Leader and Trailer will receive values. It would be incorrect to initialize LeadersCount and TrailersCount to Count[1], as was done in Example 11.1, since candidate 1 may have been eliminated.

The expressions 'Leader and Trailer have equal votes' and 'Leader has more than half the votes' can easily be expressed in terms of LeadersCount and TrailersCount.

Refinement 3.4 of CountVotes: the candidate placed in Ballot[Place] is one who has already been eliminated

```
not InContention[Ballot[Place]]
```

Level 5 of TransferableVotes

This is obtained by substituting these refinements, and one or two remaining minor ones, into Level 4, yielding the Pascal program. As a final exercise, hand-test the complete program with your own data.

```
program TransferableVotes ( Input, Output );

const
    MaxCandidates = 10;

type
    Candidates = 1 . . MaxCandidates;
    Placings = 1 . . MaxCandidates;
    Ballots = array [Placings] of Candidates;
    VoteCounts = 0 . . MaxInt;
    Outcomes = (AllTied, OverallMajority, RecountNeeded);

var
    NrCandidates: Candidates;
    Leader, Trailer: Candidates;
    Outcome: Outcomes;
    BallotFile: file of Ballots;
    InContention: array [Candidates] of Boolean;

procedure StoreValidBallots;
    var
        Ballot: Ballots;
        Valid: Boolean;

    procedure ReadAndCheckOneBallot
                (var Ballot: Ballots;
                 var Valid: Boolean);
```

```
    var
      Choice: Integer
      Place: Placings;
      AlreadyChosen: array [Candidates] of Boolean;

    begin
    Valid := True;
    for Choice := 1 to NrCandidates do
      AlreadyChosen[Choice] := False;
    for Place := 1 to NrCandidates do
      begin
      Read (Choice);
      if (Choice < 1) or (Choice > NrCandidates) then
        Valid := False
      else
      if AlreadyChosen[Choice] then
        Valid := False
      else
        begin
        Ballot[Place] := Choice;
        AlreadyChosen[Choice] := True
        end
      end;
    ReadLn
    end (* ReadAndCheckOneBallot *);

  begin (* StoreValidBallots *)
  Rewrite (BallotFile);
  while not EOF(Input) do
    begin
    ReadAndCheckOneBallot (Ballot, Valid);
    if Valid then
      Write (BallotFile, Ballot)
    end
  end (* StoreValidBallots *);

procedure SetupCounting;
  var
    Contender: Candidates;
  begin
  ReadLn (NrCandidates);
  for Contender := 1 to NrCandidates do
    InContention[Contender] := True
  end (* SetupCounting *);
```

```
procedure Eliminate (Contender: Candidates);
  begin
  InContention[Contender] := False
  end (* Eliminate *);

procedure CountVotes
        (var Leader, Trailer: Candidates;
         var Outcome: Outcomes);
  var
    Count: array [Candidates] of VoteCounts;
    Ballot: Ballots;
    Place: Placings;
    MostFavoured, Contender: Candidates;
    LeadersCount, TrailersCount: VoteCounts;
    NrValidBallots: VoteCounts;

  begin
  for Contender := 1 to NrCandidates do
    Count[Contender] := 0;
  Reset (BallotFile);
  NrValidBallots := 0;
  while not EOF(BallotFile) do
    begin
    Read (BallotFile, Ballot);
    NrValidBallots := NrValidBallots + 1;
    (* determine the most favoured candidate on this
       ballot, apart from eliminated candidates *)
    Place := 1;
    while not InContention[Ballot[Place]] do
      Place := Succ(Place);
    MostFavoured := Ballot[Place];
    Count[MostFavoured] := Count[MostFavoured] + 1
    end;
  (* determine which of the candidates still in contention
     received most votes (Leader) and least votes (Trailer) *)
  LeadersCount := 0;
  TrailersCount := NrValidBallots+1;
  for Contender := 1 to NrCandidates do
    if InContention[Contender] then
      begin
      if Count[Contender] > LeadersCount then
        begin
        Leader := Contender;
        LeadersCount := Count[Leader]
```

```
              end;
          if Count[Contender] < TrailersCount then
            begin
            Trailer := Contender;
            TrailersCount := Count[Trailer]
            end
          end;
      if LeadersCount = TrailersCount then
        Outcome := AllTied
      else
      if LeadersCount > NrValidBallots div 2 then
        Outcome := OverallMajority
      else
        Outcome := RecountNeeded
      end (* CountVotes *);

  procedure Report (Outcome: Outcomes;
                    Leader: Candidates);
    var
      Contender: Candidates;
    begin
    case Outcome of
      OverallMajority:
        WriteLn ('Winner is candidate: ', Leader:1);
      AllTied:
        begin
        WriteLn ('Tie among the following candidates: ');
        for Contender := 1 to NrCandidates do
          if InContention[Contender] then
            WriteLn (Contender: 20)
        end
      end (* case Outcome *)
    end (* Report *)

begin (* TransferableVotes *)
SetupCounting;
StoreValidBallots;
CountVotes (Leader, Trailer, Outcome);
while Outcome = RecountNeeded do
  begin
  Eliminate (Trailer);
  CountVotes (Leader, Trailer, Outcome)
  end;
Report (Outcome, Leader)
end (* TransferableVotes *) .
```

18.4 SOME GENERAL PRINCIPLES

Let us now summarize our work on methodical programming. We shall draw some lessons from the case studies, and we shall state some general principles. Refer back to the case studies from time to time to see the principles in practice.

DESIGN DECISIONS AND REFINEMENTS

Developing a program involves numerous *design decisions*. An example of a design decision is choosing a particular algorithm to perform some computation. Another example is the decision to introduce a variable. Yet another is to choose a type for that variable.

Design decisions are often interdependent. A change in one part of the design might have repercussions elsewhere. It is therefore essential to be methodical. That is the point of stepwise refinement: it encourages you to be methodical. It is also essential to record design decisions and their dependencies on one another. This is in case the design decisions have to be revised later.

Some decisions might appear very trivial, such as the choice of a simple variable or type. You might not even think of them as true design decisions. Avoid this attitude, however, because the choice of variables can have a major impact on the resulting program. In Case Study III, at one point we decided to hold the current line of output in store until it was almost filled. For this purpose we introduced a string field, Column, with a count of the number of characters in the line held in Size. This rather simple decision affected the programming of the entire Line cluster. It follows that a careless choice of variables can lead to a poorly designed program.

Consider a slightly different text formatting problem. The output lines are to be restricted to the specified line-width, but are *not* to be right-adjusted. Levels 1 and 2 would be very similar to Case Study III. At this point we have to decide about the current line of output. An inexperienced programmer might unthinkingly introduce fields Column and Size, just as in Case Study III. But there is a simple alternative here. The words and spaces can be written out immediately, instead of being held in store. This alternative decision leads to a much simpler program. Thus a decision *not* to introduce variables can also be important!

Data structures might need refinement, in much the same way as control structures. In Case Study IV, when refining Level 2 we decided to store the ballots in a file. On this basis we wrote Level 1 of StoreValidBallots and Level 2 of CountVotes. We did not at that stage decide how to represent individual ballots. We decided that the ballots file would have type **file of** Ballots, but we delayed writing a type definition for Ballots. Had we made the latter decision too early, we would have introduced too much detail into Level 3.

In fact a good general principle is to delay design decisions as long as possible. It is often possible to refine instructions before deciding exactly how the data they operate on should be structured. Indeed the delay is a positive advantage. It is only when we know what operations are required that we can choose the best data structure. Case Study IV illustrates this point. If we had decided earlier how to store the set of ballots, our choice might have been a two-dimensional array. However we delayed this decision until we were refining Level 3, and by then it was clear that the program could process the ballots in serial order. Thus a serial file became clearly the best choice.

BACKTRACKING AND THINKING AHEAD

In Case Study III we had to choose between alternative refinements. It was not clear at first which refinement was better, so we had to try both. This was done by carrying out each refinement for one or two levels. Then it became clear which was better. At that point the other refinement was abandoned.

As you become more experienced you will find it easier to choose between alternative refinements. You will be able to think ahead, down through one or two levels, and visualize roughly the consequences of each alternative refinement. Then you can choose the more promising refinement before committing yourself to paper.

Even experienced programmers, however, sometimes make refinements that later prove to be unsatisfactory (or wrong). Then the only course of action is to abandon the unsatisfactory refinements and *backtrack* to the point where the bad choice was made.

Time spent on backtracking and improving on earlier design decisions should not be considered wasted. It is part of the essential experience of every programmer. As experience is accumulated, these occasions will become less frequent.

It often happens that even when a program is complete, tested and working, the programmer will see a better way in which it could have been written. It is then that will-power is needed if excellence is to be pursued!

MODIFICATIONS

Any program good enough to be used for a long time is likely to require modification. Indeed program modification (or maintenance) is a full-time occupation for many programmers. For example, programs dealing with tax will have to accommodate periodic changes in the tax laws.

It is also common for a programmer to find that a new programming assignment resembles a previously-written program. In such a case, careful modification of the original program can save a lot of work.

Modifications should be done methodically, in the same way as correcting errors. That is to say, the necessary modifications should be located to specific refinements, and these refinements redone. It is a mistake to modify the program text alone, without regard for the way it was developed. That bad practice leads to a modified program that is harder to understand than the original program. Thus further modifications will be more difficult. Eventually it will become so difficult to perform further modifications that the only practicable course of action is to rewrite the program from scratch. This is how programs become obsolete.

PRACTICE

No-one has ever become a good programmer simply by reading about programming methods. (Nor, for that matter, by writing or teaching about them!) There is no substitute for practical experience. Attempt a variety of programming problems, from several application areas. Consciously apply our advice about methodical programming.

This book is about both methodical programming and Pascal. Really these are separate subjects. We treat them together because it is inadvisable to teach programming without any method, or to teach programming methods without a programming language! However, methodical programming is needed in any language. So if you are required to use another language, even a language that lacks the nice control and data structures of Pascal, you should continue to apply your skills in methodical programming.

18.5 SOFTWARE DEVELOPMENT AND DOCUMENTATION

Developing a computer system that truly meets the user's needs is a difficult and complex task. On the one hand there is the user, who perhaps has no understanding of the capabilities and limitations of computer systems. On the other hand there is the computer—powerful, but primitive. To exploit its potential to the full is the challenge facing you, the programmer.

(1) First comes the job of discovering exactly what the user would like the computer to do. This may involve you in interviews, market surveys, or simple introspection (when writing a program for your own use).

(2) The user's requirement is stated in the user's terms. It must now be restated in terms of computer operations, and a scheme must be devised to meet the requirement. In general a suite of programs is needed, interacting with each other through several sets of data. Once you know what data is initially available, and what must be generated by the operation of the system, you can specify each program by detailing its inputs and outputs.

This is no more than a first refinement step. It applies on a much larger scale than refinements within programs, but is no different in principle.

(3) Given the program specifications, you can design, write and test each of the programs.

(4) As soon as a system goes into operation, users will begin to discover reasons for changing it. It may be necessary to correct errors that escaped detection during testing. Just as common are requests to adapt the system to changes in the user's requirement. If the required changes are very extensive, the system has become obsolete and the whole development process repeats from step (1).

This is known as the *software life cycle.*

Step (1) is known as *systems analysis,* step (2) is *system design,* step (3) is *implementation* and step (4) is *maintenance.* Taken together steps (3) and (4) constitute what we call *programming.* It is quite common for the implementation and maintenance phases to be the responsibility of different programmers. It is also common for maintenance to absorb 50% or more of the effort in a software project.

This book is concerned almost exclusively with programming. Systems analysis and design are neglected here not because they are unimportant—quite the contrary—but because they depend on a mature understanding of the problems and possibilities of programming.

The *documentation* of a program consists of those supporting specifications and descriptions which are needed by the user and by the maintenance programmer. It is of the utmost importance to document a program well. The user of a program is dependent on the documentation for his information about it. Nothing is more annoying than discrepancies between what the documentation says and what the program actually does.

A 'User Guide' provides the information needed to exploit a program. It might contain some or all of the following sections.

(1) A brief description of the capabilities of the program. This is equivalent to the abstract of an article and its purpose is similar—to let the reader find out quickly whether the program is relevant to his needs.

(2) A detailed description. This contains a subsection for each facility of the program, giving precise descriptions of input and output requirements.

(3) Theoretical background. If the program is based on any mathematical or scientific theory, a brief summary is given. In the case of work which has been published a reference is adequate.

(4) Resources used. The amount of store and time needed to run the program are stated, relating these factors to the amount of input. If this is not practical, the resources needed to run a 'typical' job are stated.

(5) Operational description. The instructions for the computer operator and/or the operating system control program are given, including the actions to be taken on the various kinds of failure.

The maintenance programmer can have his work greatly expedited by good documentation; bad documentation is useless. It may be necessary to scrap a poorly documented program and write a well-documented replacement which is cheaper to maintain. Even when maintaining a program you wrote yourself, you will often find it difficult to understand after having set it aside for a few months to work on something else.

An 'Implementation Description' provides the information needed by the maintenance programmer. It might contain the following items.

(1) A complete program outline and refinement history, with discussion of the reasons for each design decision.
(2) A program structure diagram (e.g. Figure 7.1).
(3) The program text. Only the text of a program can lay claim to being a fully authoritative description. To assist the maintenance programmer, programs should be written with a view to readability. Consistent indentation, 'paragraphing' with additional blank lines, meaningful identifiers, informative comments—all these help the reader to understand a program.

Whatever its nature, documentation should be clearly written, complete, unambiguous, accurate, timely and up-to-date. Writing documentation to this standard is just as difficult as programming and should be undertaken with equal care. It is worth noting that many of the ideas that lead to readable programs also help in writing readable English. The principles of modularity, localization, consistency, and simplicity are particularly relevant.

EXERCISES 18

18.1. Systematically modify TextFormatter so that the procedure AppendWordToLine forms a separate cluster on its own.

18.2. Systematically enhance TextFormatter to support the following features:

(a) the special 'word' /BREAK/ is to start a new line, the current line being written without right-adjustment;
(b) the special 'word' /SPACE/ is to have the same effect as /BREAK/ and, additionally, is to leave a single blank line;
(c) the special 'word' /PAGE/ is to have the same effect as /BREAK/ and, additionally, is to start a new page;
(d) the program is to read, in addition to the line width, the maximum number of lines per page, and a new page is to be started automatically whenever the current page contains that number of lines.

18.3. Why were 'prepare to count votes' and 'eliminate the candidate with fewest votes' refined in terms of procedures in TransferableVotes?

18.4. What happens in TransferableVotes if *all* the ballots are invalid? What happens if there is only one candidate for election? Systematically amend the program to improve its behaviour in these circumstances.

PROGRAMMING EXERCISES 18

18.5. Write a program to plot the results of an experiment roughly on a line-printer page. Pairs of x- and y-values are supplied as input, one pair per line. The plot must include both the x- and y-axes. The positions of the axes and the x- and y-scale-factors must be chosen so as to use as much of the page as possible. The scales need not be marked on the axes, but the x- and y-scale-factors must be printed on the same page.

18.6. A text file Titles contains a list of book titles separated by line boundaries. A number of 'keywords' are supplied as input data, each left-justified on a line. Write a program which, for each keyword, writes a list of all the titles which contain that keyword, aligned such that the keyword always starts in a fixed column, e.g.:

```
              COMPUTER PROGRAMMING FOR ENGINEERS
                       PROGRAMMING IN PASCAL
                  SYSTEMATIC PROGRAMMING
        AN INTRODUCTION TO DYNAMIC PROGRAMMING
                         PROGRAMMING AND METHODICAL PROGRAMMING
PROGRAMMING AND METHODICAL PROGRAMMING
```

If a keyword occurs more than once in a title, the title should be repeated, as illustrated above.

18.7*. Disk files are often used for permanent storage of programs, texts, documents, mailing lists, etc. A program called an *editor* is needed to amend such files as required. Write an editor which reads a text file, OriginalFile, and writes an edited copy of this file to a second text file, UpdatedFile. The input data contains *editing directives*, one per line, whose effect is specified below (where *xyz* and *uvw* stand for any character sequences):

Directive	Effect
C'*xyz*'	Copy the current line and subsequent lines up to the next line containing *xyz*. This line becomes the new 'current line'.
S'*xyz*'	Skip to the next line containing *xyz* (i.e. do *not* copy the preceding lines). This line becomes the new 'current line'.
R'*xyz*''*uvw*'	Replace the first occurrence of *xyz* in the current line by *uvw*.

The 'current line' is initially the first line of OriginalFile. When all the editing directives have been processed, the current line and all remaining lines of OriginalFile are to be copied to UpdatedFile.

Part VI
Additional topics

19

Sets

This chapter may be omitted on a first reading. It covers:

* the mathematical concept of sets
* set types in Pascal
* typical applications of sets

19.1 SETS AND PROGRAMMING

The concept of a *set* is one of the most basic in mathematics. A set is best defined, for our purposes, as a collection of distinct objects all of the same type. The objects contained in a set are its *members*. {*June, July, August*} and {3, 5, 7, 11, 13, 17, 19} are examples of sets: the first has three members, which are months; the second has seven members, which are integers. The order in which the members are listed is of no importance: {*August, July, June*} is the same set as {*June, July, August*}. Repetition of members does not affect matters either: {3, 5, 7, 3, 5, 5, 7} is the same set as {3, 5, 7}. A set with no members at all is called the *empty set*.

The following operations are defined upon sets.

(a) Test for membership: a given value either is a member of a given set or is not. Thus *June* is a member of the set {*June, July, August*}, but *May* is not.
(b) Test for inclusion: a set A is included in a set B (alternatively, A is a *subset* of B) if and only if every member of A is also a member of B. Thus {*June, July, August*}, {*July*} and the empty set are all subsets of {*June, July, August*}.
(c) Set intersection: the intersection of two sets A and B is the set of all values

which are members of *A* and members of *B*. Thus the intersection of {*June, July, August*} and {*December, March, June, September*} is the set {*June*}.

(d) Set union: the union of two sets *A* and *B* is the set of all values which are members of *A*, or members of *B*, or both. Thus the union of {*June, July, August*} and {*December, March, June, September*} is the set {*March, June, July, August, September, December*}.

(e) Set difference: the difference of two sets *A* and *B* is the set of all values which are members of *A* but not *B*. Thus the difference of {*June, July, August*} and {*December, March, June, September*} is the set {*July, August*}.

The use of sets permits a very elegant formulation of many programming problems. The following example illustrates a common situation.

Example 19.1

Suppose we have a variable Month, and suppose that we want a statement to be executed only if Month has one of the values *April, June, September* or *November*. The 'obvious' solution is:

```
if (Month = April) or
   (Month = June) or
   (Month = September) or
   (Month = November) then
      . . . . . . . . . .
```

A much neater formulation is this:

```
if Month is a member of
      {April, June, September, November} then
         . . . . . . . . . .
```

Moreover, this formulation can easily be generalized, for example:

```
if Month is a member of MonthsOfInterest then
      . . . . . . . . . .
```

where MonthsOfInterest is a *set variable*, that is a variable whose value (in this case) will be a set of months.

19.2 SETS IN PASCAL

Unlike most other programming languages, Pascal allows the programmer to take advantage of the elegance of set notation. We can declare set variables, and we can compose set expressions using the operations defined in Section 19.1.

Example 19.2

Given the type definition:

> Months = (January,February,March,April,May,June,July,
> August,September,October,November,December)

we can declare some set variables as follows:

> MonthsOfInterest, SummerMonths: **set of** Months

This declares that the variables MonthsOfInterest and SummerMonths will take values which are sets, and that each member of these sets will be of type Months; the latter is called the *base type* of the sets. Alternatively, we may give the set type an identifier by means of a type definition:

> SetOfMonths = **set of** Months

and then declare the variables as follows:

> MonthsOfInterest, SummerMonths: SetOfMonths

The syntax of set types is summarized in Figure 19.1. **set** and **of** are both reserved words.

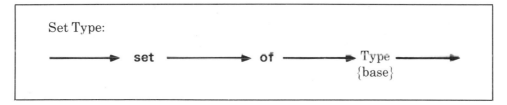

Set Type:

set ⟶ of ⟶ Type {base}

Figure 19.1. Syntax of Set Types

In order to allow an efficient implementation, Pascal imposes the restriction that the base type of every set type must be an *ordinal type*. Moreover, if the base type is Integer (or a subrange thereof), a Pascal compiler is free to impose limits on the smallest and largest values that can be used.

In Pascal we denote a set value using notation borrowed from mathematics, only replacing the curly brackets by square brackets. For example:

> SummerMonths := [June,July,August]

assigns a set value (with three members) to the set variable SummerMonths. This particular set constructor can be abbreviated. The statement:

> SummerMonths := [June . . August]

assigns to SummerMonths a set value whose members are June to August inclusive.

The form *a* .. *b* occurring in a set constructor represents all values between *a* and *b* (inclusive). If *a* is greater than *b*, *a* .. *b* denotes no values whatsoever.

We are not restricted to using constants in a set constructor. For example, if I and N are Integer variables, we can test whether the value of I lies in the range N to N+6 inclusive as follows:

if I in [N .. N+6] then .....

which is a neat alternative to the more usual:

if (I >= N) and (I <= N+6) then .....

(However the set formulation is subject to the limitations stated above.)

The empty set is denoted by [   ]. The syntax of set constructors is summarized in Figure 19.2.

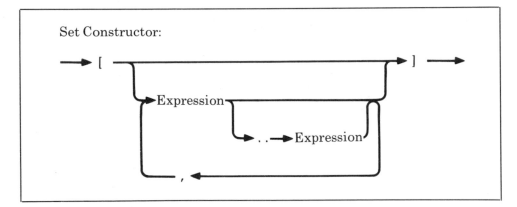

Figure 19.2. Syntax of Set Constructors

The last example has introduced the test for membership, denoted in Pascal by the operator **in**. Here is another example of its use, showing how the conditional statement of Example 19.1 would be expressed in Pascal:

if Month in MonthsOfInterest then

. . . .

in has the same priority as the comparison operators, and like them **in** yields a result which is True or False.

The comparison operators '=', '<>', '<=' and '>=' (but not '<' nor '>') may be used with set operands. Let A and B be sets. A = B yields True if and only if A and B have exactly the same members; A <> B is defined in the opposite sense. A <= B means 'A is a subset of B'; A >= B means 'B is a subset of A'.

Set expressions may be composed using the following set operators:

*   which with set operands denotes set intersection;
+   ,,   ,,   ,,   ,,   ,,   ,, union;
—   ,,   ,,   ,,   ,,   ,,   ,, difference.

A set value may be assigned to a set variable, and sets may be passed as parameters to subprograms. However, a function cannot have a set as its result.

Example 19.3

Assume the variable declaration:

> HolidayMonths, WetMonths, DryMonths: SetOfMonths

The following statements illustrate some uses of set expressions:

```
HolidayMonths := [July . . September];
(* any month which is not wet is assumed to be dry . . . *)
DryMonths := [January . . December] — WetMonths;
if HolidayMonths <= DryMonths then
    (* . . . i.e. every summer month is dry *)
    take beachwear on holiday
else if HolidayMonths * DryMonths <> [ ] then
    (* . . . i.e. some summer months are dry *)
    take an umbrella as well as beachwear
else
    (* . . . i.e. every summer month is wet *)
    stay at home
```

19.3 TYPE RULES FOR SETS

THE **in** OPERATOR

If the left operand of **in** has type A and the right operand has type **set of** B, then A and B must be the same type, or both must be subranges of the same type, or one must be a subrange of the other.

COMPATIBILITY

Two set types are *compatible* if they have the same base type, or if the base types are subranges of the same type, or if one of the base types is a subrange of the other. Two set values may be combined using the set operators, or compared, only if they are of compatible types.

ASSIGNMENT COMPATIBILITY

A set expression may be assigned only to a set variable of a compatible type, and every member of the value of the set expression must be a value of the set variable's base type.

EXERCISES 19

19.1. A group of people have been numbered 1 to N. Write down declarations of variables OldPeople, Males, Smokers and Drinkers which can take values which represent sets of people in this group. Assuming that appropriate values have been assigned to these variables, write set expressions whose values will be:

(a) the whole group;
(b) the set of non-smokers;
(c) the set of old smoking drinking males;
(d) the set of those who smoke or drink (or both);
(e) the set consisting of all the old people plus those males who smoke or drink.

Write a statement which outputs the message 'BAD INSURANCE RISK' if a given person Person is in set (e).

19.2. Write a program fragment which determines whether a given colour occurs in your national flag or not, by testing for membership of a suitably chosen set of colours.

19.3. Write a program fragment which determines whether a given character is a letter, a digit, a blank, punctuation, or other. Use sets rather than comparisons.

19.4. (Needs arrays.) Modify program TransferableVotes of Section 18.3 to use set variables instead of the Boolean arrays AlreadyChosen and InContention. Thus, for example, the condition InContention[Contender] is to be replaced by something like Contender in Contention.

PROGRAMMING EXERCISES 19

19.5. (Needs arrays.) In a strictly hierarchical organization every employee (except for the president) has a single immediate superior. Suppose a small hierarchical organization uses employee numbers in the range 1 to 40. Input is supplied in which each line contains an employee's number, the number of his immediate superior (or 0 if the employee is the president himself), and other details of no concern here. Write a program which uses this input to produce output showing, for each employee, a list of all subordinates. (Hint: use an array of sets.)

19.6. (Needs records and files.) The departments of an organization are numbered from 1 to 20 and there is a file containing a record for each employee, including the employee's name and department number. Write a program to create a new file, containing records only for those employees working in a given subset of the departments. The standard input gives the department numbers of interest, one number per line. The employee data is given in the program file parameter MasterFile, and the selected employee records are to be written to the program file parameter ExtractedFile.

20

Pointers and linked lists

This chapter may be omitted on a first reading. It covers:

* the pointer concept
* dynamically created data structures
* pointer types in Pascal
* using pointers to implement a simple dynamic data
  structure—the linked list

20.1 POINTERS

In Section 15.2 we developed a program SortNames, which sorts a series of names into lexicographic order. It works by inserting each name, immediately it is read, into its correct position in an ordered list of names. The list of names is represented by an array, List.

This program illustrates the basic idea of insertion sorting using an array. It works, but it is rather inefficient. Each time a new item is inserted, some of the items already in the array must be shifted to make room for the new item. As the list gets longer, the number of items to be shifted increases, and the program gets slower. If the list gets very long (50 items or more, say), the program will be unacceptably slow.

The shifting is necessary because the array is a rigid data structure. The first item in the list must be in List[1], the second item must be in List[2], the third in List[3], and so on. So to insert a new item between the second and third items, we must displace the item in List[3] into List[4]; that in turn displaces the item in List[4] into List[5], and so on.

A completely different way to represent the list is to make each entry in the list refer *explicitly* to the entry which follows it, as shown here by arrows:

For obvious reasons, these references are called *pointers*. The advantage of using pointers becomes apparent when we update the list by inserting a new item, for example by inserting 'Hoare' between 'Dijkstra' and 'Knuth'. This is achieved simply by: (1) creating a new entry to contain the name 'Hoare' and a pointer to the 'Knuth' entry (which will be the new entry's follower); and (2) redirecting the pointer in the 'Dijkstra' entry to refer to the new entry. The other entries in the list need not be disturbed at all:

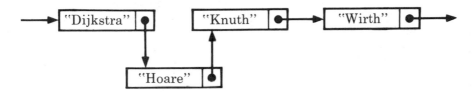

Similarly, it is easy to *delete* an item from such a list, if the problem requires this. To delete 'Knuth' from the last diagram, for example, we need only redirect the pointer in the 'Hoare' entry to refer to the 'Wirth' entry:

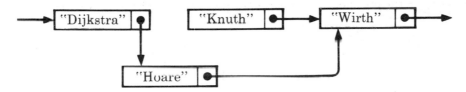

A list of records linked by pointers in this way is known as a *linked list*.

Pointers are data which can be assigned and compared. Thus lists and more complex data structures built up using pointers can be manipulated simply by redirecting the pointers, which is faster than copying bulky data structures.

20.2 DYNAMIC DATA STRUCTURES

When we declare a variable V in the declarative part of a block, we obtain a store location named V:

V [   ]

We can access this store location by quoting its name. For example, if V is a record:

```
with V do . . .
```

On the other hand, the store locations in the linked list of the previous section are anonymous. Such locations are accessed not by name, but by means of the pointers which refer to them. Thus, if P is a pointer which refers to a record, the form of the **with** statement must be:

> **with** the record referenced by P **do** . . .

A named location is created automatically on entry to the block where the variable is declared, and it is destroyed on exit from that block. Anonymous locations have the great advantage that they can be created and destroyed *at any time* while the program is running. Data structures composed of anonymous locations linked by pointers are called *dynamic data structures*, since they can expand and contract freely. A linked list is a simple example.

Thus we see a further advantage in representing a list of varying length as a linked structure instead of an array. A linked list can be made just as long as required. The size of an array, on the other hand, is chosen in advance by the programmer, so an arbitrary limit must be imposed on the number of items to be stored.

20.3 POINTERS IN PASCAL

Suppose we wish to set up a linked list containing items of some type Items. (How Items is defined is irrelevant here.) The type definition:

> ItemPointers = ↑ ItemNodes

defines ItemPointers to be a *pointer type*: each value of type ItemPointers will be a pointer to an anonymous variable of type ItemNodes. Each such anonymous variable can represent one entry of the linked list and so must contain not only an item but also a pointer to the next entry in the linked list. Therefore ItemNodes must be defined as a record type:

> ItemNodes = **record**
>   Item: Items;
>   Next: ItemPointers
>   **end**

We can make the field Item contain one of the items, and the field Next contain a pointer to the following entry in the linked list.

Each entry in the list can thus be accessed from the previous entry, but how can the first entry be accessed? For the purpose we need a variable such as:

> ListHead: ItemPointers

in which we can store a pointer to the first entry. Finally, how can we indicate that the last entry in the list has no follower? For purposes such as this, Pascal provides the special pointer value **nil**, which points to nothing at all. (**nil** is a reserved word.) Thus we can mark the last entry in the linked list by storing **nil** in its Next field:

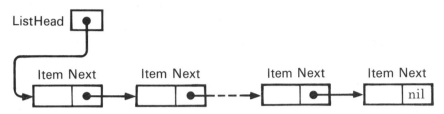

We can represent an empty linked list (i.e. one with no entries at all) simply by storing **nil** in ListHead itself:

ListHead nil

Pointer values in Pascal may be assigned, and they may be compared using the comparison operators '=' and '<>'. (Two pointer values are equal if they are both **nil** or if they point to the same anonymous variable.) Pointers may also be passed as parameters, and a function may have a pointer result.

If P and Q are pointer variables of some type ↑T, and suitable pointer values (i.e. not **nil**) have been assigned to P and Q, the anonymous variables to which P and Q point can be accessed by P↑ and Q↑ respectively. For example, if T is a record type, we can write:

with P↑ do . . .

P↑ and Q↑ are examples of *referenced variables*.

It is most important to distinguish between the pointer variable P, which contains a pointer value, and the referenced variable P↑, which denotes the anonymous variable to which P's value points (provided P's value is not **nil**). The following situation illustrates the distinction, where x and y are values of type T:

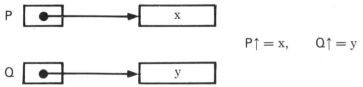

$$P\uparrow = x, \qquad Q\uparrow = y$$

(a) The assignment statement P:=Q assigns a *pointer value*, as a result of which P now points to the same anonymous variable as Q:

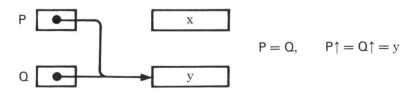

$$P = Q, \qquad P\uparrow = Q\uparrow = y$$

(b) On the other hand, the assignment statement P↑:=Q↑ assigns the value of the anonymous variable pointed to by Q to the anonymous variable pointed to by P. P still points to the same anonymous variable as before:

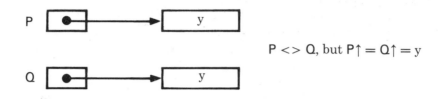

P <> Q, but P↑ = Q↑ = y

(Both P↑:=Q and P:=Q↑ are meaningless and violate the type rules of Pascal.)

The syntax of pointer types is summarized in Figure 20.1, and that of referenced variables in Figure 20.2. Each pointer type must specify a *domain type*, which is the type of the anonymous variables to which the pointers will point. (The domain type will commonly, but not always, be a record type.)

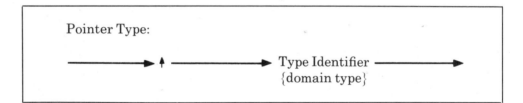

Figure 20.1. Syntax of Pointer Types

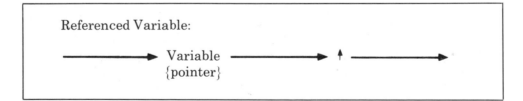

Figure 20.2. Syntax of Referenced Variables

The domain type must be given by a type *identifier*. This type identifier is an exception to the general rule that every identifier must be declared before it is used (see Example 20.3).

The variable declaration:

P: ↑T

creates a store location for P only. P may subsequently contain a pointer to an anonymous variable of type T, or it may contain the value **nil**. However, P's initial value is undefined, just like any other variable:

(This does *not* mean that P's value is **nil**.)

Anonymous variables are created dynamically using the standard procedure New. For example, New(P) creates a new anonymous variable of type T and makes P point to it:

The value of this anonymous variable is initially undefined, but a value of type T may subsequently be assigned to it.

If an anonymous variable has outlived its usefulness, for example if we are deleting an entry from a linked list, we can use the standard procedure Dispose. Dispose(P) releases the storage space occupied by the anonymous variable P↑ (so that it may later be used for some other purpose), and leaves P undefined. It must be emphasized that Dispose does nothing more than this; the redirection of pointers to delete an entry from a linked list (as described in Section 20.1) must be programmed explicitly.

(There are also special forms of New and Dispose applicable only to anonymous variables which are variant records. See Appendix 3.)

One last point: New(P) makes P point to an anonymous variable. There is no way in Pascal to make a pointer variable point to a named variable, so the following situation is *impossible*:

Nor can P ever point to an anonymous variable of any type other than P's domain type T.

20.4 LINKED LIST PROCESSING

In this section we illustrate the use of pointers by examples of linked list manipulation.

Example 20.1

Assume the definitions of the types ItemPointers and ItemNodes from the previous section. Let us write a function which, given as a parameter a pointer ListHead to the first entry of a linked list of items, returns the number of items in the linked list.

This problem is a simple illustration of serial processing of a linked list. We need a local pointer variable, say Ref, which will be made to point to each entry of the linked list in turn. Ref will be initialized to the value of ListHead. The serial processing can be performed by a loop which is terminated when Ref is nil. A **while** loop will allow for an empty list.

```
function ListLength ( ListHead: ItemPointers ): Integer;
  var
    ItemCount: Integer;
    Ref: ItemPointers;
  begin
  ItemCount := 0;
  Ref := ListHead;
  while Ref <> nil do
    begin
    ItemCount := ItemCount+1;
    Ref := Ref↑.Next
    end;
  ListLength := ItemCount
  end (*ListLength*)
```

Within the body of the loop, we can be sure that the value of Ref is not **nil**, so Ref points to a record of type ItemNodes. Therefore Ref↑ denotes the record itself, and Ref↑.Next denotes the field Next of this record. Thus the statement Ref:=Ref↑.Next advances the pointer Ref from one list entry to the next.

Example 20.2

Assume the definitions of the types ItemPointers and ItemNodes from the previous section. Let us write a procedure which, given as parameters an item Target and a pointer ListHead to the first entry of a linked list of items, returns in a variable parameter a pointer to the entry containing Target (or **nil** if there is no such entry in the linked list). We do not assume that the items in the list are in any particular order.

This problem illustrates linear search in a linked list. (Compare Example 11.7.)

```
procedure SearchList (Target: Items;
                      ListHead: ItemPointers;
                      var TargetLoc: ItemPointers);
  var
    Ref: ItemPointers;
    Located: Boolean;
```

```
    begin
    Ref := ListHead;
    Located := False;
    while not Located and (Ref <> nil) do
        with Ref↑ do
            if Item = Target then
                Located := True
            else
                Ref := Next;
    TargetLoc := Ref (* could be nil *)
    end (*SearchList*)
```

Within the body of the loop we know that the value of Ref is not **nil**, so Ref points to a record of type ItemNodes. The body of the loop processes this record. The **with** clause 'with Ref↑ **do**' allows us to abbreviate Ref↑.Item to Item and Ref↑.Next to Next.

Procedure SearchList could be recast as a pointer-valued function; see Exercises 20.

Example 20.3

Let us modify program SortNames of Section 15.2 to use a linked list instead of an array.

```
program SortNames ( Input, Output );

const
    NameLength = 20;

type
    Names = packed array [1 . . NameLength] of Char;
    NamePointers = ↑ NameNodes;
    NameNodes = record
                        Name: Names;
                        Next: NamePointers
                end;

var
    ListHead: NamePointers;
    CurrentName: Names;

procedure ReadName ( var Name: Names );
    ....................
    .................... (* as in Section 15.2 *)
    ....................
```

```
procedure WriteAllNames;
  var
    Ref: NamePointers;
  begin
  Ref := ListHead;
  while Ref <> nil do
    with Ref↑ do
      begin
      WriteLn (Name);
      Ref := Next
      end
  end (*WriteAllNames*);

procedure MakeListEmpty;
  begin
  ListHead := nil
  end (*MakeListEmpty*);

procedure Insertname ( NewName: Names );
  var
    Ref, RefPrevious, NewRef: NamePointers;
    Located                 : Boolean;
  begin
  (* find the position where the new entry will be inserted *)
  Ref := ListHead;
  Located := False;
  while not Located and (Ref <> nil) do
    with Ref↑ do
      if NewName <= Name then
        Located := True
      else
        begin
        RefPrevious := Ref;
        Ref := Next
        end;
  (* create a new entry for NewName *)
  New(NewRef);
  NewRef↑.Name := NewName;
  NewRef↑.Next := Ref;
  (* place the new entry in position *)
  if Ref = ListHead then
    ListHead := NewRef
  else
    RefPrevious↑.Next := NewRef
  end (*InsertName*);
```

```
begin (*SortNames*)
  MakeListEmpty;
  while not EOF(Input) do
    begin
    ReadName (CurrentName);
    InsertName (CurrentName)
    end;
  WriteAllNames
end (*SortNames*) .
```

The main program's statement part is unchanged, a direct consequence of the judicious choice of procedures and parameters in Section 15.2. The following changes have been made to the program.

(a) The global variables Count and List representing the list of names have been replaced by the single global variable ListHead, a pointer to the first entry in the list.

(b) Procedure WriteAllNames has been rewritten to traverse the linked list rather than an array.

(c) Procedure MakeListEmpty now initializes ListHead to nil.

(d) Procedure InsertName has also been rewritten. The test to ensure that the list is not already full is no longer necessary. The refinement of 'find the position ...' leaves Ref pointing to the entry which will *follow* the new entry. Since the pointer field Next in the previous entry must be redirected when the new entry is inserted (except in the case where the new entry is inserted at the front of the linked list), the procedure uses an additional pointer variable, RefPrevious, to point to the previous entry in the linked list. The step 'shift up the entries ...' is no longer needed, and in its place comes 'create a new entry for NewName'. The statement New(NewRef) creates a new entry to which NewRef is made to point. The two statements following it store, in the fields of this entry, NewName and a pointer to the entry which will follow it in the extended list. The refinement of 'place the new entry in position' redirects the Next field of the previous entry to point to the new entry, unless the new entry is to be inserted at the front of the list, in which case ListHead itself is redirected to point to the new entry.

Convince yourself of the correctness of InsertName by working through it by hand, choosing suitable test cases as in Section 15.2.

Example 20.4

Assume the definitions of the types ItemPointers and ItemNodes from the previous section. Let us write a procedure which deletes a given item OldItem from a given linked list pointed to by a parameter ListHead.

The procedure must first locate the list entry which contains the item to be deleted. This can be done by a linear search similar to Example 20.2. Since the pointer field Next of the *previous* entry must be redirected to bypass the deleted entry, however, we need an additional pointer variable, RefPrevious, which points to the entry preceding Ref. Also we must be careful to cater for the case where the entry to be deleted is the *first* in the linked list, for then it is ListHead itself which must be redirected. Thus ListHead must be a *variable* parameter.

```
procedure DeleteItem ( OldItem: Items;
                       var ListHead: ItemPointers);
  var
    Ref, RefPrevious: ItemPointers;
    Located: Boolean;
  begin
  (* locate the entry to be deleted *)
  Ref := ListHead;
  Located := False;
  while not Located and (Ref <> nil) do
    with Ref↑ do
      if Item = OldItem then
        Located := True
      else
        begin
        RefPrevious := Ref;
        Ref := Next
        end;
  if Located then
    begin
    if Ref = ListHead then
      (* deleting first entry — redirect ListHead *)
      ListHead := Ref↑.Next
    else
      (* redirect Next field of previous entry *)
      RefPrevious↑.Next := Ref↑.Next;
    Dispose (Ref)
    end;
  end (*DeleteItem*)
```

Dispose must always be used with great care. For example, the statements in DeleteItem which redirect a pointer to bypass the deleted entry do so by copying the pointer value Ref↑.Next into ListHead or into the Next field of the previous entry. It would be a serious error to obey Dispose(Ref) *before* copying Ref↑.Next, since Dispose(Ref) makes the record Ref↑, and therefore its field Ref↑.Next, inaccessible.

Procedure DeleteItem takes no action at all if no item in the linked list equals OldItem. As an exercise, modify the procedure to return, through a Boolean parameter, an indication of whether an entry was deleted or not.

20.5 TYPE RULES FOR POINTERS

ASSIGNMENT COMPATIBILITY

A pointer value may be assigned to a pointer variable of the same type. **nil** may be assigned to any pointer variable.

COMPARISONS

Pointer values of the same type may be compared with one another or with **nil**.

EXERCISES 20

20.1. (a) Write type definitions describing a linked list whose entries contain integers. (b) Write a function which, given a pointer to the first entry of such a linked list, returns the sum of the integers stored in the list.

20.2. What happens if procedure SearchList (or procedure DeleteItem) is supplied with a list containing duplicate items?

20.3. Write a program which reads a line of characters and writes them in reverse order. Use a linked list, and insert each character as it is read at the *head* of the list.

20.4. Program SortNames (Example 20.3) can be improved further if we can avoid searching the whole list to decide where to insert the new name. One way to do this is to have 26 linked lists, one for each initial letter. It becomes necessary to have an *array* of list heads, one for each linked list. Modify the program along these lines.

20.5. Modify Example 16.9 so that the directory is represented by a linked list rather than by an array.

PROGRAMMING EXERCISES 20

20.6. Write a program which simulates a queue of customers at an office counter or supermarket checkout. A customer on arrival joins the end of the queue. The customer at the front of the queue is served first and then departs.

The times of customers' arrivals and departures are supplied as input data to the simulation program. An arrival is indicated by a line of input data containing the letter 'A' and the time of day (hours, minutes, seconds). A departure is indicated by a line of input data containing the letter 'D' and the time of day. Assume that the input data is ordered by time of day.

The program is to output a histogram showing the distribution at intervals of one minute. It is also to compute the mean and standard deviation of the time spent by customers in the queue. (See Exercises 11 for a definition of standard deviation.)

(Hint: represent the queue by a linked list containing one entry for each customer currently in the queue. When a customer arrives, add an entry containing the time of arrival to the end of the list. When a customer departs, remove an entry from the head of the list.)

20.7*. Write a program which maintains a stock inventory held in the form of a linked list. The list must consist of one entry for each different component in stock, each entry containing the component number, the number of units in stock, and the reorder level for that component. The inventory is initially empty. Each line of input specifies an operation on the inventory, the operation being identified by the first character in the line:

Code	Operation requested	Additional data on the same line
'N'	New component	Component number, initial number of units in stock, reorder level.
'D'	Delete component	Component number.
'A'	Add to stock	Component number, number of units added.
'R'	Remove from stock	Component number, number of units removed.
'P'	Print inventory	None.

Invalid and impossible operations should give rise to suitable error messages, and operation 'R' should give rise to a warning message if the number of units in stock falls below the reorder level.

20.8. Modify your answer to exercise 20.7 so that operation 'P' lists the contents of the inventory in order of component number. (The best way to do this is to keep the list ordered at all times, by suitable implementation of operation 'N'.)

21

Advanced use of subprograms

This chapter may be omitted on a first reading. It covers:

* recursive subprograms
* mutual recursion and the **Forward** directive
* procedures and functions as parameters of subprograms
* conformant array parameters

21.1 RECURSIVE SUBPROGRAMS

Methodical development of a complicated program often leads to a program with a hierarchical structure. In other words, the main program delegates most of its work to subprograms. These in turn delegate some of their work to other subprograms. And so on to any desired depth. All this exploits the ability for one subprogram to call another.

There is another way of using subprograms. In Pascal a subprogram may call itself! It is then said to be *recursive*. At first sight this seems to be a useless idea. What could a subprogram achieve by calling itself? Yet a recursive subprogram is sometimes a very elegant solution to a programming problem. The best way to see this is to study some examples.

Example 21.1

Consider the expression A^N, where A and N are integers and N is positive. Let us write this expression in functional notation: *power(A,N)*. We could informally define this function as follows:

$$power(A,N) = A \times A \times \ldots \times A$$

where A is multiplied by itself N times. We can avoid this awkward notation by an alternative definition:

$$power(A,N) = \begin{cases} A & \text{if } N=1 \\ A \times power(A,N-1) & \text{if } N>1 \end{cases}$$

Here the function is defined in terms of itself. In fact, it is defined recursively.

The recursive definition can be transcribed easily into a Pascal function:

```
type PositiveInteger = 1 . . MaxInt;
. . .
function Power (A : Integer;
                N : PositiveInteger) : Integer;
  begin
  if N = 1 then
    Power := A
  else
    Power := A * Power (A, N−1)
  end (*Power*)
```

We now show how this function succeeds in producing a result. Firstly, note that the function will produce a result directly if N is 1. Secondly, consider what happens when N is greater than 1. Then the function does call itself, but the second parameter is one less than before (N−1). The function might call itself many times, but each time the second parameter will be smaller than before. Eventually it will be 1 and then the recursion will stop.

Take a specific example. Let us trace the action of the function as it evaluates Power(4,3). This should give $4 \times 4 \times 4$, i.e. 64.

Evaluating Power(4,3): A = 4, N = 3: must compute 4*Power(4,2).

Evaluating Power(4,2): A = 4, N = 2: must compute 4*Power(4,1).

Evaluating Power(4,1): A = 4, N = 1: result is 4.

Thus Power(4,2) = 4*Power(4,1) = 16.

Thus Power(4,3) = 4*Power(4,2) = 64.

Of course, the function Power can easily be programmed using a loop rather than recursion: see Example 6.1

For many problems either recursion or a loop can be chosen. Given a choice, most programmers prefer the loop. A recursive subprogram uses more storage space, since another set of store locations is allocated every time it calls itself. It also tends to be slower, because of overheads on entering and leaving the subprogram.

However, some computations are 'naturally' recursive. They are very awkward to program without using recursion. The following example illustrates such a problem.

Example 21.2

Finding a path out of a maze is a popular puzzle. Assume that the maze is a rectangular area divided into squares. Each square is either empty or covered by hedge. Along the perimeter all squares are hedge-covered, except for one or more exits. You are set down on any empty square, and your problem is to find your way to an exit. You may move to any adjacent square, but not diagonally. Of course, you cannot cross a hedge.

We shall develop a program to solve this problem. We must choose a data structure to represent the maze. A simple representation would be a two-dimensional character array. Here is an example, representing a maze with a single exit (near the South-East corner):

```
H H H H H H H H H H H H H
H . . H H H . . . . H H
H H . . . H . H H H . H
H . . H . H . H . . . H
H H H . . . . H H H H H
H . . . H H H . . . . H
H . H . . . . . II II . II
H H H H H H H H H H . H
```

where 'H' represents hedge
and '.' represents walkway.

Here is an outline of a computer solution to this problem:

```
(* find a path from square S to an exit *)
if square S is on the perimeter then
    exit from the maze
else
    begin
    try heading East;
    if no exit found yet then
        try heading South;
    if no exit found yet then
        try heading West;
    if no exit found yet then
        try heading North
    end
```

Let us further refine 'try heading East' (the others will be analogous):

```
(* try heading East *)
if S's eastern neighbouring square is walkway then
    find a path from S's eastern neighbouring square to an exit
```

But 'find a path from S's eastern neighbouring square to an exit' is analogous to the original problem 'find a path from square S to an exit'! So let us introduce a procedure, SeekExitFrom, with the coordinates of a square as its parameters, whose task is to find a path from that square to an exit. This procedure will be recursive.

The following is a complete solution to the problem for a 8-by-12 maze (as illustrated above), omitting only the details of reading and writing a picture of the maze. The coordinates of the starting square are read as input data.

```
program Maze ( Input, Output );

const
    NorthLimit = 1; SouthLimit = 8;
    WestLimit  = 1; EastLimit   = 12;
    Walkway    = '.';
    Hedge      = 'H';
    Footstep   = 'o';
    Pathmark   = '*';

type
    Latitudes  = NorthLimit . . SouthLimit;
    Longitudes = WestLimit . . EastLimit;
    Squares    = Char;

var
    Maze: array [Latitudes, Longitudes] of Squares;
    StartLatitude  : Latitudes;
    StartLongitude : Longitudes;
    ExitFound      : Boolean;

procedure SeekExitFrom ( Lat:  Latitudes;
                         Long: Longitudes );
    (* find a path from square (Lat,Long) to an exit *)
    begin
    if (Lat=NorthLimit) or (Lat=SouthLimit) or
        (Long=WestLimit) or (Long=EastLimit) then
            (* . . . (Lat,Long) is on the perimeter *)
        ExitFound := True
    else
        begin
        Maze[Lat,Long] := Footstep;
        (* try heading East *)
```

```
        if Maze[Lat,Long+1] = Walkway then
          SeekExitFrom (Lat, Long+1);
        if not ExitFound then
          (* try heading South *)
          if Maze[Lat+1,Long] = Walkway then
            SeekExitFrom (Lat+1, Long);
        if not ExitFound then
          (* try heading West *)
          if Maze[Lat,Long−1] = Walkway then
            SeekExitFrom (Lat, Long−1);
        if not ExitFound then
          (* try heading North *)
          if Maze[Lat−1,Long] = Walkway then
            SeekExitFrom (Lat−1, Long)
        end;
    if ExitFound then
      Maze[Lat,Long] := Pathmark
    end (*SeekExitFrom*);

begin (*Maze*)
read Maze;
Read (StartLatitude, StartLongitude);
ExitFound := False;
SeekExitFrom (StartLatitude, StartLongitude);
write Maze;
if not ExitFound then
  WriteLn ('No way out of maze')
end (*Maze*).
```

The procedure contains some necessary additional details. The statement Maze[Lat,Long]:=Footstep marks each square of the maze as it is visited; this is essential to ensure that we do not go round the maze in circles! The statement Maze[Lat,Long]:=Pathmark marks each square which lies on the path from the entrance to the exit. Thus the final picture of the maze will show this path, and also any blind alleys which were followed during the search. Here is the output obtained when the starting square is (2,2):

```
H H H H H H H H H H H
H * * H H H o o o o H H
H H * * * H o H H H . H
H . . H * H o H . . . H
H H H * * o o H H H H H
H . . * H H H * * * * H
H . H * * * * H H * H
H H H H H H H H H H * H
```

where '*' marks a step on the exit path and 'o' marks a step up a blind alley

If the starting square is (3,11), on the other hand, the program will report that no exit path exists.

From these examples we may extrapolate to the following general principles concerning recursive subprograms:

(a) A recursive subprogram must, in at least one degenerate case, perform its task without invoking itself recursively. In Example 21.1, the degenerate case is N=1. In Example 21.2, one degenerate case is when the current square *is* an exit square; in addition, the procedure will not invoke itself recursively when every neighbouring square either is hedge-covered or has already been visited.

(b) A recursive subprogram must invoke itself only in such a way as to approach one of the degenerate cases mentioned in (a). In Example 21.1, the function invokes itself with a second parameter (N) which is positive but smaller than before, i.e. it has moved closer to the case N=1. In Example 21.2, every entry to the procedure marks the current square in such a way that it will not be visited again.

One peculiarity arises from *mutually recursive* subprograms, that is, subprograms that call each other. The declaration-before-use rule of Pascal requires that a subprogram must be declared earlier in the program than any call on it. But it is not possible to abide by this rule when two or more subprograms call each other. One of them must be declared last, and the calls on it must therefore precede it. (The situation is analogous to the one that we encounter with records containing pointers—Section 20.3.)

The problem is resolved by providing a way to declare a subprogram *without its body*. The body is given in a later declaration that completes the subprogram. Since it is the bodies of mutually-recursive subprograms that contain the troublesome calls, we can first declare all of them without bodies then, quite legally, supply bodies calling them. A declaration without a body is called a *forward declaration*. It consists of the subprogram heading, followed by the word Forward.

A forward-declared subprogram must be completed by a second declaration of it in the same Declarative Part. The second declaration omits the formal parameters and the function result type (where applicable), as these have already been given in the forward declaration.

Forward is a peculiar beast. It is neither an identifier, nor a reserved word, but a *directive*—a class of word introduced into Pascal so that the subprogram facility may be extended to meet new requirements. Forward is the only directive specified by the ISO standard, but you may well encounter others (perhaps External, to declare a separately-compiled subprogram).

For the full syntax of subprogram declarations, see Appendix 1.9.

21.2 FUNCTIONAL PARAMETERS AND PROCEDURAL PARAMETERS

We have already seen that a subprogram may invoke another subprogram. Now, just as a *value parameter* allows a subprogram to work with different given values on different occasions, and just as a *variable parameter* allows a subprogram to work with different variables on different occasions, sometimes we wish to allow a subprogram to invoke different functions or different procedures on different occasions. Pascal makes this possible by providing two additional parameter mechanisms, *functional parameters* and *procedural parameters*.

We illustrate this idea with just one example.

Example 21.3

Let us write a procedure which approximately evaluates the integral of $F(x)$ between given limits A and B, where F is assumed to be a continuous finite real function with a single real parameter.

We can visualize this integral as the area bounded by the curve $y=F(x)$ and the straight lines $y=0$, $x=A$ and $x=B$.

A simple method of approximating the integral is to choose a suitable positive integer N and divide the interval $[A,B]$ into N equal intervals, each of width $W = (B-A)/N$, as illustrated. This divides the area of interest into strips which resemble right-angled trapezia, and it is easy to derive the following approximate formula for the area under the curve:

$$W (F(A)/2 + F(A+W) + F(A+2W) + \ldots + F(B)/2)$$

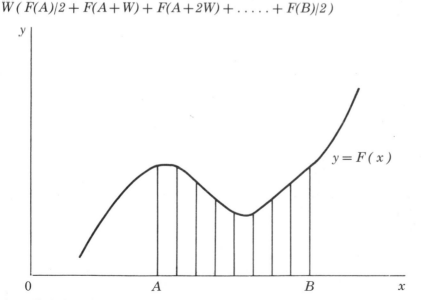

This is called the *trapezoidal rule*.

Since our procedure must deal with *any* given function *F*, *F* will be a functional parameter.

```
procedure Integrate ( function F (X:Real): Real;
                      A, B: Real;
                      var Integral: Real              );
    (* evaluates approximately the integral of F(x)
       between limits A and B, using the trapezoidal
       rule with 8 intervals *)
const
    N = 8;
var
    W, Sum: Real;
    I: 1 . . N;
begin
W := (B−A)/N;
Sum := (F(A)+F(B))/2;
for I := 1 to N−1 do
    Sum := Sum + F(A+I*W);
Integral := W * Sum
end (*Integrate*)
```

'**function** F (X:Real): Real' is a *functional parameter section*. This specifies that F is a functional parameter, that its result type is Real, and that it has itself a single Real value parameter. (The identifier X here has no significance.) Inside the statement part of Integrate, F is invoked just like an ordinary function, by function designators such as F(A) and F(A+I*W).

When we invoke Integrate by a procedure statement, the actual parameter corresponding to F must also be a function with a Real result and a single Real value parameter. For example, to integrate Tan(*x*) between limits 0 and Pi/4, we could use the procedure statement:

```
Integrate (Tan, 0, Pi/4, Area)
```

assuming that the function Tan has been declared as in Example 13.1. When this procedure statement is obeyed, the functional parameter F stands for the function Tan. Thus the function designator F(A) actually results in the evaluation of Tan(A); and the function designator F(A+I*W) actually results in the evaluation of Tan(A+I*W).

Functional and procedural parameter sections are similar in syntax to function and procedure headings; see Appendix 1.9.

Every actual parameter corresponding to a functional parameter F must be a function identifier, and that function's heading must be similar to the functional parameter section which specifies F. The only possible variation is in the identifiers chosen for the functional parameter's own formal parameters.

(These identifiers may be chosen freely.) A similar rule applies to each actual parameter corresponding to a procedural parameter.

21.3 CONFORMANT ARRAY PARAMETERS

When we declare a procedure or function, one of the most important things we specify is the type of each of its formal parameters. An actual parameter must have the same type as the corresponding formal parameter. Most of the time, this is just what we want. The compiler knows the type of every formal parameter and can check that the actual parameter supplied in a call is of the same type. Thus Pascal prevents the kind of error that can be made in less secure languages, such as FORTRAN, when a subprogram is written to expect (say) an array parameter, but on call is given (say) an integer constant instead.

There is one case where the requirements of strict type checking hinder the programmer, rather than help. It arises when we write a subprogram that operates on array parameters. An example is the procedure **ReadMatrix** in Section 15.1, which takes a variable parameter of type **Matrix**. This type is declared as a 10×10 array. If we want to read matrices of different sizes, we are forced to define a further array type for each distinct size, and a further procedure to handle a parameter of that type. Hardly convenient!

ISO Standard Pascal introduced a new language feature that solves this problem for a wide class of array parameters. In a parameter specification we now have the option to provide a *conformant array schema* instead of a type identifier. The conformant array schema:

(a) states whether the array is packed,
(b) gives the number of dimensions,
(c) for each dimension, gives a base type for the index in that dimension,
(d) states the type of the array components.

An actual parameter can be any array having the same dimensionality, the same component type, and index types that are *subranges* of the given base types. If the formal parameter is packed, so must be the actual parameter. An array satisfying these requirements is said to *conform* to the schema.

As an added facility, the schema also declares identifiers that take the values of the lower and upper bounds of each index type of the *actual* parameter, for use within the subprogram.

To see how this works, compare the following version with the original **ReadMatrix** procedure of Section 15.1.

```
procedure ReadMatrix (var M: array [L1 . . U1: Integer;
                                    L2 . . U2: Integer] of Real);
    var
        I, J: Integer;
    begin
```

```
for I := L1 to U1 do
  for J := L2 to U2 do
    Read (M[I,J]);
end (*ReadMatrix*);
```

This version of the procedure can be called in exactly the same way as before, because the actual parameters A and B are both two-dimensional arrays with Real components, and have index types that are subranges of Integer, thus conforming to the schema. While the call ReadMatrix(A) is being executed, L1 and L2 both have the value 1. Similarly, U1 and U2 both have the value 10.

So far so good. Now we can begin to exploit the full freedom offered by conformant array parameters:

(a) Any Integer value is an acceptable lower bound in either dimension. Similarly, any upper bounds may be given. For example, ReadMatrix can handle matrices indexed from 0, as well as those indexed from 1. Moreover, as the schema does not require L1 to equal L2, nor U1 to equal U2, ReadMatrix can handle non-square matrices.

(b) The bound identifiers can be used to program useful checks on the validity of the actual parameters. For example, a procedure intended to process strings might declare the formal parameter with the schema:

```
packed array [ M . . N : Integer ] of Char
```

It can ensure every actual parameter genuinely is a string by verifying on each call that the lower bound identifier, M, has the value 1. As another example, take the MultiplyMatrices procedure in the MatrixProduct program. It is possible to multiply a matrix of size $M \times R$ only with a matrix of size $R \times N$, and the result is of size $M \times N$. Using the bound identifiers it is easy to check whether this condition is satisfied.

CONFORMABILITY

The full syntax of Conformant Array Parameter Sections is given in Appendix 1.9. The rules governing conformability of actual and formal parameters have already been stated.

There are three restrictions you should be aware of. Firstly, packed conformant array parameters have only one dimension. (Of course, the component type, specified by the type identifier, may be any type including an array type.) This means, for example, that you can have a packed conformant array of Char, or a conformant array of strings, but not a packed two-dimensional conformant array of Char.

Secondly, if several formal parameters are specified with the same conformant array schema, then all of the corresponding actual parameters in a particular call must have the *same type as each other*. This can be used to advantage in (say) a procedure to add two matrices. Matrix addition requires the operands, and the result, to have the same size. Declaring all three parameters with the same schema lets the compiler check this for you.

Thirdly, a conformant array formal parameter cannot be passed on, in a further procedure call, as a value actual parameter; not even as a *value conformant array* actual parameter. However, a conformant array formal parameter can be passed on as a *variable conformant array* actual parameter. This provides another reason why you might choose to specify a **var** parameter for a subprogram, even when a value parameter seems more natural.

These restrictions probably seem rather arbitrary to you, but they had to be imposed so that conformant array parameters could be added without excessive difficulty to compilers that had been originally written without taking account of them.

EXERCISES 21

21.1. Modify function Power (Example 21.2) to allow its parameter B to be 0, returning the result 1 in that case.

21.2. The factorial function $N!$ may be defined recursively:

$$N! = \begin{cases} 1 & \text{if } N <= 1 \\ N * (N-1)! & \text{if } N > 1 \end{cases}$$

(a) Transcribe this definition into a recursive function. (b) Write an alternative non-recursive version of this function.

21.3. (a) Write a function which returns the number of True values of a given Boolean function F (which takes a single Integer parameter), between given limits Low and High inclusive. (b) Write a statement which invokes your function to compute the number of prime numbers between 2 and M inclusive. Use the prime-number function of Exercise 13.6 as an actual parameter.

21.4*. Write a procedure which traverses a given linked list of names (defined as in Example 20.3) and applies a procedure P to each entry of the linked list. P is to be a procedural parameter specified by the procedural parameter section:

```
procedure P (EntryRef:NamePointers)
```

Modify procedure WriteAllNames of Example 20.3 to make use of your traversal procedure.

21.5. Rewrite the MatrixProduct program of Section 15.1 to make full use of conformant array parameters. You should find that the procedures in the new version are far more suitable as general, library routines than the very specialized procedures in the original.

21.6. Rewrite the YearlyMaxima program of Example 13.3, so that it outputs the rainfall maximum for October to December and the temperature maximum for May to August, in addition to those for the year as a whole.

PROGRAMMING EXERCISES 21

21.7*. If you have completed Exercise 15.6, modify the procedure which reads the molecular formula so that it accepts parentheses within the formula, such as (Al2(SO4)3). (Hint: on detecting an inner '(', the procedure should invoke itself recursively to read the inner group.)

21.8*. 'The Towers of Hanoi' is a game played with three poles and a set of discs, all differently sized, which fit on to the poles. Initially all the discs are on pole 1, as shown below; the object of the game is to move all the discs on to pole 2. Only one disc may be moved at a time, and no disc may ever be placed above a smaller disc.

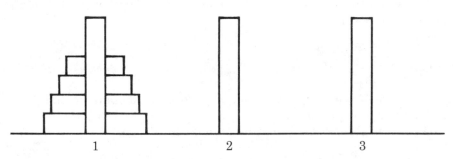

Consider the more general problem of moving N discs from pole Source to pole Destination, using pole Spare as a spare. This problem can be solved recursively by the following strategy:

(1) move $(N-1)$ discs from pole Source to pole Spare, using pole Destination as a spare;
(2) move a single disc from pole Source to pole Destination;
(3) move $(N-1)$ discs from pole Spare to pole Destination, using pole Source as a spare.

Transcribe this strategy into a recursive procedure which writes a suitable message each time a single disc is moved. Write a program which uses your procedure to solve the Towers of Hanoi problem with four discs.

22

The goto statement

This chapter may be omitted on a first reading. It covers:

* the need for irregular control flow in exceptional circumstances
* the **goto** statement in Pascal
* good and bad uses of the **goto** statement

22.1 EXCEPTIONAL FLOW OF CONTROL

The great majority of programming problems—certainly those which you are likely to encounter at this stage—can be solved satisfactorily without resorting to control structures other than sequencing, selection (**if** or **case**), repetition (**while**, **repeat** or **for**), and subprograms. Nevertheless, in certain exceptional circumstances we find that the desired flow of control is too irregular to be naturally expressed using only nested selective and repetitive statements.

Such a situation might arise in a program whose input data is somewhat complicated. A high-quality program will check its data as it reads it, and issue appropriate warning messages if it detects any errors. This helps the user to correct any such errors before running the program again. The problem is, how should the program continue after detecting and reporting an error? Some errors are so severe that the program's only recourse is to abandon the task which it is currently performing, perhaps even to halt completely. The cleanest solution in such circumstances might be a direct jump out of the piece of program which detects the error. For such purposes Pascal provides the *goto statement*.

22.2 *goto* STATEMENTS AND LABELS IN PASCAL

We shall introduce the **goto** statement by an example illustrating the kind of situation described above.

Example 22.1

The following procedure reads an $N \times N$ matrix of non-negative integers and stores it in an array of type:

```
Matrix = array [1 . . N,1 . . N] of 0 . . MaxInt
```

where N is an appropriately defined constant. If the input data is correct, it should contain exactly N^2 non-negative integers. To guard against the possibility of the input data being incomplete (or of there being too much input data), the matrix elements are followed by a negative endmarker. The procedure checks every datum and, if it detects the endmarker prematurely, it writes a warning message and returns immediately. (Compare procedure ReadMatrix of Example 15.1, which performed no error checking.)

```
procedure ReadMatrix ( var M : Matrix );
  label 9;
  var
    Datum : Integer;
    I, J : 1 . . N;
  begin
  for I := 1 to N do
    for J := 1 to N do
      begin
      Read (Datum); (* which should not be the endmarker *)
      if Datum >= 0 then
        M[I,J] := Datum
      else
        begin
        WriteLn ('Too few matrix elements');
        goto 9 (* stop reading immediately *)
        end
      end;
  Read (Datum); (* which should be the endmarker *)
  if Datum >= 0 then
    WriteLn ('Too many matrix elements');
  9:
  end (*ReadMatrix*)
```

There are three aspects to the use of a **goto** statement, which are illustrated by Example 22.1.

(a) A *label declaration* such as **label** 9 declares that 9 is to be used as a *statement label*, attached to some statement within the same block.
(b) A prefix such as '9:' attaches the statement label 9 to the statement which follows. In Example 22.1, the statement label 9 is attached to a dummy statement preceding the final **end** of the procedure's statement part.
(c) The effect of a statement such as **goto** 9 is to pass control directly to the statement whose statement label is 9, thereby abandoning whatever was being done before the **goto** statement was obeyed. In Example 22.1, the nett effect of **goto** 9 is to jump out of the nested **for** loops to the end of the procedure's statement part (thus completing the execution of the procedure).

Statement labels look like unsigned integer numbers (with at most 4 digits), but they have no inherent significance. Thus the statement label 9 in Example 22.1 could be consistently replaced by 0 or 1 or 9999 without affecting the meaning of the procedure.

All labels attached to statements in a block must be declared in a label declaration which must be placed at the very beginning of that block (before any other definitions or declarations). No statement label may be attached to more than one statement in the same block (otherwise a **goto** statement referring to the duplicated label would be ambiguous).

Any statement may be labelled, but there are restrictions on the positioning of **goto** statements referring to a given statement label.

(a) No **goto** statement may cause a jump *into* a structured statement (that is a compound, **if**, **case**, **while**, **repeat**, **for** or **with** statement), from outside. For example, the following is illegal:

```
for . . . do
   begin
   . . . . .
1: . . . . .
   . . . . .
   end;
. . . . .
goto 1
```

Such a jump would have consequences difficult to predict!
(b) No **goto** statement may cause a jump *into* a subprogram from outside. The reasoning behind this is similar to (a).
(c) A **goto** statement may jump *out of* a subprogram, but only to the outermost statement level of an enclosing block. This possibility is illustrated by Example 22.2.

Example 22.2

If the procedure of Example 22.1 were substituted into program Matrix-
Product(b) of Example 15.1, the modified program would print a warning
message on detecting an error in its input data, but then it would continue its
computation as if nothing were wrong. Its results would probably be useless.

    The procedure would be more useful if it had a second, Boolean, variable
parameter to indicate whether its input data was found to be valid or not. The
main program could then use the value returned through this parameter to
decide whether to continue the computation. (As an exercise, modify procedure
ReadMatrix, and the main program of MatrixProduct(b), along these lines.)

    An alternative solution is to make procedure ReadMatrix halt the
execution of the program when it detects an input error, instead of just
abandoning its own task. This requires the procedure to contain **goto**
statements which jump to a label at the end of the main program.

```pascal
program MatrixProduct ( Input, Output );

label 999;    (* end of program label *)

const
  N = 10;   (*say *)
type
  Matrix = array [1 . . N, 1 . . N] of 0 . . MaxInt;
var
  A, B, P: Matrix;

procedure ReadMatrix ( var M : Matrix );
  var
    Datum: Integer;
    I, J: 1 . . N;
  begin
  for I := 1 to N do
    for J := 1 to N do
      begin
      Read (Datum);   (* which should not be the endmarker *)
      if Datum >= 0 then
        M[I,J] := Datum
      else
        begin
        WriteLn ('Too few matrix elements');
        goto 999   (* halt the program immediately *)
        end
      end;
  Read (Datum);    (* which should be the endmarker *)
```

```
    if Datum >= 0 then
      begin
      WriteLn ('Too many matrix elements');
      goto 999    (* halt the program immediately *)
      end
    end (*ReadMatrix*);

  procedure WriteMatrix ( M : Matrix );
    ..........
    .......... (* as in Example 15.1 *)
    ..........

  procedure MultiplyMatrices (M1, M2 : Matrix;
                              var Product : Matrix);

    ..........
    .......... (* as in Example 15.1 *)
    ..........
  begin (*MatrixProduct*)
  ReadMatrix (A);
  ReadMatrix (B);
  MultiplyMatrices (A, B, P);
  WriteMatrix (P);
  999:
  end (*MatrixProduct*).
```

The statement label 999 is attached to a dummy statement preceding the **end** of the main program's statement part. This statement label must therefore be declared in a label declaration in the main program's declaration part.

The syntax of label declarations, **goto** statements and statement labels can be found in Appendices 1.2, 1.3 and 1.10 respectively. **label** and **goto** are both reserved words.

22.3 USE AND ABUSE OF goto STATEMENTS

The use of **goto** statements is a much-debated and controversial subject. Some people assert that they should *never* be used. Others think that occasional use is necessary. But no-one believes that they should be used indiscriminately. There is good reason for that. Overuse of **goto** statements undoubtedly makes a program hard to understand.

Compare the program fragments in the following examples. In each example the two fragments have the same effect. But which is easier to understand?

Example 22.3

```
if X > Y then goto 1;        if X <= Y then
Max := Y;                        Max := Y
goto 2;                      else
1: Max := X;                     Max := X;
2: Write (Max)               Write (Max)
```

Example 22.4

```
1: if R < N then goto 2;     while R >= N do
R := R − N;                      R := R − N;
goto 1;                      Write (R)
2: Write (R)
```

Any program can be written using only **if** ... **then** ... and **goto** to deter-mine the flow of control. We could dispense with **while, for, repeat** and **case** statements altogether. The trouble is that such a program would be extremely hard to understand. Indeed it is not easy to understand what effect even a single **goto** statement will have on the flow of control. We cannot tell from its appearance alone. We must look for the statement label it refers to. (And that could be several pages away!) In Example 22.3 the statement **goto** 1 jumps *forwards*, so it skips some statements. In Example 22.4, on the other hand, the identical statement **goto** 1 jumps *backwards,* so it causes repetition of some statements. Similarly the **if** statements containing **goto** statements are quite different from each other. The one in Example 22.4 controls a loop, although we must study the program fragment closely to see that. In a large program with many **goto** statements the flow of control is very confusing. Such programs are aptly called spaghetti programs.

By contrast, it is much easier to understand the flow of control in a program that uses only control structures such as **if, case, while, repeat** and **for** statements. In each case the opening word tells us immediately what we want to know. **if** or **case** starts a selection. **while, repeat** or **for** starts a loop.

When, if ever, is it appropriate to use a **goto** statement? Consider Example 22.1. This *could* be rewritten without any **goto** statement, if we replaced the nested **for** statements by nested **while** statements. But this turns out to be awkward. (Try it yourself, as an exercise.) And the resulting procedure is if anything *less* readable.

This brings us to the crucial point. The only purpose of good programming style is to make programs easy to read and understand. Nearly always this means that **goto** statements should be avoided. But occasionally they avoid awkwardness, for example when we must escape from a loop or subprogram. Then their use is acceptable. However they should be used sparingly and only after careful consideration.

EXERCISES 22

22.1. The input data contains a list of integers, one per line, preceded by a line containing the size of the list. Write programs to compute the sum of the integers: (a) using a **for** statement, with a **goto** statement to escape from the loop if end-of-file is reached prematurely; and (b) using a **while** statement and no **goto** statement.

Which version of the program do you think is more readable?

PROGRAMMING EXERCISES 22

22.2*. Details of transactions on a number of bank accounts have been prepared, one transaction per line, each line being of the form:

T account-number amount

where the amount is positive for a deposit or negative for a withdrawal. Details of the balances of the accounts are also available, one line per account, in the form:

B account-number balance

Assume that both sets of data have been sorted in order of account-number, and merged so that all the transaction lines for one account are immediately followed by the balance line for the same account. For example:

```
T 2001 +10
T 2001 −20
B 2001 100          (2 transactions on this account)
B 2003 0            (0 transactions on this account)
T 2008 −5
T 2008 −25
T 2008 +3
B 2008 −10          (3 transactions on this account)
```

(a) Write a program which reads this input data, assuming it to be free of errors, and outputs the updated balance for each account. (b) Modify your program to cater for the possibility that the last balance line is missing. (c) Further modify your program to cater for the possibility that transaction lines with different account-numbers occur together, or that a group of transaction lines is followed by a balance line with a different account-number.

Appendix 1

Collected syntax diagrams

Syntax diagrams defining the entire syntax of Pascal are collected together here.

1.1 THE PROGRAM

Program:

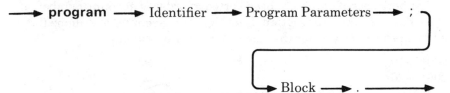

Program Parameters:

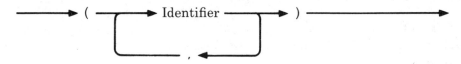

1.2 BLOCKS

Block:

```
──────► Declarative Part ──────► Statement Part ──────►
```

Declarative Part:

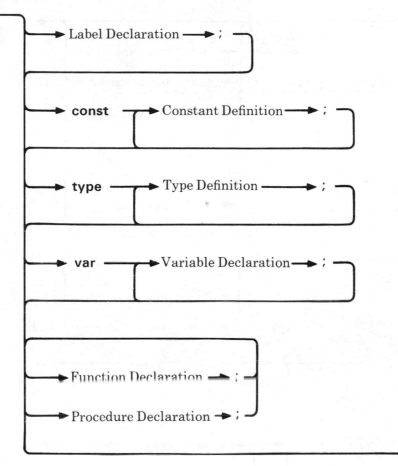

Label Declaration:

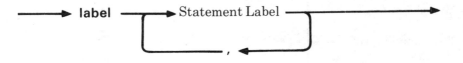

Statement Part:

Compound Statement

1.3 STATEMENTS

Statement:

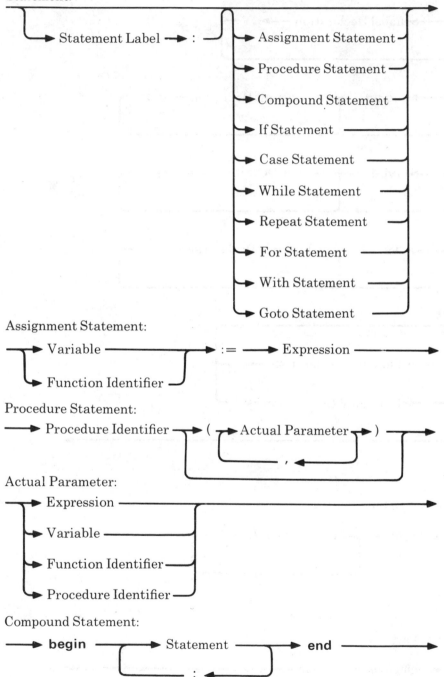

Assignment Statement:

Procedure Statement:

Actual Parameter:

Compound Statement:

If Statement:

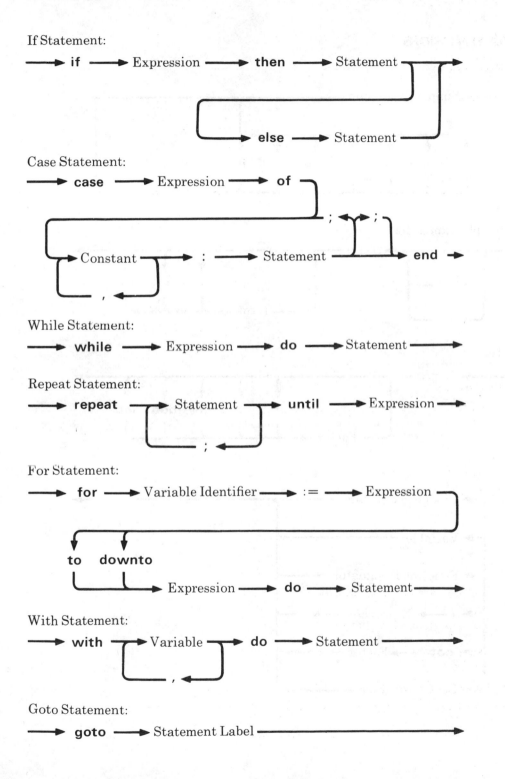

Case Statement:

While Statement:

Repeat Statement:

For Statement:

With Statement:

Goto Statement:

1.4 EXPRESSIONS

Expression:

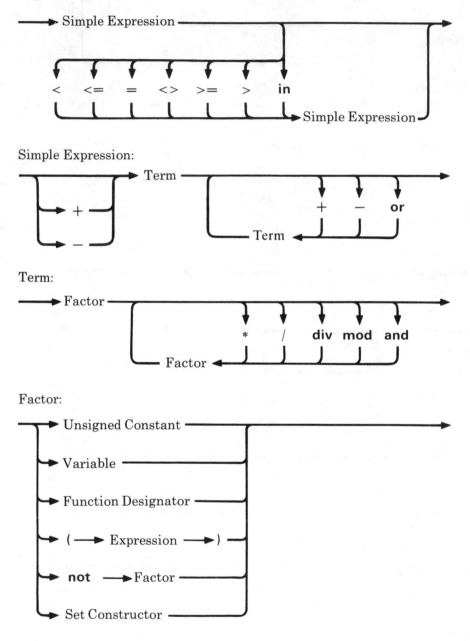

Simple Expression:

Term:

Factor:

Unsigned Constant:

Function Designator:

Set Constructor:

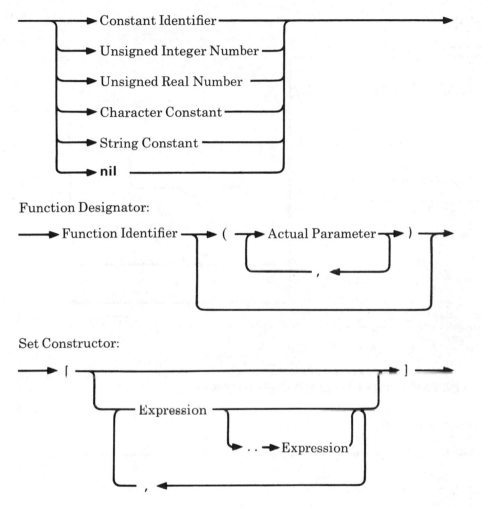

1.5 VARIABLES

Variable:

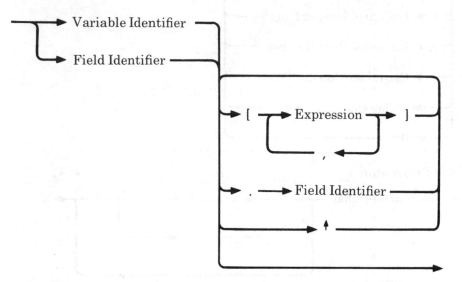

1.6 CONSTANTS AND CONSTANT DEFINITIONS

Constant Definition:

Constant:

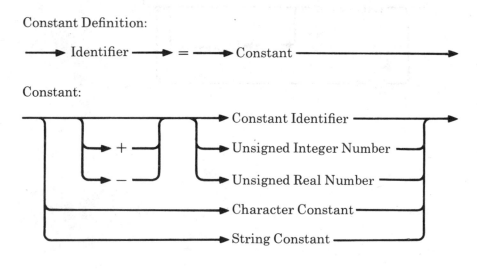

1.7 TYPES AND TYPE DEFINITIONS

Type Definition:

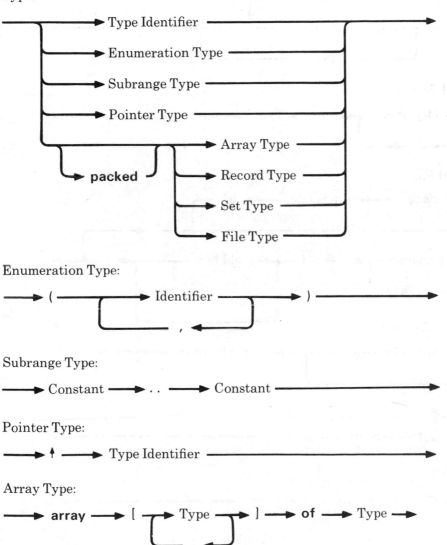

Type:

Enumeration Type:

Subrange Type:

Pointer Type:

Array Type:

Record Type:

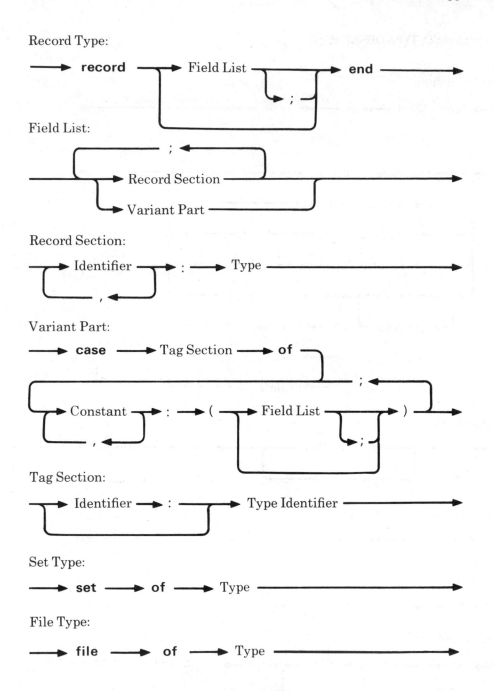

Field List:

Record Section:

Variant Part:

Tag Section:

Set Type:

File Type:

1.8 VARIABLE DECLARATIONS

Variable Declaration:

1.9 SUBPROGRAMS

Function Declaration:

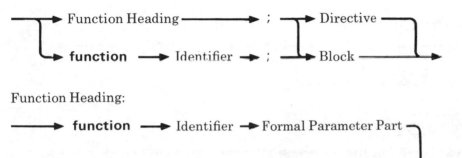

Function Heading:

Procedure Declaration:

Procedure Heading:

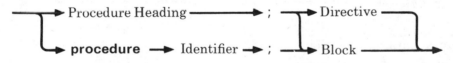

Formal Parameter Part:

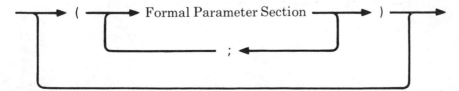

Formal Parameter Section:

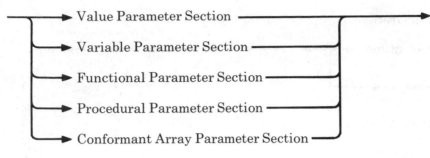

Value Parameter Section:

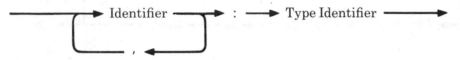

Variable Parameter Section:

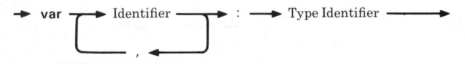

Functional Parameter Section:

→ Function Heading ————————————————————→

Procedural Parameter Section:

→ Procedure Heading ————————————————————→

Conformant Array Parameter Section:

Conformant Array Schema:

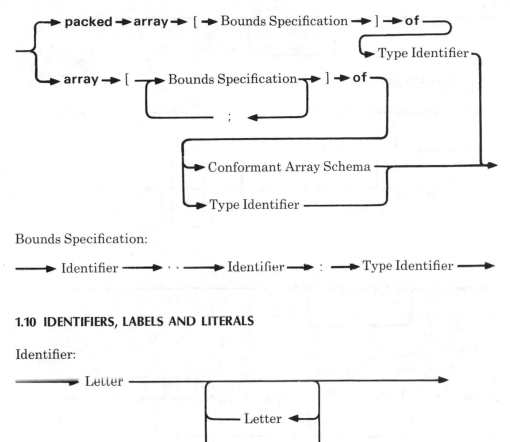

Bounds Specification:

→ Identifier ——→ · · ——→ Identifier —→ : —→ Type Identifier ——→

1.10 IDENTIFIERS, LABELS AND LITERALS

Identifier:

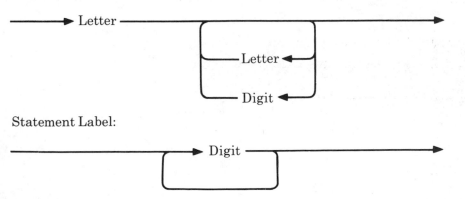

Directive:

Letter

Letter
Digit

Statement Label:

Digit

Unsigned Integer Number:

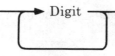

Unsigned Real Number:

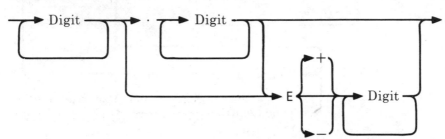

Character Constant:

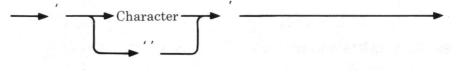

String Constant:

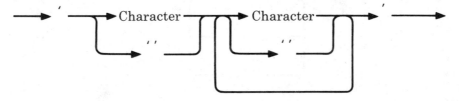

Appendix 2

Reserved words and special symbols

2.1 RESERVED WORDS

A *reserved word* is a word which has a special meaning and cannot be used as an identifier. In this book reserved words are set in boldface for emphasis. Here is a complete list of the reserved words of Pascal:

and	downto	if	or	then
array	else	in	packed	to
begin	end	label	procedure	type
case	file	mod	program	until
const	for	nil	record	var
div	function	not	repeat	while
do	goto	of	set	with

2.2 SPECIAL SYMBOLS AND THEIR REPRESENTATIONS

Here is a complete list of the special symbols of Pascal:

```
+       −      *       /
=       <>     <       <=      >=      >
(       )      [       ]       {       }
:=      .      ,       ;       :       ..      ↑       '
```

Some of these symbols have alternative representations, to allow for deficiencies in some character sets:

Symbol:	↑	{	}	[	]
Alternative representations:	^ or @	(*	*)	(.	.)

Strictly speaking, '{' and '}' are the standard representations of the comment brackets, rather than '(*' and '*)'. The latter representations have been used in this book because they are available in all character sets.

Appendix 3

Standard constants, types, functions and procedures

const
    MaxInt = the largest positive integer which can be represented in a particular computer (* see Integer *);

type
    Boolean = (False,True);
    Char   = a particular character set;
    Integer = the set of whole numbers, or integers, which can be represented in a particular computer
           (* in effect $-$MaxInt . . $+$MaxInt *);
    Real   = the set of real numbers which can be represented in a particular computer;
    Text   = files of characters subdivided into lines;

    (**** Arithmetic functions ****)

function Odd (I: Integer): Boolean;
    returns True if and only if I is odd;
function Abs (A: any arithmetic type): same arithmetic type;
    returns the absolute value of A;
function Sqr (A: any arithmetic type): same arithmetic type;
    returns the square of A;
function Trunc (X: Real): Integer;
    returns the value of X truncated to its integral part;
function Round (X: Real): Integer;
    returns the value of X rounded to the nearest integer;
function Sqrt (X: Real): Real;
    returns the square root of X;
function ArcTan (X: Real): Real;
    returns the arctangent, in radians, of X;
function Cos (X: Real): Real;
    returns the cosine of X radians;

function Sin (X: Real): Real;
   returns the sine of X radians;
function Exp (X: Real): Real;
   returns the value of *e* raised to the power of X;
function Ln (X: Real): Real;
   returns the logarithm of X to the base *e*;

   (**** Ordinal functions ****)

function Succ (S: any ordinal type): same ordinal type;
   returns the successor value of S, if such a value exists;
function Pred (S: any ordinal type): same ordinal type;
   returns the predecessor value of S, if such a value exists;
function Ord (S: any ordinal type): Integer;
   returns the ordinal number of S;
   (* The values of an enumeration type, including Boolean, have ordinal
   numbers 0, 1, 2, etc., in order of their enumeration.
   The ordinal number of a Char value depends on the character set: see
   Appendix 5.
   The ordinal number of an Integer value is itself. *)
function Chr (I: Integer): Char;
   returns the character whose ordinal number is I, if such a character exists;

   (**** File handling function and procedures ****)

function EOF (**var** F: any file type): Boolean;
   returns True if and only if F's reading/writing position is at end-of-file;
procedure Reset (**var** F: any file type);
   resets F's reading position to the beginning of F, sets EOF(F) to True if F is
   empty, otherwise copies the first component of F into F↑;
procedure Get (**var** F: any file type);
   (* permitted only if EOF(F) is False *)
   advances F's reading position by one component, sets EOF(F) to True if
   there is no next component, otherwise copies the next component into F↑;
procedure Read (**var** F: any file type;
                  var C: component type of F);
    begin
    C := F ↑ ; Get (F)
    end;
(* Read (*f,c1,c2,* ...) is equivalent to:
    begin Read (*f,c1*); Read (*f,c2*); ...... **end** *)
procedure Rewrite (**var** F: any file type);
   makes F empty and ready to be rewritten;
procedure Put (**var** F: any file type);
   appends the contents of F↑ to F, leaving F↑ undefined;

```
procedure Write ( var F: any file type;
                        C: component type of F);
    begin
    F↑ := C; Put (F)
    end;
```
(* Write (*f,c1,c2,* ...) is equivalent to:
    begin Write (*f,c1*); Write (*f,c2*); . . . . . **end** *)

(* For text file handling functions and procedures, see Appendix 4. *)

(**** Dynamic storage allocation procedures ****)

```
procedure New ( var P: any pointer type );
```
   creates a fresh anonymous variable and makes P point to it;
   (* If *p* is a pointer to a variant record type which has a case label *l*, New(*p,l*)
   creates an anonymous variant record which will be constrained to the
   variant specified by *l*. (The tag field is not initialized by New.) This
   constraint allows the storage space allocated to the variant record to be
   minimized.
   The extended form New(*p,l1,l2,* ...) is available for a record with nested
   variants corresponding to case labels *l1, l2,* ... *)
```
procedure Dispose ( var P: any pointer type );
```
   discards the anonymous variable P↑, leaving P undefined;
   (* Dispose (*p,l*) must be used to discard an anonymous variant record
   created by the form New(*p,l*), and thus constrained to the variant
   specified by *l*.
   Similarly for the extended form Dispose(*p,l1,l2,* ...). *)

(**** Packing and unpacking procedures ****)

```
procedure Pack (      U: any unpacked array type;
                      I: index type of U;
                  var P: any packed array type with
                          same component type as U);
```
       copies U[I], U[Succ(I)], ... into all the components of P;

```
procedure Unpack (      P: any packed array type;
                    var U: any unpacked array type with
                            same component type as P;
                        I: index type of U);
```
       copies all the components of P into U[I], U[Succ(I)], ...

Appendix 4

Text input and output

Legible input and output is achieved through text files, which are character files subdivided into lines by end-of line markers (see Sections 8.2 and 17.3).

The standard file handling function EOF and procedures Reset, Get, Read, Rewrite, Put and Write, as described in Appendix 3, are all applicable to text files, and are similar in effect. However, when the reading position in a text file t is moved to an end-of-line marker, by Reset, Get, Read (or ReadLn), a *blank* is stored in $t\uparrow$ and EOLn(t) becomes True.

4.1 THE PROCEDURE Read

In this and the following section, t denotes a text file, and v, $v1$, $v2$, ... denote variables of type Char or Integer (or a subrange thereof), or Real.

(a) Read ($v1,v2,...$) means Read (Input,$v1,v2,...$).

(b) Read($t,v1,v2,...$) means:

   begin Read ($t,v1$); Read ($t,v2$)... **end**

(c) Read(t,v), where v is a Char (or subrange of Char) variable, means:

   begin $v := t\uparrow$;   Get(t) **end**

(d) Read(t,v), where v is an Integer (or subrange of Integer) variable, reads a sequence of characters from t, consisting of zero or more blanks and end-of-line markers followed by an integer number (possibly signed). This signed integer number is converted to its internal representation, then assigned to v. Afterwards, $t\uparrow$ contains the character immediately following the number.

(e) Read(t,v), where v is a Real variable, is similar to (d) except that the number may be either real or integer.

4.2 THE PROCEDURE ReadLn

(a) ReadLn(*v1,v2,...*) means ReadLn(Input,*v1,v2,...*). ReadLn with no parameters means ReadLn(Input).

(b) ReadLn(*t,v1,v2,...*) means:

begin Read(*t,v1*); Read(*t,v2*);... ReadLn(*t*) **end**

(c) ReadLn(*t*) advances the reading position of *t* just beyond the next end-of-line marker in *t*, i.e. to the beginning of the next line. EOF(*t*) becomes True if there is no next line.

4.3 THE PROCEDURE Write

In this and the following section, *t* denotes a text file, and *p1, p2, . . .* denote *write-parameters*. Each write-parameter has one of the forms:

$$e{:}w \qquad e \qquad e{:}w{:}d$$

where *e* is a Char, string, Integer, Real or Boolean expression, and where *w* and *d* are Integer expressions with positive values.

(a) Write(*p1,p2,...*) means Write(Output,*p1,p2,...*).

(b) Write (*t,p1,p2,...*) means:

begin Write (*t,p1*); Write (*t,p2*) ... **end**

(c) Write (*t,e:w*) writes to *t* an external representation of the value of *e*, preceded by as many blanks as necessary to ensure that at least *w* characters are written. If *e* is Char or string, its value is written without surrounding apostrophes. If *e* is a string whose length exceeds *w*, only the first *w* characters of the string are written. If *e* is Integer, its value is written as an integer number, signed if negative. If *e* is Real, its value is written in scientific notation, preceded by a sign if negative, or by a blank otherwise; with one digit before the decimal point; and with as many digits after the point as the field can accommodate. If *e* is Boolean, either the string 'false' or the string 'true' is written.

(d) Write (*t,e*) is similar to (c), except that a suitable default value is taken for *w*. In particular, a Char or string value is written without any preceding blanks.

(e) Write (*t,e:w:d*), where *e* must be Real, writes the value of *e* in fixed-point notation, with *d* digits after the decimal point.

4.4 THE PROCEDURE WriteLn

(a) WriteLn(*p1,p2*, ...) means WriteLn(Output,*p1,p2* ...).
    WriteLn with no parameters means WriteLn(Output).

(b) WriteLn(*t,p1,p2,* ...) means:

begin Write (*t,p1*); Write (*t,p2*); ... WriteLn(*t*) **end**

(c) WriteLn(*t*) appends an end-of-line marker to *t*.

4.5 THE FUNCTION EOLn

(a) EOLn with no parameter means EOLn(Input).
(b) EOLn(*t*) returns True if and only if the reading position of text file *t* is at an end-of-line marker.

4.6 THE PROCEDURE Page

(a). Page with no parameter means Page(Output).
(b) Page(*t*) forces subsequent output on text file *t* to continue on a new page, should *t* subsequently be printed.

Appendix 5

Character sets

The two most common computer character sets are ASCII (or ISO) and EBCDIC. These are tabulated below, each character set in order across the rows. In each table 'ｶ' denotes the blank character, and empty slots are 'control characters', which cannot be printed. The ordinal number of each character may be determined by adding the numbers on its row and column.

5.1 THE ASCII CHARACTER SET

	0	1	2	3	4	5	6	7	8	9	10	11	12	13	14	15
0																
16																
32	ｶ	!	"	#	$	%	&	'	(	)	*	+	,	-	.	/
48	0	1	2	3	4	5	6	7	8	9	:	;	<	=	>	?
64	@	A	B	C	D	E	F	G	H	I	J	K	L	M	N	O
80	P	Q	R	S	T	U	V	W	X	Y	Z	[	\	]	^	—
96	`	a	b	c	d	e	f	g	h	i	j	k	l	m	n	o
112	p	q	r	s	t	u	v	w	x	y	z	{	|	}	~	

5.2 THE EBCDIC CHARACTER SET

	0	1	2	3	4	5	6	7	8	9	10	11	12	13	14	15
0																
16																
32																
48																
64	♭										¢	.	<	(	+	
80	&										!	$	*	)	;	|
96	–	/										,	%	—	>	?
112											:	#	@	'	=	"
128		a	b	c	d	e	f	g	h	i						
144		j	k	l	m	n	o	p	q	r						
160			s	t	u	v	w	x	y	z						
176																
192		A	B	C	D	E	F	G	H	I						
208		J	K	L	M	N	O	P	Q	R						
224			S	T	U	V	W	X	Y	Z						
240	0	1	2	3	4	5	6	7	8	9						

Appendix 6

Implementation variations

Ideally, any Pascal program which runs successfully on one computer should run on any other computer, with identical results. This is not always the case, for two principal reasons. Firstly, different Pascal compilers are not always consistent in their interpretation of the Pascal language. Secondly, there are factors which are determined by the computer system and are beyond the control of the compiler, such as the character set, the range of integer numbers which can be stored, and the representation of real numbers.

A summary of variations from one Pascal implementation to another is given in this appendix, keyed to the chapters in the main text. Gross language variations and extensions are excluded from this list. Before using a Pascal compiler, it may be worthwhile to check these points in the user guide.

Chapter 1

- Many compilers ignore all but the first 8 characters of an identifier, so HydrogenFlowRate and HydrogenTemperature would both be treated as Hydrogen. Some other compilers ignore all but the first 10 or 12 or 32 characters.
- Some implementations do not provide both upper- and lower-case letters, or do not treat them as equivalent.

Chapter 3

- The value of MaxInt, and hence the range of Integer values, vary from one implementation to another.
- Some implementations interpret **div** and **mod** wrongly with negative operand(s), for example (−5) **div** 3 might yield −2 instead of −1. Many implementations allow **mod** to have a negative right operand.

Chapter 4

- See notes on text input/output (Chapter 8, below).

Chapter 8

- The character set, and its ordering, vary from one system to another.
- The default field widths for writing Boolean, Integer and Real values vary from one implementation to another.
- Some implementations are very non-standard in their treatment of text input/output.

Chapter 9

- The ordinal numbers of Char values depend on the character set in use.
- The control variable of a **for** statement should be a local variable (see Section 13.3), but some compilers do not enforce this restriction. Also, many compilers do not prevent illegal assignments to the control variable.
- Some implementations do not treat it as an error for the value of the case index not to match any of the case labels of a **case** statement.

Chapter 10

- The range of Real values, the number of significant digits and the set of real numbers represented exactly all vary from one system to another.
- Some computers round the results of Real operations, others truncate.

Chapter 11

- Some compilers use a more liberal definition of equivalence of array types.

Chapter 12

- Some compilers ignore **packed** altogether.
- String ordering depends on the character set ordering.

Chapter 14

- Some compilers apply the scope rules incorrectly in certain obscure situations, for example allowing the following (and setting D = 7) instead of reporting a violation of the definition-before-use rule:

```
const C = 7;
procedure P;
  const D = C;
        C = 2;
  ..........
```

Chapter 16

- Some compilers do not require *all* possible values of the tag field to be present as case labels in a variant part.
- Some compilers ignore **packed** altogether.
- Some compilers use a more liberal definition of equivalence of record types.
- Some compilers do not implement tagless variant parts.

Chapter 17

- See notes on text input/output (Chapter 8, above).
- The requirements placed on interactive programs vary from one implementation to another. Some implementations have special features to cope with interactive input/output.

Chapter 19

- Each implementation imposes its own limits on the range of values of a set's base type. Some compilers restrict all base types (not just Integer), in some cases excluding even **set of** Char.

Chapter 20

- Some implementations do not allow Dispose. Some others allow it but ignore it, so that storage space is not reclaimed.

Chapter 21

- Some compilers do not implement functional and procedural parameters.
- Some others do not allow the functional or procedural parameter's own formal parameters to be specified explicitly, and restrict the latter to value parameters only.
- Some compilers do not implement conformant array parameters.

Chapter 22

- Some compilers do not prevent **goto** statements from jumping into structured statements.
- Some compilers forbid **goto** statements to jump out of blocks. Others allow this, but do not restrict the jumps to the outermost statement level of a block.

Further reading

PASCAL

Wilson, I.R. and Addyman, A.M.:
  A Practical Introduction to Pascal—with BS6192. Macmillan, 1982.

SOFTWARE ENGINEERING

Jackson, M.:
  Principles of Program Design. Academic Press, 1975.
Kernigan, B.W. and Plauger, P.J.:
  The Elements of Programming Style. McGraw-Hill, 1978.
Kernigan, B.W. and Plauger, P.J.:
  Software Tools in Pascal. Addison-Wesley, 1981.
Myers, G.J.:
  The Art of Software Testing. Wiley, 1979.
Myers, G.J.:
  Software Reliability. Wiley, 1976.
Pressman, R.S.:
  Software Engineering: a Practitioner's Approach. McGraw-Hill, 1982.
Watt, D.A., Wichmann, B.A. and Findlay, W.:
  Ada: Language and Methodology. Prentice-Hall, 1985.
Yourdon, E. and Constantine, L.:
  Structured Design. Prentice-Hall, 1979.

SYSTEMS ANALYSIS

De Marco, T.:
  Structured Analysis and System Specification. Prentice-Hall, 1979.
Gane, C. and Sarson, T.:
  Structured Systems Analysis. Prentice-Hall. 1979.

WHAT ACTUALLY HAPPENS!

Brooks, F.P.:
  The Mythical Man-Month. Addison-Wesley, 1974.
Kidder, T.:
  The Soul of a New Machine. Atlantic-Little, Brown, 1981.

Answers to selected exercises

Specimen solutions to most of the exercises (but not the programming exercises) are given here. Many of the exercises have alternative, equally satisfactory, solutions.

ANSWERS 1

1.1. (a), (b), (c), (e) and (g) are valid.

1.3. (a), (c) and (f) are valid.

1.5. For example: *C1H4, Li1H1, B1H3, He99, C2H4, (C2H2)4C1Li2*.

Note that (e.g.) *CH4* is *not* allowed by the syntax given, which requires every component to end with an integer number. (What alteration to the diagrams is needed to allow *CH4*?)

ANSWERS 2

2.1. (a) For example: 'is even', 'is zero', 'is prime'.

(b) For example: 'is a letter', 'is a vowel', 'is a punctuation-mark'.

2.2. (a) Real, (b) Char and (c) Integer.

2.3. (a), (f), (g), and (l) are legal.

2.4. Variables are represented by words of storage, and values by bit-patterns. A variable is undefined if the corresponding bit-pattern is not specified by the rules of the Pascal language.

ANSWERS 3

3.1.

```
const
    DaysInWeek = 7;
    InchesPerFoot = 12;
    CmPerMetre = 100;
    YardsPerMile = 1760;
    MetresPerKm = 1000
```

3.2.

```
var
    GrossPay, Tax, UnionDues, NettPay: Integer
```

3.3.

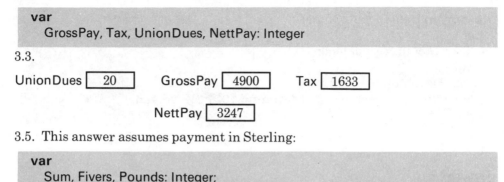

UnionDues ⎡ 20 ⎤   GrossPay ⎡ 4900 ⎤   Tax ⎡ 1633 ⎤

NettPay ⎡ 3247 ⎤

3.5. This answer assumes payment in Sterling:

```
var
    Sum, Fivers, Pounds: Integer;
    P50, P20, P10, P5, P2, P1: Integer;
    . . . . . . . . . .
Fivers := Sum div 500; Sum := Sum mod 500;
Pounds := Sum div 100; Sum := Sum mod 100;
P50 := Sum mod 50; Sum := Sum mod 50;

(* . . . . . and so on . . . . . *)
```

ANSWERS 4

4.1.
```
    8000  −3000  −1000  9000
```
4.3. For example:

```
Write ('Hugh McSporran'); WriteLn;
Write ('13 Auchenshuggle Road'); WriteLn;
Write ('Campbeltown'); WriteLn;
Write ('Scotland'); WriteLn
```

4.4.

```
program Powers ( Input, Output );
var
    Z, SqrZ: Integer;
begin
Read (Z);
SqrZ := Sqr(Z);
Write ('Number':12, 'square':12, 'cube':12, '4th power':12);
WriteLn;
Write (Z:12, SqrZ:12, SqrZ*Z:12, Sqr(SqrZ):12);
WriteLn
end.
```

4.5.

```
program Date ( Input, Output );
var
   Day, Month, Year: Integer;
begin
Read (Day, Month, Year);
Write (Day:2, '/', Month:2, '/', (Year mod 100):2); WriteLn
end.
```

ANSWERS 5

5.1.

```
Positive := Number > 0;
Zero := Number = 0;
Negative := Number < 0
```

5.2. Either of the following equivalent statements:

```
Left := not Odd(PageNumber)
Left := PageNumber mod 2 = 0
```

5.3. Either of the following equivalent statements:

```
Monoglot := (English and not French) or
            (French and not English)
Monoglot := English <> French
```

5.4.

```
program Multiple (Input, Output);
var
   I, J: Integer;
begin
Read (I,J);
Write (I mod J = 0); WriteLn
end.
```

5.5.

```
program Christmas (Input, Output);
const
   December = 12;
var
   Month, Day: Integer;
```

```
begin
Read (Month, Day);
Write ((Month=December) and (Day=25)); WriteLn
end.
```

5.6. (a)

```
LeapYear := Year mod 4 = 0
```

(b) The following answers are equivalent. Can you see why?

```
LeapYear := ((Year mod 4 = 0) and (Year mod 100 <> 0))
            or (Year mod 400 = 0)
LeapYear := (Year mod 4 = 0) and
            ((Year mod 100 <> 0) or (Year mod 400 = 0))
```

5.7.

$x < y$ is equivalent to **not** x **and** y

$x >=$ y is equivalent to x **or not** y

$x > y$ is equivalent to x **and not** y

$x = y$ is equivalent to **not** x **and not** y **or** x **and** y

$x <>$ y is equivalent to $(x$ **or** $y)$ **and** (**not** x **or not** $y)$

5.8.

$x =$ True is equivalent to x

$x =$ False is equivalent to **not** x

$x <>$ True is equivalent to **not** x

$x <>$ False is equivalent to x

Conclusion—use the simplified forms only, they are easier to read, to write and to compute.

5.9. (a) $(a$ **and** b **and** $c)$ **or** x

(b) True

(c) $(a$ **or** b **or** $c)$ **and** $(x$ **or** y **or** $c)$

{Hint: use the fact that c is equivalent to $(c$ **and** $c)$ to make the expression symmetrical.}

ANSWERS 6

6.1.

```
    *****
    *****************
    *********
    ******
  0
    *
```

6.2. It writes bars of excessive length, which may not fit on a single line. Some computer systems will treat this as an error.

```
program Display ( Input, Output );
const
  MaximumWidth = 72; (*say *)
var
  StarCount, WidthOfBar: Integer;
begin
Read (WidthOfBar);
while WidthOfBar >= 0 do
  begin
  if (WidthOfBar = 0) or (WidthOfBar > MaximumWidth) then
    Write (WidthOfBar:8)
  else
    begin
    Write ('   ':8);
    StarCount := 0;
    while StarCount < WidthOfBar do
      begin
      Write ('*');
      StarCount := StarCount + 1
      end
    end;
  WriteLn;
  Read (WidthOfBar)
  end
end (* Display *).
```

6.3. Assume the declaration 'Factorial, I: Integer'.

```
Factorial := 1;
I := 2;
while I <= N do
  begin
  Factorial := Factorial * I;
  I := I + 1
  end
```

6.4. Assume the declaration 'PowerOf10, NrDigits: Integer'.

```
NrDigits := 1;
PowerOf10 := 10;
while PowerOf10 <= N do
  begin
  NrDigits := NrDigits + 1;
```

```
    PowerOf10 := PowerOf10 * 10
    end
```

6.5.

```
if N > 0 then
    Write ('positive')
else if N < 0 then
    Write ('negative')
else
    Write ('zero')
```

6.6. Assume the declaration 'ThisDay, ThisMonth, ThisYear, BirthDay, BirthMonth, BirthYear, Age: Integer'.

```
if BirthMonth < ThisMonth) or
    (BirthMonth = ThisMonth) and (BirthDay <= ThisDay)
then
    Age := ThisYear — BirthYear
else
    Age := ThisYear — BirthYear — 1
```

6.7. (a)

```
program LargestByCount ( Input, Output );
var
    Number, Largest, Size, Count: Integer;
begin
Largest := 0;
Count := 0;
Read (Size);
while Count < Size do
    begin
    Read (Number);
    if Number > Largest then
        Largest := Number;
    Count := Count+1
    end;
Write ('The largest was ', Largest); WriteLn
end.
```

(b)

```
program LargestToMarker ( Input, Output );
var
    Number, Largest: Integer;
```

```
begin
Largest := 0;
Read (Number);
while Number >= 0 do
  begin
  if Number > Largest then
    Largest := Number;
  Read (Number)
  end;
Write ('The largest was ', Largest); WriteLn
end.
```

(c)

```
program LargestToEOF ( Input, Output );
var
   Number, Largest: Integer;
begin
Largest := 0;
while not EOF(Input) do
  begin
  Read (Number);
  if Number > Largest then
    Largest := Number;
  ReadLn
  end;
Write ('The largest was ', Largest); WriteLn
end.
```

6.8. (a)

```
program LargestByCount ( Input, Output );
var
   Number, Largest, Size, Count: Integer;
begin
Read (Size);
if Size <= 0 then
  begin
  Write ('The input list is empty'); WriteLn
  end
else
  begin
  Largest := 0;
  Count := 0;
  repeat
```

```
      Read (Number);
      if Number > Largest then
         Largest := Number;
      Count := Count+1
      until Count = Size;
   Write ('The largest was ', Largest); WriteLn
   end
end.
```

ANSWERS 7

7.2.

Level 1b outline

```
program Traffic (Input, Output);
declarations;
begin
prepare to process signals;
while not end of data do
   process a signal or interval and read the next signal;
output the results
end.
```

As an exercise, hand-test Level 1b with the same test data as before.

Refinements from Level 1b

If the signal on hand is a vehicle or an error signal, it is to be processed individually. If it is a timing signal, it is to be treated as the first of an interval, and the whole of the interval is to be processed. Since this will involve reading the next signal, the processing of vehicle and error signals must do likewise. Thus we do not have a separate step to read the next signal.

Refinement 1.1b: process a signal or interval and read the next signal

```
begin
if it is a vehicle signal then
   process a vehicle signal and read the next signal
else
if it is an error signal then
   process an error signal and read the next signal
else
   time a vehicle-free interval and read the next signal
end
```

Level 2b is obtained by substituting this in Level 1b. As an exercise, write out Level 2b and hand-test it with your test data.

Refinements from Level 2b

There is explicit provision in this version of the program for timing the intervals, so processing a vehicle signal or an error signal involves no more than incrementing the appropriate tally. As before we use Integer variables Vehicles and Errors.

Refinement 2.1b: process a vehicle signal and read the next signal

```
begin
Vehicles := Vehicles + 1;
Read (Signal)
end
```

Refinement 2.2b: process an error signal and read the next signal

```
begin
Errors := Errors + 1;
Read (Signal)
end
```

To time an interval we must note its beginning, process all the timing signals in the interval, and note its end.

Refinement 2.3b: time a vehicle-free interval and read the next signal

```
begin
note the start of an interval;
while it is a timing signal do
   process a timing signal and read the next signal;
note the end of an interval
end
```

Inserting these refinements in Level 2b gives us Level 3b. As an exercise, write out Level 3b and hand-test it with your test data.

Complete program for Traffic(b)

```
program Traffic (Input, Output);
const
    Terminator      = 0;
    TimingSignal    = 1;
    VehicleSignal   = 2;
```

```
var
    Vehicles, Errors, Seconds, StartTime, Longest, Signal: Integer;
begin
(* prepare to process signals *)
Vehicles := 0;
Errors := 0;
Seconds := 0;
Longest := 0;
Read (Signal);
while Signal <> Terminator do
  begin (* process a signal or interval and read the next signal *)
    if Signal = VehicleSignal then
      begin (* process a vehicle signal and read the next signal *)
      Vehicles := Vehicles + 1;
      Read (Signal)
      end
    else
    if Signal > VehicleSignal then
      begin (* process an error signal and read the next signal *)
      Errors := Errors + 1;
      Read (Signal)
      end
    else
      begin (* time a vehicle-free interval and read the next signal *)
      (* note the start of an interval *)
      StartTime := Seconds;
      while Signal = TimingSignal do
        begin (* process a timing signal and read the next signal *)
        Seconds := Seconds + 1;
        Read (Signal)
        end;
      (* note the end of an interval *)
      if Seconds − StartTime > Longest then
        Longest := Seconds − StartTime
      end
  end;
(* output the results *)
Write ('        No. Of      No. Of     Elapsed    Longest');
WriteLn;
Write ('        Vehicles    Errors      Time       Gap');
WriteLn;
Write (Vehicles:12, Errors:12, Seconds:12, Longest:12);
WriteLn
end (* Traffic(b) *).
```

Traffic (b) is more efficient because the interval processing is done only between intervals, rather than at every signal.

7.3. Traffic (a):

Refinement 2.3a': process an error signal

```
Errors := Errors + 1
```

Traffic (b):

Refinement 1.1b': process a signal or interval and read the next signal

```
begin
if it is a vehicle signal then
    process a vehicle signal and read the next signal
else
    time a vehicle-free interval and read the next signal
end
```

Refinement 2.3b': time a vehicle-free interval and read the next signal

```
begin
note the start of an interval;
while it is a timing or error signal do
    process a timing or error signal and read the next signal;
note the end of an interval
end
```

Refinement 3.2b': process a timing or error signal and read the next signal

```
begin
if it is an error signal then
    Errors := Errors + 1
else
    Seconds := Seconds + 1;
Read (Signal)
end
```

Refinement 3.4b': it is a timing or error signal

```
(Signal=TimingSignal) or (Signal > VehicleSignal)
```

7.4. Traffic (a):

Refinement 2.3a': process an error signal

```
begin
Errors := Errors + 1;
Seconds := Seconds + 1;
Interval := Interval + 1
end
```

Traffic (b): As Answer 7.3(b), except:

Refinement 3.2b': process a timing or error signal and read the next signal

```
begin
if it is an error signal then
    Errors := Errors + 1;
Seconds := Seconds + 1;
Read (Signal)
end
```

7.5. Traffic (a):

Refinement 2.3a': process an error signal

```
begin
Errors := Errors + 1;
Consecutives := Consecutives + 1;
if Consecutives = 8 then
    begin
    Write ('There have been eight consecutive error signals');
    WriteLn;
    Consecutives := 0
    end;
check the length of the interval;
Interval := 0
end
```

Refinements 2.1a, 2.2a and 3.7a must all include Consecutives:=0. Refinement 3.8a must declare Consecutives an Integer variable.

Traffic (b)

Refinement 1.1b': process a signal or interval and read the next signal

```
begin
if it is a vehicle signal then
    process a vehicle signal and read the next signal
else
if it is an error signal then
```

```
    process a run of error signals and read the next signal
else
    time a vehicle-free interval and read the next signal
end
```

Refinement 2.2b': process a run of error signals and read the next signal

```
begin
note the start of a run of error signals;
while it is an error signal do
    process an error signal and read the next signal
end
```

Refinement 3.4b': process an error signal and read the next signal

```
begin
Errors := Errors + 1;
Consecutives := Consecutives + 1;
if Consecutives = 8 then
    begin
    Write  ('There have been eight consecutive error signals');
    WriteLn;
    Consecutives := 0
    end;
Read (Signal)
end
```

Refinement 3.5b': note the start of a run of error signals

```
Consecutives := 0
```

Refinement 3.8a must declare Consecutives an Integer variable. Of the amended versions, Traffic (b) is significantly more modular.

ANSWERS 8

8.1. Replace the body of the loop by:

```
begin
Read (Character);
if Character = '.' then
    PeriodCount := PeriodCount+1
else if Character = ',' then
    CommaCount := CommaCount+1
```

```
else if Character = ';' then
  SemicolonCount := SemicolonCount+1
else if Character = ':' then
  ColonCount := ColonCount+1
else if ('A' <= Character) and (Character <= 'Z') then
  LetterCount := LetterCount+1
else if ('0' <= Character) and (Character <= '9') then
  DigitCount := DigitCount+1
end
```

and insert declarations and initializations of the Integer variables PeriodCount, CommaCount, SemicolonCount and ColonCount.

8.2. Assume the variable declarations 'Character: Char; Length: Integer'.

```
Length := 0;
while not EOLn(Input) do
  begin
  Read (Character);
  Write (Character);
  Length := Length+1
  end;
WriteLn;
while Length > 0 do
  begin
  Write ('−');
  Length := Length−1
  end;
WriteLn
```

8.3.

```
program CutSpacing (Input, Output);
const
  Blank = ' ';
var
  This, Previous: Char;
begin
while not EOF(Input) do
  begin
  Previous := '*'; (* any non-blank character would do *)
  while not EOLn(Input) do
    begin
    Read (This);
```

```
      if (This <> Blank) or (Previous <> Blank) then
         Write (This);
      Previous := This
      end;
    WriteLn;
    ReadLn
    end
 end.
```

ANSWERS 9

9.1. (a), (b), (c), (f), (g), (h), (i), (j), (k), (l), (m), (n), (p), (r), (t), (u), (v), and (x) are legal.

9.2. (a)

Faculty: (Science,Medicine,Law,Arts)

(b) Assume the declaration 'Code: Char'.

```
Read (Code);
if      Code = 'S' then Faculty := Science
else if Code = 'M' then Faculty := Medicine
else if Code = 'L' then Faculty := Law
else if Code = 'A' then Faculty := Arts
else
   WriteLn ('Invalid faculty code: ', Code)
```

(c)

```
case Faculty of
   Science:  Write ('Science');
   Medicine: Write ('Medicine');
   Law:      Write ('Law');
   Arts:     Write ('Arts')
   end
```

9.3. (a)

Write (Day:2, '/', 1+Ord(Month):2, '/', Year:4)

9.4. Assume the declaration 'NrDaysInMonth: 28 . . 31'.

```
(* determine the number of days in this Month and Year *)
case Month of
  Jan, Mar, May, Jul, Aug, Oct, Dec:
    NrDaysInMonth := 31;
  Apr, Jun, Sep, Nov:
    NrDaysInMonth := 30;
  Feb:
    if Year is a leap year (* see Exercises 5 *) then
      NrDaysInMonth := 29
    else
      NrDaysInMonth := 28
  end;
(* update Day, Month, and Year to tomorrow's date *)
if Day < NrDaysInMonth then
  Day := Day+1
else
  begin
  Day := 1;
  if Month < Dec then
    Month := Succ(Month)
  else
    begin
    Month := Jan;
    Year := Year+1
    end
  end
```

9.6.

```
for StarCount := 1 to WidthOfBar do
  Write ('*')
```

9.8. Insert Write('£') in the initialization sequence. Replace the Write statement in the loop body by:

```
if Remainder = Number then (* leading zero *)
  Write ('*')
else
  Write (Chr(Quotient+Ord('0')))
```

9.10. Assume the declaration 'Group: 1 . . 5'.

```
if Weight > 60 then
  Group := 5
```

```
  else
    Group := (Weight+14) div 15;
  case Group of
    1: Charge := 12;
    2: Charge := 22;
    3: Charge := 31;
    4: Charge := 36+2 * (Distance div 1000);
    5: Charge := 40 + 3 * (Distance div 1000)
  end
```

ANSWERS 10

10.3. (A+B)+C evaluates to 0.00. (B+C)+A evaluates to 0.004. (A+B is rounded to 1.00.)

   X*Y/Y evaluates to 3.89. (The value of X*Y, 15.054, is rounded to 15.1 before division.)

   Z+Z+Z+Z+Z+Z+Z+Z+Z+Z evaluates to 3.31. 10*Z evaluates to 3.33. (Cumulative rounding error occurs in the former case.)

10.4. (a) 4/3 * Pi * R * Sqr(R)
      (b) 2 * (A*B + B*C + C*A)
      (c) Sqrt(Sqr(X)+Sqr(Y)) and Arctan(Y/X)
      (d) Sqr(V)/R

10.5. Assume the declaration 'S, AreaSquared: Real'.

```
  S := (A+B+C)/2;
  AreaSquared := S*(S−A)*(S−B)*(S−C);
  if AreaSquared >= 0.0 then
    WriteLn ('Area of triangle is ', Sqrt(AreaSquared))
  else
    WriteLn ('No such triangle exists')
```


ANSWERS 11

11.1. (a)

Free: **array** [1 . . NrRooms] **of** Boolean

(b) Assume the variable declarations
'NrFreeRooms: 0 . . NrRooms; Room: 1 . . NrRooms'.

```
NrFreeRooms := 0;
for Room := 1 to NrRooms do
  if Free[Room] then
    NrFreeRooms := NrFreeRooms+1
```

11.3. Assume the variable declarations 'Year: 1901 .. 1999; MinRainFall, MaxRainFall: Real'.

```
MinRainFall := YearlyRainFall[1900];
MaxRainFall := YearlyRainFall[1900];
for Year := 1901 to 1999 do
  if YearlyRainFall[Year] > MaxRainFall then
    MaxRainFall := YearlyRainFall[Year]
  else if YearlyRainFall[Year] < MinRainFall then
    MinRainFall := YearlyRainFall[Year];
WriteLn ('Yearly Rainfall range: ',
        MaxRainFall−MinRainFall)
```

11.5. Replace the constant definition by 'MaxCandidates = 10' and insert the variable declaration 'ActualNrCandidates: 1 .. MaxCandidates'. Replace NrCandidates by MaxCandidates throughout the program's *declaration part*, and by ActualNrCandidates throughout the program's *statement part*. Insert ReadLn(ActualNrCandidates) as the first statement of the program.

11.8. (a) Assume the declarations 'Symmetric: Boolean; Row, Col: 1..N'.

```
Symmetric := True;
Row := 1; Col := N;
(* traverse the rows from right to left above the main
   diagonal, comparing each element with its mirror-image
   in the diagonal *)
while Symmetric and (Row < N) do
  if Matrix[Row,Col] <> Matrix[Col,Row] then
    Symmetric := False
  else
    begin
    Col := Col−1;
    if Col = Row then
      (* hit the main diagonal, go on to next row *)
      begin Row := Row+1; Col := N end
    end
```

(b) Similar to (a).

ANSWERS 12

12.3. (a) Assume the variable declarations 'Character: Char; Length: 0 . . MaxInt'. N.B.: the following solution reads up to and including the blank or end-of-line marker following the string.

```
Length := 0;
Read (Character);
while Character <> ' ' do
  begin
  Length := Length+1;
  if Length <= L then
    String[Length] := Character;
  Read (Character)
  end
for Length := Length+1 to L do
  String[Length] := ' '
```

(b) Insert:

```
while Character = ' ' do
  Read (Character);
```

immediately before the **while** statement in (a).

12.4. In the declarations of List and Target, replace Integer by **packed array** [1 . . 10] of Char. No change at all to the program fragment!

12.5. (a) Assume the variable declarations 'Hrs: 0 . . 23; Mins: 0 . . 59; TotalMins: 0 . . 1439'. N.B.: the following assumes that TimeString has already been checked for correct format.

```
Hrs := (Ord(TimeString[1])−Ord('0')) * 10 +
       (Ord(TimeString[2])−Ord('0'));
Mins := (Ord(TimeString[4])−Ord('0')) * 10 +
        (Ord(TimeString[5])−Ord('0'));
TotalMins := Hrs*60 + Mins
```

(b) Assume the same variable declarations.

```
Hrs := TotalMins div 60; Mins := TotalMins mod 60;
TimeString[1] := Chr(Hrs div 10 + Ord('0'));
TimeString[2] := Chr(Hrs mod 10 + Ord('0'));
TimeString[3] := ':';
```

```
TimeString[4] := Chr(Mins div 10 + Ord('0'));
TimeString[5] := Chr(Mins mod 10 + Ord('0'))
```

ANSWERS 13

13.1.

```
N := NrDaysIn (ThisMonth, ThisYear+1)
```

13.2. (a)

```
function FourthPower ( X: Real ): Real;
   begin
   FourthPower := Sqr(Sqr(X))
   end (* FourthPower *)
```

(b)

```
Write (FourthPower(A+B))
```

13.3

```
program CharacterCount ( Input, Output );
. . . . . . . . . .
function Alphabetic ( Ch: Char ): Boolean;
   begin
   Alphabetic := ('A' <= Ch) and (Ch <= 'Z')
                 or ('a' <= Ch) and (Ch <= 'z')
   end (*Alphabetic*);

function Numeric ( Ch: Char ): Boolean;
   begin
   Numeric := ('0' <= Ch) and (Ch <= '9')
   end (*Numeric*);

begin (*CharacterCount*)
. . . . . . . . . .
   if Alphabetic(Character) then
      LetterCount := LetterCount+1
   else if Numeric(Character) then
      DigitCount := DigitCount+1

. . . . . . . . . .
end.
```

13.4. (a)

```
function Prime ( Number: Integer ): Boolean;
   var
      Divisor: 0 . . MaxInt;
      NoFactor: Boolean;
   begin
   Number := Abs(Number); (* allows for Number < 0 *)
   Divisor := Round(Sqrt(Number));
   NoFactor := True;
   while NoFactor and (Divisor > 1) do
      if Number mod Divisor = 0 then
         NoFactor := False
      else
         Divisor := Divisor−1;
   Prime := NoFactor
   end (* Prime *)
```

(b) Assume the declaration 'N: Integer'.

```
Read (N); Write (N:1, ' is ');
if Prime(N) then
   Write ('prime')
else
   Write ('non-prime')
```

13.9. Assume the type definition 'Names = **array** [1 . . Length] **of** Char'.

```
function Initial ( FullName: Names): Char;
   const
      Blank = ' ';
   var
      I: 1 . . Length;
   begin
   (* locate the end of the surname *)
   I := Length;
   while FullName[I] = Blank do
      I := I−1;
   (* locate the beginning of the surname *)
   while FullName[I−1] <> Blank do
      I := I−1;
   Initial := FullName[I]
   end (* Initial *)
```

ANSWERS 14

14.2.

```
procedure Swap ( var X, Y: Items);
  var
    XCopy: Items;
  begin
  XCopy := X; X := Y; Y := XCopy
  end (*Swap*)
```

14.3.

```
procedure ReadBoolean ( var B: Boolean );
  const
    Blank = '  ';
  var
    Ch: Char;
  begin
  (* skip any blanks preceding the Boolean representation *)
  Read (Ch);
  while Ch = Blank do
    Read (Ch);
  if Ch = 'F' then
    B := False
  else if Ch = 'T' then
    B := True
  else
    WriteLn ('Invalid input on reading Boolean: ', Ch)
  end (*ReadBoolean*)
```

14.5. Assume the type definition 'Strings = **packed array** [1 . . L] **of** Char'.

```
procedure ReadLine ( var Line: Strings );
  var
    Col: 1 . . L;
  begin
  for Col := 1 to L do
    if EOLn(Input) then
      Line[Col] := '  '
    else
      Read (Line[Col]);
  ReadLn
  end (*ReadLine*)
```

14.6. (a)

```
procedure MaxMin ( Profile: Profiles;
                        var MaxCentre, MinCentre: Centres );
   var
      Centre: Centres;
   begin
   MaxCentre := Frankfurt; MinCentre := Frankfurt;
   for Centre := London to Zurich do
      if Profile[Centre] > Profile[MaxCentre] then
         MaxCentre := Centre
      else if Profile[Centre] < Profile[MinCentre] then
         MinCentre := Centre
   end (* MaxMin*)
```

(b) Assume the variable declaration 'SellCentre, BuyCentre: Centres'.

```
MaxMin (CurrencyValue[Sterling], SellCentre, BuyCentre);
WriteLn ('Profit on sterling deal is ',
           ((CurrencyValue[Sterling,SellCentre]
            /CurrencyValue[Sterling,BuyCentre]
            − 1.0) * 100):5:1, '%')
```

ANSWERS 15

15.2. In MatrixProduct (b), replace the statement part of procedure ReadMatrix by:

```
begin
for I := 1 to N do
   for J := 1 to N do
      if I >= J then
         Read (M[I,J])
      else
         M[I,J] := 0
end (*ReadMatrix*)
```

In MatrixProduct (a), the refinements of 'read matrix A' and 'read matrix B' must separately be modified in the same way.

The refinement of 'make P the matrix product of A and B' could be modified to be more efficient for the special case of triangular matrices.

15.3. The refinement of 'read a name' becomes simply Read(CurrentName). Replace the type definition by 'Names = Integer'. No other changes are needed.

ANSWERS 16

16.1. (a) Similar to the declaration of **OneEmployee** in Example 17.4.

(b)

```
with One Employee do
  begin
  Write (Name, Number:8, '   ':4);
  case Grade of
    Manual: Write ('manual');
    Skilled:  Write ('skilled');
    Clerical: Write ('clerical');
    Managerial: Write ('managerial')
    end;
  WriteLn ('£':5, PayRate:1)
  end
```

16.2.

```
program Dates ( Input, Output );
type
  Dates = . . . .; (* as in Example 16.1 *)
var
  Today, ThatDay: Dates;

procedure WriteDate ( Date: Dates );
  begin
  with Date do
    Write (Day:2, '/', Month:2, '/', (Year mod 100):2)
  end (* WriteDate *);

begin
with Today do
  Read (Day, Month, Year);
WriteDate (Today); WriteLn;
(* determine the date exactly nine months hence *)
ThatDay := Today;
with ThatDay do
  if Month <= 3 then
    Month := Month + 9
  else
    begin
    Month := Month − 3;
    Year := Year + 1
    end;
```

```
WriteDate (ThatDay); WriteLn
end (* Dates *).
```

16.3. (a)

```
type
   Degrees = Real;
   Places  = record
                  Latitude, Longitude: Degrees
             end
```

(b)

```
type
   Hours = Real;
   . . . .

function SolarTimeDiff (Place1, Place2: Places): Hours;
   const
      DegreesPerHour = 15;
   var
      LongitudeDiff: Degrees;
   begin
   LongitudeDiff := Abs(Place1.Longitude − Place2.Longitude);
   SolarTimeDiff := LongitudeDiff/DegreesPerHour
   end (* SolarTimeDiff*)
```

(c)

```
procedure ReadPosition (var Place: Places);
   begin
   with Place do
      Read (Latitude, Longitude)
   end (* ReadPosition *)
```

(e) Assuming the declaration 'A, B: Places':

```
ReadPosition (A); WritePosition (A);
ReadPosition (B); WritePosition (B);
WriteLn (' have time difference of ', SolarTimeDiff(A,B), ' hr.')
```

16.5. (a)

```
Shapes = (Circle,Rectangle,Triangle);
Figures = record
            case Shape: Shapes of
              Circle:
                ( Radius: Real );
              Rectangle:
                ( X, Y: Real );
              Triangle:
                ( A, B, C: Real )
          end
```

(b)

```
function Area ( Figure: Figures ): Real;
  const
    Pi = 3.14159265;
  var
    S: Real;
  begin
  with Figure do
    case Shape of
      Circle: Area := Pi * Sqr(Radius);
      Rectangle: Area := X * Y;
      Triangle: begin
                  S := (A+B+C)/2;
                  Area := Sqrt(S*(S−A)*(S−B)*(S−C))
                    (* ... assuming the triangle exists! *)
                end
    end (*case*)
  end (* Area *)
```

ANSWERS 17

17.2.

```
program Concatenate ( In1, In2, Out );
type
  Items = ....;
  FileOfItems = file of Items;
var
  In1, In2, Out: Fileofitems;
```

```
procedure Append (var Source, Destination: FileOfItems);
  var
    Item: Items;
  begin
  Reset (Source);
  while not EOF(Source) do
    begin
    Read (Source, Item);
    Write (Destination, Item)
    end
  end (* Append *);

begin (* Concatenate *)
Rewrite (Out);
Append (In1, Out);
Append (In2, Out)
end (* Concatenate *).
```

17.3. Assume the type definition 'IntFiles = **file of** Integer'.

```
procedure SearchFile ( var IntFile: IntFiles;
                            Target: Integer;
                        var Found: Boolean );
  var
    Int: Integer;
  begin
  Reset (IntFile);
  Found := False;
  while not (Found or EOF(IntFile)) do
    begin
    Read (IntFile, Int);
    if Int = Target then
      Found := True
    end
  end (* Search *)
```

17.6.

```
program Hypocrites ( DrinkersFile, TemperanceFile, Output );
type
  Members = record
```

```
                  Name: packed array [1. .16] of Char
                  (*.....................
                  address and other details
                  .....................*)
            end;
var
   DrinkersFile, TemperanceFile: file of Members;
begin
Reset (DrinkersFile);
Reset (TemperanceFile);
while not (EOF(DrinkersFile) or EOF(TemperanceFile)) do
   if DrinkersFile↑.Name < TemperanceFile↑.Name then
     Get (DrinkersFile)
   else
   if DrinkersFile↑.Name > TemperanceFile↑.Name then
     Get (TemperanceFile)
   else
     begin
     WriteLn (DrinkersFile↑.Name, ' is a member of both.');
     Get (DrinkersFile);
     Get (TemperanceFile)
     end
end.
```

ANSWERS 18

18.2. (a,b,c) Replace the **if** statement in Level 1 by:

```
case kind of token of
   word:
     append the word followed by a blank . . . .;
   paragraph mark:
     start a new paragraph;
   break mark:
     write the current line without adjustment;
   space mark:
     write the current line without adjustment,
        followed by a blank line;
   page mark:
     start a new page
   end
```

Add ABreakMark, ASpaceMark and APageMark to the enumeration type
TokenKinds, each corresponding to an empty variant in the record type Tokens.
'Write the current line without adjustment' is refined to:

```
WriteLine (Unadjusted)
```

'Write the current line without adjustment, followed by a blank line' is refined
to:

```
WriteLine (Unadjusted);
WriteLn
```

'Start a new page' is refined to:

```
WriteLine (Unadjusted);
Page
```

18.4. If all the ballots are invalid, procedure CountVotes will set its parameter
Outcome to RecountNeeded, but Leader and Trailer will be left undefined; thus
procedure Eliminate will fail.

If there is only one candidate, procedure CountVotes will incorrectly set
Outcome to Alltied, and that result will be reported.

To correct these errors, replace the statement part of Level 1 of the
program by:

```
begin
prepare to count votes;
read all the ballots, storing the valid ones;
if there is only one candidate then
    report that candidate the winner
else if there are no valid ballots then
    report that the election is null
else
    begin
    count the votes;

    . . . . . . . . . .

    report the outcome of the election
    end
end
```

'Report that candidate the winner' is refined to:

```
Report (OverallMajority, 1)
```

The condition 'there are no valid ballots' can be refined to NrValidBallots=0
provided that the counting of valid ballots is transferred from procedure
CountVotes to procedure StoreValidBallots and that NrValidBallots is made a
global variable.

ANSWERS 19

19.1.

```
type
  People = 1 . . N;
var
  OldPeople, Males, Smokers, Drinkers: set of People;
. . . . . . . .
```

(a) [1 . . N]
(b) [1 . . N] — Smokers
(c) OldPeople * Smokers * Drinkers * Males
(d) Smokers + Drinkers
(e) OldPeople + Males * (Smokers+Drinkers)

```
if Person in OldPeople + Males * (Smokers+Drinkers) then
  WriteLn ('bad insurance risk')
```

19.3. The following solution assumes that the upper-case letters are contiguous, and the lower-case letters likewise. Assume the type definition:

```
type CharClasses = (Letter,Digit,Blank,Punctuation,Other)

function Class ( Ch: Char ): CharClasses;
  begin
  if Ch in ['A' . . 'Z', 'a' . . 'z'] then
    Class := Letter
  else if Ch In ['0' . . '9'] then
    Class := Digit
  else if Ch = '   ' then
    Class := Blank
  else if Ch in ['.', '!', '?', ':', ';', ',', '(', ')', '''', '-'] then
    Class := Punctuation
  else
    Class := Other
  end (* Class *)
```

ANSWERS 20

20.1. (a)

```
IntPointers = ↑ IntNodes;
IntNodes    = record
                Int: Integer;
                Next: IntPointers
              end
```

(b)

```
function ListSum (Head: IntPointers ): Integer;
  var
    Sum: Integer;
    Ref: IntPointers;
  begin
  Sum := 0;
  Ref := Head;
  while Ref <> nil do
    with Ref ↑ do
      begin
      Sum := Sum+Int;
      Ref := Next
      end;
  ListSum := Sum
  end (*ListSum*)
```

20.2. Procedure SearchList locates (and DeleteItem deletes) the *first* matching entry.

20.3.

```
program Reverse ( Input, Output );
type
  CharLinks = ↑ CharNodes;
  CharNodes = record
                  Character: Char;
                  Next: CharLinks
                end;

var
  First, This: CharLinks;
  Ch: Char;

begin
First := nil; (* make the list of characters empty *)
while not EOLn(Input) do
  begin
  Read (Ch);
  (* insert Ch at the front of the list *)
  New (This);
  This ↑ .Character := Ch;
```

```
      This ↑.Next := First;
      First := This
      end;
(* write all characters in the list *)
This := First;
while This <> nil do
  begin
  Write (This↑.Character);
  This := This ↑.Next
  end
end.
```

20.4. Replace the variable declaration 'ListHead: NamePointers' by:

```
Head: array ['A' . . 'Z'] of NamePointers
```

Replace all occurrences of ListHead in procedure InsertName by Head[NewName[1]]. Modify procedure MakeListEmpty as follows:

```
procedure MakeListEmpty;
  var
    Initial: 'A' . . 'Z';
  begin
  for Initial := 'A' to Z do
    Head[Initial] := nil
  end (*MakeListEmpty*)
```

Modify procedure WriteAllNames as follows:

```
procedure WriteAllNames;
  var
    Ref: NamePointers;
    Initial: 'A' . . 'Z';
  begin
  for Initial := 'A' to 'Z' do
    begin
    Ref := Head[Initial];
    while Ref <> nil do

    . . . . . . . . .
    . . . . . . . . .
    end
  end (*WriteAllNames *)
```

ANSWERS 21

21.2. (a)

```
function Factorial ( N: Integer): Integer;
  begin
  if N <= 1 then
    Factorial := 1
  else
    Factorial := N * Factorial(N—1)
  end (*Factorial*)
```

21.3. (a)

```
function TrueCount ( function F (X:Integer): Boolean;
                     LowLimit, HighLimit: Integer )
            : Integer;
  var
    I, Count: Integer;
  begin
  Count := 0;
  for I := LowLimit to HighLimit do
    if F(I) then
      Count := Count+1;
  TrueCount := Count
  end (* TrueCount *)
```

(b)

```
WriteLn ('Number of primes between 2 and ', M:1,
         ' is ', TrueCount(Prime,2,M))
```

21.4.

```
procedure TraverseList
            ( ListHead: NamePointers;
  (*applying*) procedure P (EntryRef:NamePointers) );
  var
    Ref: NamePointers;
  begin
  Ref := ListHead;
  while Ref <> nil do
```

```
      begin
      P (Ref);
      Ref := Ref ↑ .Next
      end
  end (*TraverseList*)
```

(b)

```
  procedure WriteAllNames;

    procedure WriteName ( At: NamePointers );
      begin
      WriteLn (At↑.Name)
      end (*WriteName*);

    begin (*WriteAllNames*)
    TraverseList (ListHead, WriteName)
    end (*WriteAllNames*)
```

21.6.

```
    SummerTemp: array [May . . Aug] of Real;
    WinterRain: array [Oct . . Dec] of Real;

    . . .

  function Maximum (Stats: array [First. .Last: Months] of Real): Real;
    var
      Max: Real;
      Month: Months;
    begin
    Max := Stats[First];
    if First < Last then
      for Month := Succ(First) to Last do
        if Stats[Month] > Max then
          Max := Stats[Month];
    Maximum := Max;
    end (*Maximum*);
    . . .

    WriteLn('Maximum summer temperature:',
            Maximum (SummerTemp):4:1);
    WriteLn('Maximum winter rainfall:',
            Maximum (WinterRain):4:1);
```

ANSWERS 22

22.1. (a)

```
program SumIntegers ( Input, Output );
label 1;
var
   Sum, Size, Summand, Count: Integer;
begin
Sum := 0;
ReadLn (Size);
for Count := 1 to Size do
   begin
   if EOF(Input) then
      begin WriteLn ('Too few numbers'); goto 1 end;
   ReadLn (Summand);
   Sum := Sum+Summand
   end;
1:
WriteLn ('Sum of numbers read: ', Sum)
end.
```

(b)

```
program SumIntegers ( Input, Output );
var
   Sum, Size, Summand, Count: Integer;
begin
Sum := 0;
ReadLn (Size);
Count := 0;
while (Count < Size) and not EOF(Input) do
   begin
   Count := Count+1;
   ReadLn (Summand);
   Sum := Sum+Summand
   end;
if Count < Size then
   WriteLn ('Too few numbers');
WriteLn ('Sum of numbers read: ', Sum)
end.
```

Index